Advance Praise for *The Sales Advantage*

"This book, in black and white, paints a colorful picture of a success model for sales professionals. If you struggle with tough prospects, hidden buyers, and the effort to generate leads, *The Sales Advantage* will reveal how thousands of successful pros have put this system to use. Read the book, follow the leaders, and make more money!"

—DAN SEIDMAN
SPEAKER AND AU THOR,
THE DEATH OF 20TH CENTURY SELLING

"Our salespeople love the Dale Carnegie Sales Advantage. It teaches them to project, in the minds of our buyers, an image of a place where they have never been, but would like to be! This approach opens up opportunities to talk about solving their business issues, placing a prospect in a receptive and positive mode. Best of all, it really works! *The Sales Advantage* is a truly valuable part of our sales curriculum."

—HAL JOHNSON
VICE PRESIDENT EXECUTIVE RESOURCES,
ADT SECURITY SERVICES, INC.

"*The Sales Advantage* is filled with "real-world" examples that salespeople can immediately apply on the job. It a wonderful guide for the salesperson of the future."

—MARSHALL GOLDSMITH
CO-EDITOR OF THE BESTSELLING BOOK
THE LEADER OF THE FUTURE, AND
THE ORGANIZATION OF THE FUTURE

"In the last 100 years, two words have defined business, personal, and sales advantage: Dale Carnegie. This book will help you learn, and earn."

—JEFFREY GITOMER
AUTHOR OF *THE SALES BIBLE*

"Dale Carnegie's principles are exemplified in this wonderful book, which shows how to build effective long-term relationships with one's customers. The real-life stories demonstrate that when we practice these principles, both parties win."

—JOANNE SHAW
PRESIDENT AND CEO
THE COFFEE BEANERY

THE SALES ADVANTAGE

How to Get It,
Keep It,
and Sell More
Than Ever

DALE CARNEGIE & ASSOCIATES, INC.

J. OLIVER CROM

MICHAEL CROM

THE FREE PRESS

NEW YORK · LONDON · TORONTO · SYDNEY · SINGAPORE

*f*P

THE FREE PRESS
A Division of Simon & Schuster Inc.
1230 Avenue of the Americas
New York, New York 10020

For information about special discounts for bulk purchases,
please contact Simon & Schuster Special Sales:
1-800-456-6798 or business@simonandschuster.com

DESIGNED BY KEVIN HANEK

Manufactured in the United States of America

10   9   8   7   6   5   4   3   2   1

Library of Congress Cataloging-in-Publication Data
The sales advantage : how to get it, keep it, and sell more than ever /
    Dale Carnegie & Associates, Inc., J. Oliver Crom, Michael Crom.
        p.   cm.
    Includes index.
    1. Selling.   2. Sales Management.   3. Sales personnel—Training of.
    I. Crom, J. Oliver.   II. Crom, Michael A.   III. Dale Carnegie & Associates.
  HF5438 .S152 2003
   658.85—dc21   2002075237
ISBN 978-0-7432-4468-8

Contents

Preface   vii

Introduction   I

CHAPTER 1   **New Opportunities**   19
Finding Prospects

CHAPTER 2   **Pre-approach**   38
Doing Our Homework

CHAPTER 3   **Initial Communication**   50
Gaining the Prospect's Attention

CHAPTER 4   **The Interview**   75
Building Trust

CHAPTER 5   **Opportunity Analysis**   120
Determining Prospect Potential

CHAPTER 6   **Solution Development**   125
Giving Customers What They Want

CHAPTER 7   **Solution Presentation**   147
Sharing Our Recommendations

CHAPTER 8   **Customer Evaluation**   166
Moving Toward Commitment

CHAPTER 9   **Negotiation**   186
Finding Common Ground

CHAPTER 10   **Commitment**   211
Moving from Prospect to Customer

CHAPTER 11   **Follow-up**   225
Keeping Our Commitments

CHAPTER 12   **Objections**   236
Opportunities to Communicate

CHAPTER 13   **The Biggest Sales Advantage**   261
Our Attitude

Our Thanks   273
Index   275

Preface

The two key questions that sales professionals most often ask us are: 1) How can I close more sales? and 2) What can I do to reduce objections?

After more than sixty years in the sales training business, we've learned the answer to those questions is pretty straightforward. Frankly, you learn how to sell.

That's not the answer most people expect to hear, but it's one we truly believe. No matter how much we want to find otherwise, there's no magic formula that eliminates objections or increases closing ratios. Overcoming objections and gaining commitment are both logical outcomes of a successful sales process. You want to meet a good closer? Find a good salesperson who truly understands *how* to sell.

It's often hard to believe that top performers need to learn how to sell. Yet we have encountered an extraordinary number of experienced and successful sales professionals who have discovered our statement to be true. In fact, by consistently practicing and applying proven principles, they've been able to increase sales and earn more money than they ever thought possible.

That tells us the Sales Advantage process is a proven way to build relationships and enhance your sales career, no matter how long you've been selling.

Don't get us wrong. We're not saying that learning the sales process is easy. And we're certainly not implying that we can sell today the same way we sold ten years ago—we can't. It's a different world out there. Customer attitudes have changed. Technology is breaking down barriers between nations but creating different kinds of barriers between our customers and us. Companies are downsizing. Territories are expanding. We're being asked to generate more sales with fewer resources. And it doesn't stop there.

These issues represent a variety of daily challenges. For example, it's tough when a customer promises a signed contract on Wednesday and she buys from a competitor on Tuesday. It's frustrating to handle service issues on a day when we plan to do nothing but prospect for new opportunities. It's hard to realize that, after months of building a relationship with a "decision-maker," the actual decision-maker is someone we've never met. Sure, technology and globalization are changing the world of selling. But honestly, most of us are more concerned about how to overcome the hurdles we face on the job every day.

Learning how to sell using the Sales Advantage tools and principles will increase the odds that we'll overcome these challenges successfully. How? By learning to see the buying and selling process from the customer's point of view. With that ideal as our foundation, we'll then learn to use timeless and proven tools. These tools will help us build credibility, uncover the customer's Dominant Buying Motive, and develop strong business relationships that lead to referrals and repeat sales. In the end, when we offer a solution to a customer, we'll be more confident that it is the *right* solution, instead of just *hoping* it is.

Look at it this way: How can we sell the total value of our products and services if we haven't learned how to gather information in a way that tells us what's important to the customer? How can we maximize our prospecting efforts without a strategic approach for finding and evaluating new opportunities? How can we get past frustrating barriers, such as voice mail, if we don't know the basics of good account penetration? How can we be prepared to address objections if we don't fully understand the customer's primary interest and buying criteria? When we consider these questions, it becomes pretty evident why a thorough understanding of the entire buying and selling process is a critical element in any successful sales career.

As you embark on your voyage to improve your sales skills, you will understand why learning how to sell using an effective process gives you an edge in the marketplace. If you become committed to making these tools and principles a part of your selling strategy, you will stand out from thousands of salespeople who simply sell on instinct. Your prospects and customers will view you differently when you meet with them. Instead of thinking, "Here's another salesperson," they'll think, "Here's someone who can help me. Here's someone I trust."

As you read this book, we would like to offer four suggestions to help you get the maximum benefit for your time invested:

KEEP AN OPEN MIND

Our real life examples come from people who live in the selling trenches every day. They know what it's like to leave twenty messages for someone and never get a return phone call. They were once skeptical about trying a new approach, but did it anyway and got results. They've hit sales plateaus and found ways to overcome them. The bottom line: Every successful selling tool mentioned in these examples has been tried and proven by a sales professional somewhere in the world. If they can do it, so can you. Open your mind to the possibilities.

AIM FOR EVOLUTION, NOT REVOLUTION

Because the Sales Advantage covers the entire sales process, it contains numerous principles and tools. We're not asking you to try all of them at once. In fact, we encourage you to apply them at a pace that's realistic for you. Try one new thing. Get comfortable with it. Then try another. And another. And continue until you eventually evolve your selling skills to a higher level of performance. Dale Carnegie always said, "The 'sure thing' boat never gets far from the shore." In other words, don't be afraid to take a chance and try something new. At the same time, don't overwhelm yourself by making too many changes too fast.

TRY THE ACTION STEPS AND SELLING TIPS

We all like a little immediate gratification—things we can do right away that might have a positive impact on our results. To that end, this book contains action steps and helpful tips you can realistically apply in your job today. Whether you sell products, services, or ideas, we hope you will find these suggestions useful.

All the while, don't lose sight of how these ideas fit into the process as a whole. The bullet point lists are helpful, but they alone will not help you build the kinds of relationships necessary to develop unique customer solutions and sustain a lucrative sales career. Your long-term success largely depends upon your commitment to understanding the process and your ability to consistently practice using the Sales Advantage tools in every selling situation.

BE YOURSELF

Many of our graduates tell us that a major benefit of the Sales Advantage is being able to use their own styles and abilities in line with our proven processes. With that in mind, remember that these principles and methods are not about a mechanical approach to selling. They are about making the sales process second nature for you, so you do them intuitively—just like driving a car.

If you become mechanical in applying the principles, it will be obvious to your prospects and customers. Your style of selling is the right style for you. Be confident in your own abilities. It's the process we want you to understand and apply. Ultimately, the specific tools and language you use are your decision. Even though the way you sell and the way your coworker sells may be totally different, you can both apply what you learn here and become even more successful.

No matter who you are, what you sell, or how long you've been selling, understanding and consistently applying these concepts has the potential of making a tremendous difference in your sales career.

It won't be easy to make changes in your routine. But if you want to increase your sales effectiveness, offer better solutions to your customers, advance your career, and maximize your income potential, you must make the commitment to step out of your comfort zone and do something different.

As Mr. Carnegie himself said: "To raise yourself to a better position, you've got to do something special. Make some extra effort. It won't be pleasant all the time. It'll mean hard grueling work while you're at it, and it will pay off in the long run."

Sincerely,

J. Oliver Crom
VICE-CHAIRMAN OF THE BOARD

Michael Crom
EXECUTIVE VICE-PRESIDENT

THE SALES
ADVANTAGE

Introduction

> I don't think anybody is cut out to be a salesperson or anything else. I
> think we've got to cut ourselves out to be whatever we want to be.
>
> —FRANK BETTGER

When it comes to the importance of sales professionals in today's marketplace, Red Motley sums it up best: "Nothing happens until somebody sells something."

That may seem like a bold statement, but look at it this way: Would the driver for an international freight company have a job if somebody hadn't sold the products being delivered? Would the construction worker have a job if a site developer hadn't sold the City Council on the idea of a retail store? Would the aerospace engineer have a job if an account executive hadn't secured a new contract for commercial jets?

Those are just a few examples of how powerful the sales professional's role is in driving the world economy. You could say the same thing about virtually any business. In fact, next time you see a truck on the highway, drive past a construction site, or board an airplane, you can smile and think to yourself: "All of this activity around me is happening because of what I do."

To us, that's exciting. Salespeople are leaders. They truly make things happen. In the minds of customers, they are the face of the company. And those who succeed in building strong business relationships are often paid very well for their efforts.

Despite the impressive rewards that await top sales performers in most industries, many salespeople don't reach their full potential. Why? Because they don't understand the fundamental process of buying and selling.

Think about the game of golf: A lot of people play, but very few really know how. We can even draw the same comparison when it comes to photography. Most of us can take pictures, but not many of us have the knowledge or skills to become a published photographer.

Selling is the same way. A lot of people know just enough about selling to make a decent living. But most people don't know enough about the buying and selling process to truly excel in a sales career.

That's where the Sales Advantage comes in.

If you've been selling for many years, perhaps by instinct rather than structure, this book can help you realize why you're succeeding. At the same time, it shows you what you're not doing—or doing unnecessarily—that's keeping you from achieving your full potential. If you're new to sales, this will give you an essential foundation upon which to build a successful and lucrative sales career.

We'll share numerous tools that can enhance your relationship with the customer. Will we use all of these tools in every sales discussion? Absolutely not. Every selling situation is different.

Keep in mind that selling is not about manipulating people into buying. It's about creating an atmosphere that's conducive to customers making a favorable decision for everyone involved. After all, nobody likes to be sold. But we all like to make good buying decisions. That is why our philosophy for selling is one of Dale Carnegie's most quoted human relations principles:

Sales Philosophy

"Try honestly to see things from the other person's point of view."

Sounds like common sense doesn't it? But common sense is not always common practice. It is often very difficult for salespeople to see things from a buyer's perspective. We often don't know their internal policies, politics, challenges, and processes. Many salespeople do not actually use the products and services they sell. In fact, many of the people who influence the buying decision don't use them either. Purchasing agents are a good example. So, it is critical for us to really understand the perspectives of everyone who has a role in buying.

This philosophy improves the customer's trust, enhances your reputation, and builds solid customer relationships. Selling according to this philosophy, in conjunction with your personal selling style, will energize you. It will significantly enhance your results and help you feel proud about being a sales professional.

Most salespeople who are successful ultimately realize that selling is a process. A proven process will give us predictable results. The process outlined below has been proven and can help any salesperson improve results.

The Sales Process

1. New Opportunity
2. Pre-approach
3. Initial Communication
4. Interview
5. Opportunity Analysis
6. Solution Development
7. Solution Presentation
8. Customer Evaluation
9. Negotiation
10. Commitment
11. Follow-up

Successful salespeople tell us that one of the keys to their performance is to follow a repeatable, proven process that gets consistent, positive results. The process outlined here has been tested extensively in a wide variety of products, industries, and cultures. It works. Adjust and adapt the process for your business and you can see the results.

The first three elements of the sales process represent every activity that leads up to that all-important first meeting. We must identify the new opportunity, do our homework through pre-approach, and initiate communication with the prospect before gaining an interview. These are essential activities in the sales process, and they take place in almost every selling situation. If we don't do these activities effectively, we haven't really earned the right to take our prospect's time.

Once we get into the interview, we must know how to build rapport and find out specifically what people need and want. As simple as that sounds, many salespeople don't understand their customers' true issues. Why? They don't know how to ask the right questions.

When they interview customers, they only ask surface-level questions. Consequently, most salespeople don't uncover the primary interest areas and the Dominant Buying Motive (the emotional reason people buy). These two key pieces of information are critical to developing a truly unique solution that stands apart from the competition.

While the interview is the heart and soul of the sales process, there are many things we have to do after that meeting in order to develop solid customer relationships. So beyond the interview, the selling process represents the activities necessary to turn our prospects into customers. We develop the solution, present it to our prospects, help them evaluate it, gain commitment, and follow up to ensure satisfaction. This part of the sales process is when we truly demonstrate our ability to step into our customers' worlds. We see things from their point of view and provide solutions that no other salesperson can provide.

Which part of the process is most important? All of them. Look at it this way: If we can't get the discussion started, how can we present a solution? If we get the first meeting but don't gather information effectively, how can we be sure we've offered the right solution? If we gain commitment but don't follow up, what are the chances of repeat business? Clearly, if any piece of the process fails, the relationship can collapse. Does every sale go through these phases? Not necessarily. But most of them do. In fact, selling is often repetitive and, in many cases, very predictable.

SOME ELEMENTS OVERLAP

We'll find that many elements of the sales process overlap into more than one part of the sales discussion. For example, it's likely that we will use effective questioning techniques several times in our interaction with the customer. And in virtually every part of the process, we'll find Dale Carnegie's human relations principles to be a critical element in our success.

THE PROCESS IS PREDICTABLE, BUT THE SITUATION ISN'T

If we're selling in an industrial environment with long sales cycles, the pre-approach may take place over several weeks. Not only that, we may have several interviews with a customer before we actually present a solution. On the other hand, in retail situations, there's very little—if any—pre-approach work that can be done. And, in contrast to large equipment sales, we may never have contact with the same customer again beyond the initial meeting.

The point is, we need to recognize that each selling situation is unique. Some salespeople will go through each element of the process several times a day. Others may only go through them a few times a year. The key is to understand how the eleven parts apply in your unique situation, and then act accordingly.

UNDERSTANDING THE WHOLE PROCESS IS ESSENTIAL FOR SUCCESS

Mastering one or two skills alone won't generate the same results as understanding and mastering the entire sales process. Even though we want to practice them one step at a time, the power of the Sales Advantage is fully realized when we pull them all together.

Let's say we're stranded on a deserted island. The good news: There's an old airplane on the island that actually flies. The bad news: We have no idea where we are, and no map to help us reach our final destination. Even though we have tools available to get off the island, we don't know where to go once we get in the air. If we decide to leave, we merely fly on chance and hope for the best. We may eventually get home; we may not.

The same theory applies to selling. Understanding and applying the principles of the entire buying and selling process leaves nothing to chance. Just as we wouldn't fly an airplane without a flight plan, we shouldn't try to sell without developing a sales strategy that encompasses every relevant part of the sales process.

Kevin McCloskey, sales representative with Quantum EDP in Toronto, Ontario, Canada, talks about how applying the Sales Advantage principles makes a difference in his selling strategy.

"I had been in sales for three years and never had a template to follow when approaching potential clients," said Kevin. "This unorganized approach quite often left me tongue-tied and unable to communicate effectively to the client what my services are.

"Now that I understand selling as a process, I am able to understand the customer's true requirements and expectations and then communicate effectively the value-added service I can offer. As a result, my success ratio has increased considerably. I feel I can now control and understand the sales cycle, which inevitably makes me a better, more professional salesperson."

McCloskey's success speaks for itself: Only six weeks into practicing the Sales Advantage principles, his activity increased so dramatically he had to hire an assistant.

Jack Maloy, northeast district manager with Tetra in Blacksburg, Virginia, says that applying the sales process and relieving "the pressure" on the customer enabled him to get significant additional shelf space for his company's products. He also says he created a new kind of excitement in a family-owned retail account.

"Treasure Island Aquarium and Pet Center is a family-run business that has three locations. Over time, I had slowly gained their trust in regards to the pet business, but had not had any luck in getting them to implement Tetra's full 'Nutrition System.' The customer has always been very cautious in reviewing new products and programs. So I realized that if I continued to ask for the sale on each visit, I might risk losing his trust.

"So instead of thinking about closing, I decided to review the entire sales process. I started by making an unannounced visit to one location, just to stop by and say hello and see how things were going. No selling involved. I began to ask probing questions, knowing the customer's answer would most likely be positive.

"Because I was listening and was truly interested in his opinion, the customer then became interested in what I had to say, especially in how he could increase sales with current customers. I then provided him with the 'solution': our full Nutrition System. He had a few objections. But, because I was following the steps of a logical buying process, I was prepared for them and we quickly overcame them. I was able to secure his commitment. Both Treasure Island and Tetra will benefit from this partnership."

Entrepreneur Bruce Hughes, vice president of Repro Tech, Inc., in Wauwatosa, Wisconsin, believes learning the sales process has taught him how to "overcome anything."

"After leaving corporate America, I decided to purchase part ownership in Repro Tech, Inc. Besides me, there was one employee at the time—my business partner Deborah Bruss. Her expertise was administrative and mine was service and repair. Neither of us had any previous sales experience. Needless to say, I didn't know that selling had a process to it.

"Since we had very few customers, along with bills to pay and families to support, I needed to have a customer base. How did I plan on getting customers? You got it—cold calling.

"For the next six months, I experienced something I never had in the past: rejection. As we all know, rejection is part of selling, but at that time, I was not prepared for this new experience. I got to the point where I thought something was wrong with me. I started to fear knocking on doors or picking up the telephone to make appointments. But I kept at it. I kept saying to myself, 'There has got to be a better way.'

"Then, I came across the Sales Advantage. I learned that with proper training and attitude, I could become a very successful salesperson. I began to implement the process. Soon, I started seeing less and less rejection. Learning and understanding the sales process taught me how to overcome any objection, from the initial cold call all the way to getting the order signed.

"Our company continues to grow. We now have several employees and we serve many counties in the area. I have achieved goals that were once only a dream. I do not fear rejection or objections, but often welcome them. I still cold call every day, but now I enjoy it. I have the greatest job in the world. I love being a salesperson!"

Kevin, Jack, and Bruce are just three people out of thousands who have seen a significant boost in their sales results after they began applying the timeless fundamentals of the Sales Advantage.

Here's the bottom line: Learning and applying the right skills can increase your activity level, decrease your stress level, help you develop stronger customer relationships, and put more money in your pocket. Anybody who really understands how to sell will tell you the same thing.

While the sales environment has changed, the buyer's mind goes through the same process it always has. Nobody's going to buy anything unless he or she has a reason to buy. And when that reason becomes significant, we need to be there ready to provide solutions that meet that person's unique needs and wants.

The Sales Advantage: A Big Impact on Big Challenges

Our tools and principles have specific applications when it comes to the toughest challenges faced by today's sales professionals. Here are some of the most common challenges identified by our participants and trainers, along with an explanation of how the tools and principles can help us achieve better results.

CHALLENGE: INFORMATION OVERLOAD

In today's marketplace, customers are inundated with direct mail, telephone solicitation, faxes, voice mail, and e-mail—everything we can imagine to make that first point of contact. For that reason, customers know more about our products and services than ever before.

The Internet presents other challenges. For example, a customer in the United States can get online and hire a consultant from Europe. Consequently, instead of competing only against local companies, we're competing against organizations from all over the world.

RESULT

One of the best things that has happened for salespeople is a more informed customer. Why? In most cases, we aren't spending our valuable time educating our customers. Therefore, we can focus more on the application of our products and services in the customer's environment rather than simply sharing features and benefits. Today's informed customer wants to know, "What's it going to do for me?" The salesperson who understands how to sell at the application level can answer that question effectively.

CHALLENGE: WORKING WITH GATEKEEPERS

Getting past a secretary or receptionist has been a challenge for sales-people from the beginning. But today, the popularity of voice mail brings yet another challenge: getting through to a human being. The combination of human and electronic gatekeepers makes it more diffi-cult than ever to reach our customers.

RESULT

True, customers do not want to be deluged with people trying to sell them goods and services. That'll never change. But they are willing to talk to people who can offer realistic solutions to the challenges they face.

Sales professionals who apply the Sales Advantage principles find ways to penetrate those walls by talking in terms of the customer's in-terest. With that ideal as a foundation, we build strategies to work with gatekeepers. Then, no matter what happens, we implement the strategy we have prepared. We'll see why voice mail can be a bridge instead of a barrier for sales professionals who know how to use it. After all, instead of risking that our messages be thrown away or written inaccurately, we can now leave our own compelling message, with our own excitement level. We actually have more opportunities than ever before to speak di-rectly to the customer, even if it is through a voice recording.

CHALLENGE: THE DARK SIDE OF TOTAL QUALITY

Total quality management did great things for internal processes and employee empowerment, but it presents challenges for salespeople. Team-based decision making often means longer buying cycles. It also means that an increasing number of the actual decision-makers are re-moved from the buying process.

Nowadays, it's rare that we find a selling situation in which we deal with one buyer and one set of buying motives. In many cases, when we're dealing with project teams, we're dealing with information gatherers. Often they appear to be, or even assume themselves that they are, the ultimate decision-makers. But most of the time, we'll find out there's another layer in the organization, someone we haven't even spoken to. And it doesn't matter how smart we are or how many probing questions we ask, we still may be surprised to find the real decision-maker is someone with whom we've never met.

RESULT

In applying the Sales Advantage principles to our selling strategy, we'll learn to identify different levels of prospects, which, in turn, helps us analyze whether the person with whom we're meeting is the decision-maker. If we aren't able to discover who the actual decision-maker is, we will work to identify the major influencer on the buying team. In either case, the Sales Advantage gives us an edge by showing us how to develop a solution around that person's Dominant Buying Motive—the emotional reason he or she will buy.

CHALLENGE: MERGERS AND ACQUISITIONS

Every time we turn around, it seems as if we're hearing about mergers and acquisitions. Just when we think we've built a good relationship, our customer informs us that she's no longer the decision-maker. This is especially tough for salespeople who aren't in headquarters towns.

RESULT

The Sales Advantage gives us insight into ways in which we can extend our reach within our customer's organization. We'll learn about developing internal champions and the importance of networking and referrals. Most important, however, are the customer-focused relationships we'll develop by practicing the tools and principles in every selling situation. These relationships will help ensure that our customers remain loyal and helpful to us even in the midst of organizational change.

CHALLENGE: PRICE BUYERS

With competition on the rise in almost every business, price seems like a bigger issue than ever before. In the competitive environment in which we are selling, to compete on price alone puts us in a dangerous position.

RESULT

In some cases, price is a legitimate concern. But in almost every selling situation, price is a miserable place to sell. Many times, if the difference between gaining or losing commitment is based solely on price, we may not be effectively communicating the value of our products and services.

The Sales Advantage is designed to support our skills in selling products and services that are designed to meet our customer's needs and wants—not just to meet a price. When we learn how to effectively gather information, we can determine a customer's primary interest and Dominant Buying Motive. With that information, we are better prepared to provide relevant solutions unique to the customer's application. As a result, price usually becomes less of an issue.

CHALLENGE: TIME

Everyone in our society is time-sensitive. In the past, it was a lot easier to meet with customers for lunch or dinner. But today, they typically don't have time for such meetings. And when we do get to talk with customers, they are more inclined to establish time parameters that can be meaningless and arbitrary. Why do they do it? Not only are they perceiving a time crunch, they're anticipating that a meeting with us could be a waste of their valuable time.

RESULT

Can we really blame customers for feeling that way? After all, most of the sales presentations they hear are not focused on them, but on what the salesperson wants to say to them.

Through the Sales Advantage, we learn to plan our meetings in a way that interests the customer. We learn that if we get our customers to do most of the talking, they quickly realize that something's different. When we engage people intellectually and emotionally in a meaningful conversation, time often becomes less of an issue.

CHALLENGE: COMPLEX PRODUCTS AND SOLUTIONS

In old models of selling, salespeople usually knew everything they needed to know to make a sales call. If they didn't, they had a catalog with them to help answer the customer's questions.

Today, many of us are selling products that are so complex, it's almost impossible to know everything. Some salespeople, especially those in highly technical fields, often get caught in "analysis paralysis." In other words, they try to learn everything possible about their company's products and services before they go out and sell. This often holds them back and keeps them from being productive salespeople.

In addition, solutions today are much more customized. Often, we have to rely on an engineer, supplier, sales manager, or someone from the research and development department to help us answer questions and develop solutions.

RESULT

Virtually none of the customers we encounter, not even technical buyers, make purchases on facts alone. They buy what the products and services will do for them in their unique business environment. By learning how to sell the application of a product, and by appealing to the customer's Dominant Buying Motive, we can gain a significant edge in today's marketplace. This is especially true with industries in which the products themselves are complex, yet similar among competitors.

When we learn how to talk in the customer's language and demonstrate an understanding of how our product or service will work in his or her environment, we move to a level of selling that distinguishes us from the competition.

CHALLENGE: INTERNAL SUPPORT

In today's selling environment, most of us don't handle all of our customer contacts. Our companies want us out there selling. So, once we gain commitment, it's up to the people on the inside to deliver. The problem: If we walk away and say our part is done, we could be asking for trouble. Inside support groups are often understaffed and overbooked. For that reason, we must have good relationships and a solid communication process with the internal people who are responsible for ultimately delivering to our customers.

RESULT

In the follow-up portion of the sales process, we'll discuss how our human relations principles apply when we interact with others in our organization. We'll also look at reasons why it might be hard to engage the internal team. If we learn to understand those reasons and see things from the team's point of view, we are better equipped to motivate them toward the common goal of customer satisfaction.

Five Drivers for Sales Success

When we understand how basic principles and methods can help us overcome some of our biggest selling challenges, our first reaction is usually, "Wow, that's so logical. Why doesn't everyone do it?"

We can answer that question based on the literally hundreds of thousands of salespeople who have come through our sales training over the years. What we've found is this: While many of the tools and principles are based on common sense, they are not common practice. Why? Simply, most people don't put forth the extra time and effort.

That sounds rather harsh, yet, unfortunately, it's true. It's human nature. After all, learning the Sales Advantage tools and principles is one thing. But consciously and consistently applying them every day is another.

It's just like anything in life we know we "should" do, but choose not to. We know we should eat a balanced diet, but many of us don't. We know we should exercise, but many of us won't.

Thomas Edison once said: "Opportunity is missed by most people because it's dressed in overalls and looks like work." We sometimes say: "Sales is a lot of luck. That's luck, spelled W-O-R-K."

Without a doubt, hard work and dedication at applying the Sales Advantage principles truly separate the amateurs from the professionals. But there are also certain qualities—or drivers for sales success—that are inherent in the personality and work habits of top achievers.

ATTITUDE CONTROL

Keeping a positive attitude isn't easy. But the saying, "If you can't change the situation, change your attitude about it," is almost a survival skill in the world of selling. After all, customers can hear a bad attitude in our voice, see it on our face, and even sense it in the things we do or say. Yet, we are constantly asked to do more, do it better, do it faster, and look happy doing it.

Eric Larson from North Aurora, Illinois, talks about a lesson he learned in attitude control.

"During my first month as a new sales representative for Varian Vacuum Technologies, my goal was to personally visit each major account. As I hurriedly met my twenty-second prospect of the day, I noticed that he was particularly uninterested in what I had to say. At one point in the conversation, he turned to me and said, 'I know about your company. I purchased some of its products over six years ago and they failed miserably. As far as I'm concerned, I'll never buy from your company again!'

"Fortunately, no one was around to see my jaw hit the floor. I graciously fumbled my way out of his office and spent a fair bit of time thinking about his remarks during the three-hour drive home that night. My pride, ego, and self-confidence took another hit when I investigated his claims and found they were true!

"A year later, I received a call from this gentleman. He was inquiring about some new products our company had developed. Even though I still felt somewhat negative toward him, I decided to put the experience out of my mind and focus on treating this person as though the past had never occurred. He cordially met with me. After another six months of developing trust and rapport, he purchased the first of two new systems.

"I learned to let go of the past, both my mistakes and those of my predecessors. I changed my attitude. I no longer see 'problem customers.' Instead I see 'customers with problems to solve.' "

Kathleen Nugent, account manager for Simco Electronics in Santa Clara, California, echoes Eric's viewpoint.

"I had an upset customer who called me and was angry over what appeared to be a misunderstanding. In his rage, he was threatening to never do business with us again. In the past, I might have become defensive. But I listened, and when he finally took a breath, I supported him. I said that I understood how he could feel that way. He quieted down a little and we hung up.

"The next morning he called back and apologized for being upset. He asked me how we could correct this situation. I came up with a solution and he is still doing business with us. This might not have been the result if I had not been able to control my attitude with him."

SELLING SKILLS

When was the last time you had the oil changed in your car? Why did you do it? What happens if you don't change the oil? Will your car continue to run properly? Or will you risk having more problems down the road by skipping this simple bit of routine maintenance?

The answers to those questions are fairly obvious. Most of us can relate to the reasons why we change the oil in our cars. Yet, we don't often recognize the importance of performing a little routine maintenance on our own selling skills.

Because the selling environment continues to change rapidly, the product peddler of the past is no longer acceptable. Today, we must understand technology, use electronic contact management systems, and have an innate ability to develop and deliver viable solutions. All the while, we must also provide after-sale service and maintain customer relationships.

Just as our car might break down if we don't change the oil, we risk that our sales career might run into problems over the long term if we aren't committed to continually improving our selling skills.

COMMUNICATION SKILLS

What happens if we have the right solution for a customer, but we don't communicate it effectively? We risk losing the relationship. That's why the ability to communicate through diverse media is a skill that successful sales professionals must possess. Increased limits on our customers' time usually means they spend less time talking with us, and for that reason, it is imperative that we know how to communicate clearly and concisely.

ORGANIZATIONAL SKILLS

Most of us are being asked to do more with less. With that in mind, the ability to do multiple tasks in one day—and do them efficiently—is an absolute must for today's salesperson. This not only means we know how to organize our time well, it also means maintaining an effective contact management system. If customers call with questions and we can't readily locate information about their business, we might damage our credibility. What's more, for salespeople who travel, being organized on the road is often a matter of survival. Regardless of where they are, whether it's behind a desk or in the airport with a briefcase, they must have a solid and predictable process in place to handle customer communications and concerns.

PEOPLE SKILLS

Strong people skills go hand in hand with creating an atmosphere of trust and respect with customers, and that's a critical component of building lasting business relationships. Successful sales professionals realize that selling is about people and problem solving, not about pushing products.

Carl Ross, founder and former president of Lynx Golf Company, relates a story about using his people skills to exceed the expectations of an angry customer.

"I got a call one day from one of my customers, a golf pro, who had just received a box of four clubs he had ordered. Only, instead of getting four right-handed clubs as he had requested, we had sent him two right-handed clubs and two left-handed clubs. I was surprised we had done this, because we're very careful in our quality control. However, I verified with my customer that this was, indeed, the case. So I went to the factory personally, got him four right-handed clubs, and mailed them immediately, along with a couple dozen golf balls. I told him to just send me the other clubs when he had a chance and gave him my private phone number in case he had any future problems.

"That golf pro is my buddy now, and it's because of the relationship I sought to have with him. I didn't let his problem fester for six weeks. I didn't pass the problem to someone else and say, 'You take care of it.' I took personal responsibility for my customer's satisfaction. I'll make sure that a second mistake never happens. My solution may seem obvious, but I'm surprised at the number of salespeople who don't want to solve problems for their customers."

Carl's ability to build relationships comes naturally to him. For others of us, it requires a little more work on our people skills. Sometimes, we need to get out of our comfort zone and look for ways to be more customer-focused.

The Sales Advantage gives us those kinds of tools. And our ultimate success is determined by the commitment we have to using the appropriate tools in every selling situation.

You could be selling complex telecommunication solutions to a large company in Melbourne, Australia, or to the United States federal government in Washington, D.C. Perhaps you're selling Internet/intranet systems for a multinational company based in Manchester, England, or Taipei, Taiwan. Maybe you're a financial advisor in Mexico City, Mexico, or a staffing consultant in Brussels, Belgium. Or possibly you own your own website development business in a small town outside of Paris, France. Wherever you are and whatever you sell, understanding the buying and selling process can help improve your people skills and make an impact in your customer relationships. The key is, you can't be afraid to try new things.

Dale Carnegie said, "The difference between a successful person and a failure often lies in the fact that the successful man will profit by his mistakes and try again in a different way."

By using the Sales Advantage to your advantage, you can become more successful. Even if you make mistakes along the way, don't dwell on them. Learn from them and move forward. If you do, you'll discover a whole new world of selling—one that excites you, energizes you, and puts you in control of your own destiny.

CHAPTER 1

New Opportunities
Finding Prospects

> Hard work alone will accomplish remarkable results. But hard work
> with a method and system will perform seeming miracles. No one can
> profit more by a realization of these truths than the person who sells
> for a living.
>
> —W. C. HOLMAN

For most salespeople, prospecting is a task that's greeted with very
little enthusiasm. Why? Because it usually takes place behind a
desk, at a computer, or somewhere else that's not in front of our
customers.

Of course, we all know that prospecting is to sales what seeds are to
a garden. If we don't plant seeds, we won't get flowers. And the more
seeds we plant, the more flowers we get. The same is true when it comes
to the relationship between new selling opportunities and satisfied customers. Without prospects, we won't have customer relationships.
That's why prospecting is so crucial for our success.

WHY WE DON'T PROSPECT

If we all agree that prospecting is important, why do we tend to make it
a low priority?

Fear is one factor. When salespeople don't have a good system of
prospecting and merely view it as cold calling, they're often faced with
rejection. And it stands to reason, the more times we get rejected, the
harder it becomes to start prospecting all over again.

Another issue is often the value we place on the time we spend
prospecting. If we leave the office one afternoon to go to the library and

research electronic databases, it may feel as if we're neglecting elements of our job that have a seemingly higher priority, especially if our efforts turn up very few legitimate leads.

Still another reason we might avoid prospecting is our perception that we're intruding on someone's time. Often, when we look for new opportunities, we must do some networking to gain information about potential business contacts. We know many of the people we're calling are busy. So, we convince ourselves that they don't really welcome our interruption when, in fact, that may not be true.

For many of us, prospecting is really hit-and-miss at best. Sometimes we're successful, and sometimes we're not. That's why it can be so frustrating. But in reality, a true system of prospecting creates a set of tools we can use to build a pipeline of new opportunities straight to our door. That's right—a good prospecting system brings customers to us.

CHANGING OUR VIEW OF PROSPECTING

For top sales performers in all industries, prospecting for new opportunities is actually fun. It's a treasure hunt—an adventure that ultimately leads to the pot of gold at the end of the rainbow. Why do they view it that way? They've acquired the skills to make prospecting more efficient and productive.

Tips for Overcoming Prospecting/Call Reluctance

Add Some Pep to Your Prospecting

Most sales professionals would rather do anything than prospect. But the fact remains, the more prospecting we do, the more customer relationships we'll have. Here's how to stay energized about prospecting.

1. Give yourself a pep talk.

Sell the idea of prospecting to yourself. Affirm that you are eager to meet more prospects because that will lead you to more sales. Don't expect to feel better after just one pep talk. You may have to resell yourself five to ten times a day until your subconscious mind takes over and does the job for you.

2. Set a goal and force yourself to work toward it.

The unsolved problem of all time is how to make ourselves do what we know we ought to do. So don't worry about beginning to make more contacts. Don't put it off. Just do it. Help yourself by setting a manageable goal. For example, depending on your situation, you might set a goal to make five more contacts per week. Think about it: After one year, you've made over two hundred more connections to potential customers, simply by making a few more calls each week. Or set a goal of attending one community or business function each month and meeting five new people at each event. By the end of the year, you've met about sixty new people. How many more customer relationships will that bring your way?

3. Stop making excuses.

It's likely that we've all used reasons such as these at some point in our career: "I can't do any prospecting on Friday afternoon, no one's there. It's no use to find new opportunities in July and August because everyone's on vacation. I can't make phone calls on rainy days, no one's in the mood to hear me." We need to stop rationalizing our inactivity.

4. Overcome the fear of wearing yourself out.

If some salespeople survive one hundred calls a day, it's possible to survive ten more a day, or whatever is realistic in your business.

Author Ralph Waldo Emerson said: "Do the thing you fear, and the death of fear is certain." In other words, if we acquire the necessary skills and make a commitment to prospecting consistently, any fear we have about it will most likely disappear. Then we improve the odds that we'll increase our sales, because we'll have enough leads to avoid the selling slumps that most average salespeople experience.

Think of it this way: If we are learning to play a musical instrument for the first time, it probably won't be much fun at first. But once we start improving, we start liking it more. Instead of dreading the practice time, we begin viewing it as relaxing and enjoyable.

For most of us, prospecting will probably never be as much fun as strumming a guitar or playing a piano. But when we see how an increase in prospecting results in more customer relationships and higher income, we'll see it in a whole new light.

In today's selling environment, the quality of each opportunity tends to be more important than the quantity of opportunities. Still, it makes sense that the more prospects we have, the more customers we can ultimately help.

A timeless classic, *The 5 Great Rules of Selling*, validates this theory. Author Percy Whiting reports that one organization, when faced with a shutdown, challenged its sales force to contact ten extra prospects each day. Ten percent of those calls resulted in so many sales that, instead of shutting down, the factory went into twenty-four-hour production.

Where to Find New Opportunities

There are many people who can benefit from our products or services. Yet not all of them are customers. Why? Sometimes, it's because we don't know about them. Other times, it's because they don't know about us. The idea behind prospecting is to find those people who can benefit from what we have to offer—no matter where they are or who they're currently doing business with.

The following are some ways to find new opportunities and generate leads. Not all of them may apply to your particular product or service, but that doesn't mean you should ignore them. Remember: Top sales performers are open to all ideas for getting new opportunities. They try as many as possible. So add these to your list. Most likely you will discover a whole new realm of possibilities you never considered.

EXISTING CUSTOMERS

Often, our best new opportunities for increasing business start with satisfied customers. Unfortunately, we tend to spend most of our prospecting time knocking on doors of people who don't know us or our company. Why? We typically convince ourselves that calling existing customers is not an important part of prospecting.

When it comes to current customers, we tend to assume that they know everything about what we have to offer. After all, they have our brochures and we've told them about our full range of products and services. But when we take for granted that current customers will remember everything about our company, we aren't showing them the same courtesy we would show to new customers. That leaves the door open to the competition. How? Well, ask yourself this question: What if our competitor comes in and uncovers a need that we don't know about, because we took for granted that the customer would call us if the need arose? What potentially happens to our good account?

Why not help our customers—and help ourselves at the same time—by using a tool called the opportunity chart? Simply, the opportunity chart helps us graphically depict the truth about our relationship with each of our existing customers, as well as past customers we've lost over time. In turn, we can identify new opportunities within those particular accounts. Complete an opportunity chart like the one on the next page for your current accounts. You'll almost certainly find selling opportunities.

The opportunity chart method works no matter how long you've been in sales. If you're new in sales or have changed jobs, completing an opportunity chart before an introductory call is an effective way to familiarize yourself with the customers in your territory. For more experienced sales professionals, the chart forces you to think creatively about accounts you've been serving for years. While the opportunity chart doesn't work for all businesses, it will work for most.

Robert Priganc, a financial advisor with the Mony Group in Pittsburgh, Pennsylvania, uses the opportunity chart successfully in offering additional financial products to his existing customers.

"It's always challenging for me to make my clients aware of all the products and services we offer. In fact, since they aren't aware of them, I find out that many of them are purchasing these products from our competitors.

"So I list all the products and services we offer. I photocopy the list many times. Then before making calls, I write my client's name on a chart and review it. I look at what they're already buying and what additional products and ideas might be helpful.

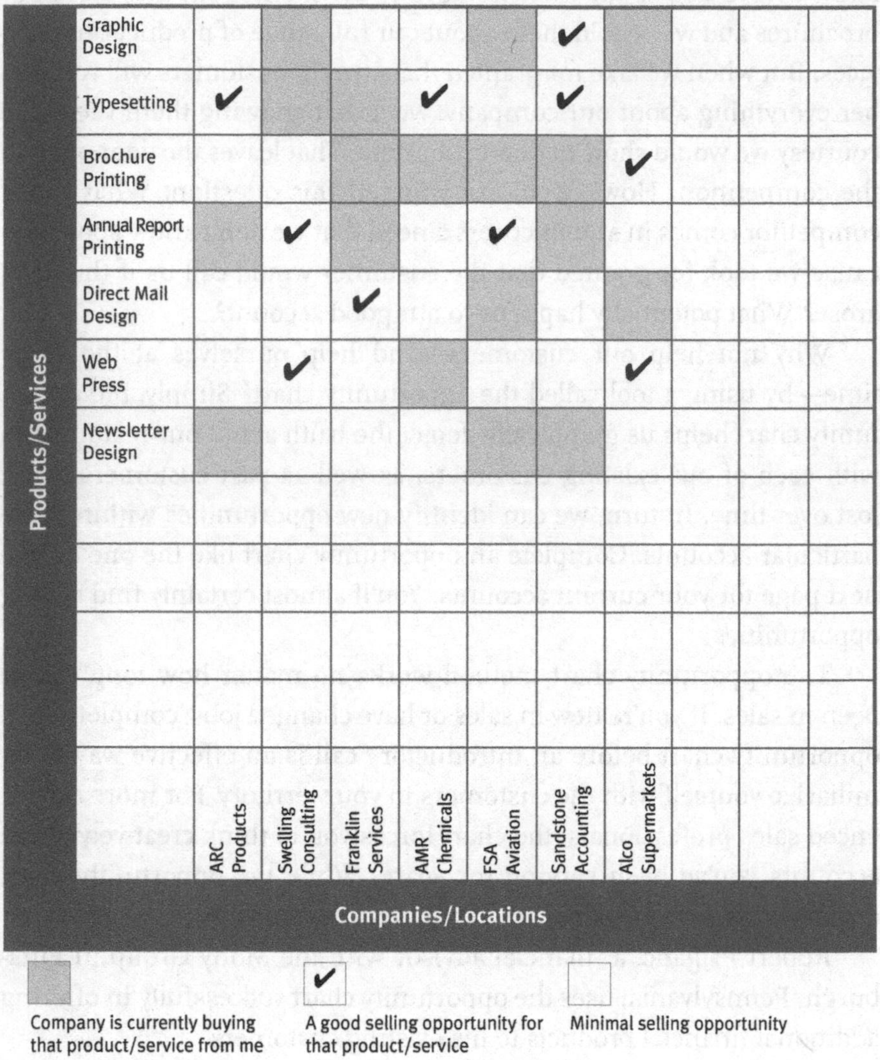

Products/Services	ARC Products	Swelling Consulting	Franklin Services	AMR Chemicals	FSA Aviation	Sandstone Accounting	Alco Supermarkets
Graphic Design						✔	
Typesetting	✔			✔		✔	
Brochure Printing							✔
Annual Report Printing		✔			✔		
Direct Mail Design			✔				
Web Press		✔					✔
Newsletter Design							

Companies/Locations

- ▨ Company is currently buying that product/service from me
- ✔ A good selling opportunity for that product/service
- ☐ Minimal selling opportunity

Figure 1: The Opportunity Chart

"In one particular situation, I was managing a customer's life insurance and retirement account. I noticed he didn't have disability coverage. Knowing he was the type of person who really cared about his family's well-being, I brought this to his attention. He agreed it was a smart idea and appreciated my concern about the situation.

"I really do care about making sure my customers are prepared for the future. By using the opportunity chart, I have a systematic way to know what products a customer might need. It's also been fun to see how my sales have increased as a result."

Robert's example demonstrates why increasing account penetration can be so effective. After all, the relationships are already in place. In environments where large capital is involved, the cost structures are often in place. We're dealing with a known entity. And we know the customer is financially reliable. So not only do we enhance our customer relationships, we typically see a more immediate impact on our own company's bottom line.

Remember, we can't expect our customers to buy what they don't know we offer. So let's help them out. And let's not give business away to our competitors because we're taking our customers for granted. The more products and services our clients depend on us to deliver, the less likely it is they will consider buying from the competition.

There are countless ways in which opportunity charts can be used throughout the sales process. You can use it in your pre-approach with new prospects. You can adapt it for re-entry into lost or neglected accounts. Some sales managers even revise it and use it to track the performance of their salespeople. The point is, the uses for the opportunity chart are limited only by your creativity. If you can find a way to take advantage of this powerful tool, do it.

DEVELOP CHAMPIONS

Champions in existing accounts also can be valuable resources for new business opportunities. Typically, a good champion is someone in an existing account who is well respected within the company and among peers. He or she is articulate and dynamic and understands what makes your products or services effective. Champions may not always have decision-making authority, but they can influence a buying decision or help us meet key decision-makers.

Andrew Winter, business development manager for Ignition Group in Toronto, Ontario, Canada, prospects daily. His main responsibility is to develop new business for Ignition Group.

Throughout his career, Andrew has worked with champions to help link him to new business opportunities.

"In one case, I had built a strong rapport with a customer at a division office in St. Louis, Missouri, by offering a high level of service from initial order through to completion.

"As the result of the trust we developed and our strong business relationship, this customer eventually became my friend. In turn, he became my champion. He spoke highly of our services to his Chicago, Illinois, Dallas, Texas, and Atlanta, Georgia, offices. Most important, he talked to the corporate office in San Francisco, California. Thanks to his help, I was able to increase sales to all divisions of his company, including the corporate office. In a six-month time frame, sales to this customer grew from thirty to eight hundred thousand dollars.

"My champion then moved from St. Louis to Chicago. Although we were already in business discussions with the Chicago office, we had been talking to a different marketing manager. As a result of my champion's transfer, we had the opportunity to do twice the business in the Chicago office. In addition, I am still working with his original division. Had I not had this relationship, it would've been more difficult to keep the business going after my client moved.

"Never underestimate the power of rapport and trust, because that's the first step in finding a champion. Our goals should always include the establishment of a quality relationship with our customers; a relationship built on honesty and integrity. Then, no matter what happens, whether they get transferred or their company merges with another, we are in a much better position to continue the business relationship. If we respect them as people first and customers second, they will return that respect tenfold, or in this case, 280-fold."

ASK FOR MORE REFERRALS

While champions take it upon themselves to promote our company, referrals typically require us to take the initiative in asking for additional business contacts. Even though referrals are one of the most powerful door openers, most salespeople don't use them. Why? For a variety of reasons: 1) We're afraid to ask; 2) we feel we don't have a good enough relationship to ask; 3) we're not confident in ourselves or our product; and 4) we simply forget.

Normally, it's most effective to ask for referrals after we've developed rapport with a prospect or after we've established a trusting business relationship with a customer.

There are cases, however, when it makes sense to ask for referrals early on in the sales discussion. This depends largely on the type of products and services we sell. Keep in mind, we should only ask for referrals right away if we are confident that our prospect is feeling good about the interaction. We can never take for granted that a prospect will automatically provide us with referral information just because we showed up for a meeting or made a phone call.

During his securities sales career, Dale Carnegie and Associates' vice chairman Ollie Crom had a way to remind himself to ask for referrals. On the underside of his briefcase, he attached four raised letters: AFAR. Every time he finished a sales call, he reached down and felt these four letters. Then, if the timing was appropriate, he remembered to "Ask For A Referral." We'll cover referrals in more detail in the follow-up element of selling.

USE LISTS

In many situations, our company will provide us with lists of current and past customers. A word of caution: Don't assume the lists are up-to-date unless you've discovered for yourself that they are.

As experienced sales professionals will testify, it's not uncommon to have deceased people listed as key contacts, or addresses and phone numbers that no longer exist. If you are fortunate enough to have an assistant, it's a good idea to have that person update the list for you. If you're on your own, you can always phone the specific company and try an introduction similar to this: "I need some help. I'm updating my mailing list and want to make sure I get the right information to the right person in your company." Most receptionists are happy to oblige or will connect you with the person who can help you. Then, you can proceed with verifying the information and using it as part of your pre-approach, which we discuss in the next chapter.

Finding New Opportunities

Existing Customers
- New products/projects with current customers (opportunity chart)
- Champions
- Referrals
- Lists

New Customers
- Drive time
- Building directories
- Telephone directories
- Community organizations
- Chambers of Commerce
- Business/social functions
- Trade shows
- Alternate calls
- Industry leads in publications
- The Internet
- Personal referral networks

NEW CUSTOMERS

As we mentioned at the beginning of this chapter, finding new opportunities through existing customers is usually the best way to spend our time prospecting. But the fact remains that new business is also an important part of most sales strategies.

Finding opportunities with brand-new customers often presents the biggest challenge for most salespeople. Without a system of generating leads, we have a tendency to view new-customer prospecting as nothing more than cold calling. Of course, in most sales jobs, there's no avoiding the cold call, whether it's in person or on the phone. Later in this book, we've dedicated a whole section to telephone skills. And in the next chapter, we'll be learning about pre-approach methods. Together, these skills will help you turn cold calls into "warm" calls and ultimately make your new-business prospecting time more rewarding.

Prospecting for new customers is a lot more than picking up the phone or knocking on doors. With a little creativity and planning, we can use a variety of tools to ensure that our time spent prospecting is effective and productive.

USE DRIVE TIME AS A PROSPECTING TOOL

For some sales professionals, prospecting for new customers is as simple as driving down the street.

Some people like to keep voice-activated tape recorders in their cars, or leave themselves voice mail, to make verbal notes of companies they see driving to and from appointments. Still others like to vary their routes, so they increase the possibilities of discovering new businesses in an area they previously hadn't seen.

Often, the advertisements we see and hear while on the road can provide potential prospects. For example, if you sell radio advertising, listening to stations besides your own can let you know firsthand what companies are buying airtime on other stations. In fact, no matter what you sell, radio ads can alert you to new and existing businesses in the area that may have a need for your products or services. The same theory applies to billboard advertising. One salesperson even reports getting leads from company information printed on the sides of trucks and delivery vans. Whatever the case, simply keeping your eyes and ears open to your surroundings can make a huge difference in your prospecting efforts.

CONSULT BUILDING DIRECTORIES

Often, a few minutes spent in the lobby of an office building can result in solid sales opportunities.

Jeff Hanlon, a sales professional in Phoenix, Arizona, used this approach to secure a long-term contract with a new customer. "After a sales call at a large state government agency, I noticed a directory of other state agencies in the building. An unlikely prospect was the Board of Funeral Directors and Embalmers. No one from our industry ever thought to contact them or even knew they existed. Knowing that government agencies have similar needs and procurement processes, I saw this as a potential opportunity.

"After asking some questions and identifying the need, we delivered the solution to their situation. This relationship led to additional referrals within the state government. I would have never known this agency existed had I not stopped for thirty seconds to look for new opportunities on the building directory."

LOOK THROUGH TELEPHONE DIRECTORIES

Whether we have a local territory or we fly across the ocean to conduct business, telephone directories provide a great resource, especially if we want to do business with smaller companies that may not be on the Internet or listed in industry publications.

We also can use our computer to investigate some of the online phone directories on the Internet. Many of them allow us to search by industry category within a specific city. We never know what might turn up in just a few minutes of browsing.

BECOME ACTIVE IN COMMUNITY ORGANIZATIONS

Professional salespeople become successful through building strong relationships. Getting involved in community activities sends a clear message that we care about more than just making a sale.

Peter Legge, president and publisher of Canada-wide Magazines and Communications Ltd., believes that community involvement is essential on the part of the successful salesperson.

"I think it is absolutely mandatory that, if you're looking for any kind of success in business, you should put something back into the community. You may not have the money to put into the community, but you can make the time if you really try. I believe in the ancient law of sowing and reaping: The more you sow, the more you reap. Frankly, I get involved because I love doing it. And I've noticed, the more I do, the more it comes back to me in a positive way."

Bill Bertolet, a Dale Carnegie sponsor in southern New Jersey, became the general campaign chairman for his community's United Way. His involvement throughout the year with 220 volunteers led to a more productive workplace charitable effort.

After a year's worth of work, Bill's record-breaking results earned him a great deal of publicity and media coverage. On a subsequent sales call, the prospect brought up Bill's accomplishments. By discussing their common interest in the United Way, they formed an immediate bond that led to a stronger relationship. Bill found that asking for the prospect's commitment was easier due to his charitable work.

CHAMBERS OF COMMERCE

Ted Owen, president and publisher of the *San Diego Business Journal*, became involved in his Chamber of Commerce when he made the transition from military to civilian life. In so doing, he established relationships within the business community at the very highest level. When Ted decided to go into business for himself, these contacts were invaluable.

Ollie Crom also found the Chamber of Commerce a worthwhile association early in his career as a securities salesman. When he moved to Alliance, Nebraska, he immediately visited the chamber. When he asked about projects that needed volunteer support, the chamber director put him to work. Ollie's job? Personally contacting thirty influential people in the community who had contributed to an industrial development project. These introductions proved a tremendous source of clients and, ultimately, more referrals for Ollie.

Networking Guidelines

- Always offer to help. End every meeting or phone call with, "What can I do to help you?"
- Share your unique abilities and knowledge with others.
- Share your own contacts and network with others.
- Be approachable and be yourself.
- Follow through on commitments.
- Write personal thank-you notes.

ATTEND BUSINESS/SOCIAL FUNCTIONS

Sometimes, we'll find appropriate events in the newspaper or hear about them on the television or radio. However, if you're Baek Sook

Hyun, you create your own. In fact, Sook Hyun—a top salesperson with Daewoo Electronics in Korea—is known for sponsoring events and clubs that bring people together. People come to her events and get to know her. When they need the products she sells, they buy from her.

For example, she once organized a club for taxi drivers because, in Korea, taxi drivers work two days and then take one day off. She understood their lifestyle pattern made it difficult to make friends easily. So she organized clubs focused on activities such as mountain climbing, soccer, football, and badminton. Through these clubs, they got to know her as a person, as well as a businessperson.

The company's reputation grew as Sook Hyun's reputation grew. Customers gave her numerous referrals. In fact, she organized so many clubs she ultimately had about eighty events per year.

Sook Hyun's schedule is very ambitious, but it shows what we can do if we get creative. Even if we try just one or two events, it might make a difference. For example, what about putting together a tennis league or golf tournament? What about organizing a charity event for a nonprofit group that's important to you? No matter what you decide, sponsoring events is a great way to turn a passion into new business opportunities.

Networking Rule

To be successful in sales, it's not really who you know. It's who wants to know you.

When it comes to attending business functions organized by someone else, consider finding a unique way to separate your product or service from the others. Randall K. Huntimer, certified financial planner and vice president of a financial planning firm, found a creative way to stand out from the crowd.

"I came across this approach by accident. I got into an elevator and recognized someone I knew. On the way up to the meeting, we began talking. We didn't have time to finish our conversation, so we pushed the button to go back down. We continued to ride the elevator while people got on and off. After a number of trips and conversations, people noticed I was still on the elevator.

"I realized then this was a great opportunity to meet just about everyone attending the event. People couldn't help but notice the 'elevator operator.' It became a great conversation-starter. After spending two hours in the elevators, the contacts I made represented about 10 percent of my new business that year. This was the most profitable and fun event I've ever attended."

GO TO TRADE SHOWS

Although trade shows are a viable, effective way to find new opportunities, they also present some challenges. Companies spend thousands of dollars on exhibits and brochures, yet it's often difficult to set us apart from everyone else. Not only that, salespeople often wait for people to come to them.

For those reasons, it is important to do something different. Consider putting your brochures at the back of your booth so prospects have to pass by you to pick one up. Engage your prospects with creative attention-getters at the front of the booth. Offer maps to help people find their way around. Try to do something unique to get their attention.

Also, if your company does not exhibit at every trade show, consider attending as a participant instead. This gives you an opportunity to walk the aisles and circulate to different booths. In addition to making new contacts, you may be able to learn more about your competition in the process.

MAKE ALTERNATE CALLS

It's our first appointment of the morning. We get to our destination, only to discover that the people we are supposed to see aren't available to see us. Then what? There we sit, thirty minutes from our office, two hours from our home, or one hour from the airport. What do we do now?

That's when we have an opportunity to make an alternate call—contact with someone in the vicinity who might have a use for our product or service. In some sales situations, making alternate calls simply means knocking on the next door or visiting the next office building. In others, it means using the telephone and calling other prospects in the area.

A Peoria, Illinois, salesperson makes it a habit to call on the businesses on either side of an appointment he just conducted. "I simply mention that I was next door and I thought they might like to take advantage of the same opportunity as their neighbor. I figure if I have five appointments every day, I make ten new contacts every day. That means five hundred contacts each year for no additional expense."

FOLLOW INDUSTRY LEADS IN PUBLICATIONS

These include:

- Newspapers
- Magazine articles and advertisements
- Trade journals
- New business licenses
- Departments of Commerce

TAKE ADVANTAGE OF THE INTERNET

Many online resources provide an incredible amount of information regarding potential customers from all over the world. You may have to pay for some information you download, but the time you save is most likely worth it. Or you might try using your favorite search engine and type in keywords, such as "sales leads."

Company websites can also be a great source for contact information. Often, home pages might contain business wires, stock updates, message boards, and access to user groups—all of which can be great resources. Many company Internet sites also contain links to suppliers, strategic alliances, and maybe even competitors. In some cases, they allow us to do a real-time search of similar industries.

Depending on the product or service you sell, you may want to set aside a certain amount of time for Internet prospecting each month. In fact, it's a good idea to set a maximum amount of time for Internet research as well. After all, the Internet contains vast amounts of information. If we're not careful, it's easy to get distracted. At that point, one hour of prospecting potentially turns into several hours of unproductive time.

BUILD A PERSONAL REFERRAL NETWORK

Networking among business acquaintances and friends is one of the most effective ways to meet people who might need our products or services. A personal referral network can consist of relatives, doctors, lawyers, accountants, neighbors, hairdressers, and your local grocer— you name it. Everyone with whom we come in frequent contact should know something about how we add value to our customers.

For example, how many times have you referred people to your doctor, dentist, mechanic, insurance agent, or attorney? Yet how many referrals have you received from them? If you're not getting referrals from these people in your life, it might be because they don't know enough about what you do for a living.

Keep in mind, a personal referral network is different from a group of champions. Champions are people within existing accounts who may or may not be our personal friends. The people in our personal referral network most likely do not use our products or services, but might know of others who would.

This prospecting method requires no time or energy. Educating people on what we do should be a normal part of our conversation. Over the long term, having a group of people who want to introduce us to their friends and business acquaintances can unlock many doors that might otherwise be closed.

In business-to-business sales, we don't necessarily need to have years of experience to use a personal referral network. Say, for example, we have twenty target companies with which we'd like to do business, but we don't have contact names. Why not make a note of these companies, show that document to our friends or business acquaintances, and see if they know anyone in these target organizations?

In business-to-consumer sales, where we're selling directly to the end user, our personal referral network may be our lifeline. Maybe we're selling something like vacation packages, computers, or wireless phones. Whatever the case, our friends and acquaintances are the perfect candidates to refer business our way.

Personal referral networks are also critical for entrepreneurs, especially those in consulting roles. Most small business owners and self-employed people find it difficult to market their products and make money at the same time. It's much more productive for them to have a personal network of people referring business their way.

MANAGING OUR CONTACTS

One of the most valuable assets we have is our contact list. Building and maintaining relationships throughout the sales development process requires us to keep an accurate record of events, actions, comments, and expectations of prospects, our customers, and us. Maintaining those records in a system that is accurate and accessible is critical to the long-term customer relationship. Why?

When a customer calls, our ability to readily access information about past conversations demonstrates competence and shows that we place a high priority on customer issues. What's more, the accuracy of the information gives customers added confidence that we are organized enough to manage their business and follow through on our solutions.

Traditional approaches to contact management primarily have been paper-based. They consist of personal organizers, tickler files, and even note cards. As many salespeople will testify, finding information in paper-based systems is both difficult and time-consuming.

On the other hand, personal information managers, such as Palm Pilots, can keep records of the same kind of information electronically. They help us organize information such as appointments, goals, and addresses. However, they provide little integration of this information. In other words, while these methods may store some of the things we need, the information is not typically linked to our contacts. For that reason, both personal information managers and paper-based systems lack the flexibility and features of a true contact manager.

Electronic contact managers, which are typically software packages, are designed specifically for relationship-driven professionals who need to manage day-to-day contact information in an individual or small-group environment. They provide fast and easy access to prospect and customer information, providing an excellent solution for people who work with outside contacts and have the need to track all of their communications.

A contact manager ensures a constant flow of accurate information by managing all tasks and information related to developing and maintaining customer relations. It also provides complete and comprehensive tracking of all customer and prospect information, including meetings, phone calls, correspondence, and notes.

Contact managers automate and streamline routine communication and reporting activities, as well as the activities required to find and target new prospects and ensure the satisfaction of current customers. They minimize the time spent on routine administrative tasks, increasing a sales professional's effectiveness in building business relationships. Sales professionals become more effective in managing relationships and interactions with customers, clients, and business partners through the use of these tools.

AVOID THE SLUMPS: COMMIT TO PROSPECTING

No matter how we choose to prospect for new opportunities, it's essential to do something we've never done before. It's also important to use more than one method. If we depend too much on one system of prospecting, we risk not having a continuous pipeline of opportunities. For example, if we only rely on customer lists and trade shows, we ignore the possibilities that exist elsewhere. Then, when the list runs out and the trade shows aren't happening, we aren't prospecting. The result? Our activity slows down because we aren't generating enough potential opportunities by prospecting to keep creating satisfied customers.

CHAPTER 2

Pre-approach
Doing Our Homework

> Now, let's see. We've been together ten minutes. I can tell that you know
> nothing about me, my company, our products, our competition, our
> market or our challenges. What was it you were trying to sell me again?
>
> —A BUYER'S POINT OF VIEW

I f we all agree that we are living in the information age, then why do
many salespeople choose to remain uninformed when they approach
potential customers? And why do we have a tendency to move directly from finding new opportunities into the sales discussion without
taking time to learn about our prospect's basic wants and needs?

We all have different answers to those questions based on our individual situations. But there's really no answer that provides a good
enough excuse for ignoring pre-approach. The sooner we develop a consistent strategy for pre-approach and start valuing what it brings to the
business relationship, the better we can serve our customers.

Why We Ignore Pre-approach

Overeager to gain commitment

Inadequate training

Don't know where to get information about the prospect's needs and
  wants

Complacency

Don't view it as important part of sales planning

Can't find enough time

WHAT IS PRE-APPROACH?

Pre-approach is the next logical and necessary action after we've identified our new opportunities. At this point, we need to 1) determine which opportunities represent true prospects, 2) gather information that allows us to talk in terms of the prospect's interests once we initiate communication, and 3) develop a plan for our first contact. Effective pre-approach improves the odds that we're calling a qualified prospect and that we'll successfully schedule a meeting with that person.

Pre-approach is a lot more than research—it shows consideration for our prospects. It's preparing a clear and concise message for phone calls and letters. It's knowing the name of the person we're going to contact, not just the job title. It's about understanding the prospect's industry. What's more, pre-approach provides us with valuable knowledge we might use later in the sales process. For example, we can use pre-approach information when we're creating a meeting agenda, building credibility, developing solutions, and even handling objections.

In some respects, approaching a business relationship without pre-approach is much like going on a blind date: We won't know what to expect when we go to the door. On the other hand, if we have done pre-approach, we will minimize surprises and help ensure that time with a prospect is time well spent for both of us.

PRE-APPROACH PREPARES US FOR THE INITIAL COMMUNICATION

Many salespeople are inclined to think of pre-approach as part of the sales call. But remember, this is one of the three steps leading up to our first interview. At this point, we've only identified an opportunity. We have little, if any, information about the prospect's wants and needs. And we haven't even determined if and when the person will talk to us.

It's helpful to view pre-approach as a way to improve the chance that our initial communication will be successful. How? If we've done our homework, we increase our chances of talking directly to the decision-maker, which usually increases our chances for a meeting. What's more, effective pre-approach helps us prepare our initial conversations in a way that gets the prospect's attention and sets us apart from the competition.

Look at it this way: We're telephoning one of our ideal prospects. We finally get her on the line, rather than voice mail, after many attempts. But in the first fifteen seconds of our conversation, we fail to grab her attention. We aren't clear in the purpose of our call. Even if we are, we aren't sure what questions to ask because we don't know much about her company. What happens? We resort to talking about our products and our company, just like virtually every other salesperson.

An effective pre-approach before we begin initial communication with a person earns us the right to initiate conversation, as opposed to just calling for the sake of calling.

PRE-APPROACH SAVES US FROM MAKING MISTAKES

A strong pre-approach strategy helps us avoid embarrassing situations. While the following story is not a business example, we can use a simple analogy about gift giving to illustrate how pre-approach helps us be more successful.

Let's say your coworkers nominate you to buy a holiday gift for your boss. You're in a pinch to make year-end numbers and you're working hard to gain as many last-minute commitments as possible. To save time, you get on the Internet, find an online gift company, and arrange for an extravagant box of chocolates to be delivered in time for the office party.

The box arrives beautifully wrapped and you're excited about giving it. But right before the party, in a casual discussion with a coworker, you learn that your boss is highly allergic to chocolate. So even though you were successful in accomplishing your task of buying the gift, the end result wasn't successful.

The same goes for pre-approach. Pre-approach is not about giving gifts and boxes of chocolate, but it is about knowing something about our prospects' needs and wants before we ask for their valuable time.

Certainly, by doing a little homework, we can avoid the mistakes many salespeople make. We often hear about salespeople who assume a prospect's gender based on the name alone. Or the ones who start calling people on an outdated contact list, only to discover that one or more of them is deceased. Granted, most people are forgiving in these situations. But even so, there's no way to hide the fact that we haven't prepared.

Mike McClain, a sales professional in Ohio, recalls a customer and human resources manager known as "JW." By choice, JW did not use periods between the initials. If he received a letter addressed to "J.W." he wouldn't open it. And if someone telephoned and asked for him by any name other than JW, he wouldn't accept the call. He wasn't trying to be rude. He just wanted to work with people who cared enough to know his preferred name.

Here's another mistake pre-approach helps us avoid: Have you ever had a meeting with someone who, after twenty minutes or so, reveals that he is not the decision-maker? When this happens, we have to find a tactful way to tell this person that he's not the person with whom we want to speak. In other words, we make the person on the other side of the desk pay for our lack of preparation.

PRE-APPROACH HELPS US QUALIFY PROSPECTS

Not all prospects are alike. That's another reason why we need pre-approach. In this part of the sales process, we can determine which opportunities have the highest probability for success. That way, we won't spend hours of our valuable time trying to interest so-called prospects who aren't really prospects at all. In turn, we save time for our prospects, too. If they aren't qualified, we won't take up their valuable time trying to interest them in products and services they don't need.

What exactly is a qualified prospect? Someone who has a clearly defined need and the capacity with which to fill it. In other words, he or she would make a good customer for our company. It's important to understand this definition, because not everyone who needs our products is a qualified prospect.

For example, a company might want to do business with us. But if it has a bad credit history or lacks the revenue to support the investment, we may not want to do business with it.

For most of us, qualifying prospects can be a challenge. While there are no absolute characteristics for qualifying prospects, here are some guidelines for understanding the types of people you might encounter.

Known need, willing to talk. This person typically calls and requests a meeting. He might already have a specific need or solution in mind. Prospects with known needs who are willing to talk might be calling numerous suppliers and they could be price buyers.

Known need, unwilling to talk. In this scenario, we typically have learned about the prospect's need from someone else. However, he is unwilling to talk to us because he had a previous negative experience with our company or a positive experience with our competitor. In some cases, he might not want to acknowledge the need because it requires some kind of change. In this case, it's even more important to stand out from the crowd. We must have enough pre-approach information to talk in terms of his needs and wants and, hopefully, encourage meaningful conversation.

Unknown need, don't know if willing/not willing to talk. These prospects are perhaps the most challenging for salespeople. Many times, it's our own insight and experience that help us recognize a need, but we have difficulty getting the prospect to explore that need. The good news is, if we do succeed at building a relationship with this person, he typically becomes a loyal customer who also sends us referrals. Again, pre-approach information is essential in developing an initial communication that gains his attention.

No need, willing to talk. Prospects with these characteristics are usually warm and friendly. They are always open to see us and typically engage in comfortable discussion. The danger: We enjoy the warm atmosphere so much that we spend our time with people who won't ever need our products and services. That's not to say we shouldn't be cordial. But we should be careful in spending time with prospects who have no possibility of becoming customers.

Later in the selling process, there's an element called opportunity analysis. It's important not to confuse this with prospect qualification. The difference: When we qualify prospects during pre-approach, we are merely trying to determine if they have the potential to do business with us. On the other hand, in opportunity analysis, we are prioritizing prospects in terms of when we should pursue doing business with them. Both activities are important elements of a successful sales process.

PRE-APPROACH DEMONSTRATES COMPETENCE

If we had the chance to talk with professional buyers who interact with salespeople on a daily basis, we'd learn how not to approach prospects. Chances are we'd hear many stories about salespeople who make little effort to learn about the buyers or their businesses before initiating communication. This lack of effort on the salesperson's part is often perceived as incompetence by the buyer.

On the other hand, if we care enough to do our homework, our prospects are more likely to have a favorable impression. This potentially opens the door for future communications.

Rob Maxwell, a Denver, Colorado, training consultant, recalls a situation in which pre-approach demonstrated his competence and opened an important door for him.

"I wanted to meet the new president of a public service company. I found out he was coming to Denver," says Rob. "I started reading the public service employee newsletters. I saw his picture. In reading about him, I discovered he had written a book and I started reading it. Shortly thereafter, I happened to be on another appointment in the building where this man's company was located. I was walking into the lobby when the new president walked by and smiled. I recognized him from his picture on the book jacket. I walked up to him and introduced myself.

"He was pleased to be recognized. I mentioned that I had started reading his book. This piqued his interest and he was impressed that I even knew he had written a book. We started talking casually. Finally, I said, 'I know you're new here. I'd sure love to get to know you better, since I've enjoyed reading your book. Would you like to go to lunch?' "

Rob and his prospect had lunch and began a new business relationship—one that could not have happened as easily without pre-approach.

When John Hei, president of Yu-Ling Enterprises in Taiwan, was asked to give a new-product presentation to a major international company, he had only seventy-two hours to prepare. His pre-approach strategy? He gathered background information from people within his own organization by sending e-mail to other salespeople across the company. Within a few hours of sending his e-mail, he began to receive responses from around the world. As a result, he walked into the appointment prepared to talk in terms of the prospect's interests. This differentiated him from his competitors from the very beginning. He ultimately gained commitment.

PRE-APPROACH HELPS MAINTAIN OUR COURAGE

For most sales professionals, the first communication requires a lot of courage. And if the prospect doesn't demonstrate a desire to work with us, further communications require even more. But if we're armed with pre-approach information, we are prepared to talk in terms of the other person's interests. This can greatly increase our confidence, along with the chances that the prospect will eventually speak with us.

A sales representative in the medical equipment business relates how pre-approach helped her maintain confidence in pursuing a business relationship with one of her hard-to-see prospects.

"There was one particular doctor I'd been trying to see for some time, and I knew he would be a good prospect for our product. But I never got to spend very much time with him. I was lucky if he gave me five minutes on any given day. But in doing some pre-approach, I learned about a symposium the doctor had attended the week before. I brought this topic up with the doctor during my next visit with him. I started listening intently and let him do the talking. The result: I got over forty-five minutes of his time. He even came looking for me at one point and we continued our conversation. He enjoyed talking and I enjoyed listening. Since then, when I go back to the hospital, he has always given me more time than before."

For doctors and salespeople, time is money. Because this salesperson got more time with her prospect, she eventually got to tell him how her company's products could meet his specific needs. Even though her company's product is higher-priced than her competitors', she came to know his business well enough that she could demonstrate the value of buying from her company. Of course, part of that value comes from the trust that's developed between the salesperson and the customer. And it all started with pre-approach.

The method you select for pre-approach and the time it takes will vary depending upon the product or service and the prospect. It stands to reason that someone who's selling a completely new harbor development in an undeveloped part of South America will spend a lot longer on pre-approach than someone selling a new power boat in a retail showroom.

Sources for Pre-approach Information

- Annual reports
- Association offices
- Better Business Bureaus
- Chambers of Commerce
- City directories
- Company newsletters
- Company websites
- Credit bureaus
- Departments of Commerce and Industry
- Databases (such as Dun & Bradstreet)
- Internet business directories
- Magazines
- Newspapers
- News releases
- Other sales representatives/other customers
- People in the industry
- Retail merchants' associations
- Trade journals

FOUR THINGS TO LEARN ABOUT PROSPECTS
DURING PRE-APPROACH

Let's say we decide to buy some new trees and shrubs for our yard. On a whim one Saturday afternoon, we go to the nursery. We choose a few plants that we like. A few days later, we have them delivered to our home. But now what? Where are we going to plant them? Sunlight or shade? Front yard or back? How far apart? And the list goes on. Imagine how much more efficient the landscaping project would be if we had a plan from the very beginning.

Pre-approach, just like many aspects of the sales process, is more efficient and productive when we have a plan of action. Of course, the information we want to gain during pre-approach varies based on the prospect, the product or service, and the selling cycle. Here are some suggestions. Be sure you adapt this list to your individual selling situation.

1. *Get a complete and accurate record of the prospect's name, phone number, and title.* Verify this information and make sure you spell and pronounce the prospect's name correctly. You also might want to assess the value the person places on his or her title. For example, not all Ph.D.s like to be called "doctor," but some do.

2. *Determine a general idea for how the prospect would use your product or service.* To develop an effective initial communication, it's important that you have a general idea about the application of your product or service in the prospect's environment. Keep in mind, you won't necessarily be providing solutions based on this information. As you go through the sales process, you will learn to identify buying criteria and the Dominant Buying Motive—and that's what you'll use to develop a unique solution.

3. *Gauge the competition.* Does the prospect do business with a competitor? In some businesses, you may easily find this information. For example, someone who sells television adver-

tising can easily see whether a prospect advertises on a competitor's channel. In other businesses, it may be more difficult to gain this information. But do what you can to see where the competition stands. This will not only help you in approaching the prospect, it helps as you develop solutions down the line.

4. *Find out if the prospect is in a position to buy.* Someone once wisely said, "Many a sale is lost because a misinformed salesperson either underestimated or overestimated the prospect's buying intentions and purchasing power." Remember, an increase of team-based organizations means the team leader may not be the decision-maker. Nevertheless, that person can still help you gain commitment. Just be sure he can put you in touch with the appropriate people.

One of the biggest challenges of pre-approach is managing the information we gain. If we don't have pre-approach information readily available and accessible, we'll be at a disadvantage when we're competing against other salespeople who do. It's absolutely essential to have a predictable, viable, and accessible contact management system at our fingertips.

> *Failure to prepare is preparing to fail.*
> —Benjamin Franklin

PREPARING FOR THE INITIAL CONTACT

We now have a solid foundation of information. We've recorded it in our contact management system. Now what? At this point, it's a good idea to organize pre-approach information in such a way that it helps us prepare for our first letter or phone call to the prospect.

This is the final step of pre-approach, and it's rather simple if we organize it around six basic questions:

Who am I calling on?
This includes the prospect's name, position, company, and any other relevant information about her. Often, information about her industry, market, and competition is also helpful. What's more, use any information you have about who makes buying decisions. Can she make the buying decision or is she someone who can give you that information?

What are my call objectives?
Refer to the information you have about the prospect's general needs. The answer to this question should be realistic (something that can be accomplished), positive (contribute to moving the relationship ahead), and specific (saying you want to move forward isn't enough).

What issues/needs do I recognize to be selling opportunities?
Identify what challenges this person is facing. Know where her company is going and where it's been. Know her markets. The more we understand her issues and needs before we make contact, the better chance we have of taking the relationship beyond the initial communication.

What common ground or contacts might be helpful?
Think about mutual contacts or referrals you can use to break the ice. Even if you haven't been referred, you may be involved in similar community or professional organizations that provide common ground.

What commitment do I want to obtain today?
Know what you want to accomplish. This, of course, can be affected by what happens during the call. But it never hurts to plan for a possible next step. For example, do you want to set up a meeting? Do you want permission to send more information? Are you inviting the prospect to an industry event? You need to be very clear and concise about your request. If you're not clear, how can you expect her to understand what you want?

What will I say first?
Immediately tell the prospect why she should meet with you. Again, you'll need to refer to the information you have about her general needs. In the next chapter, we'll cover in detail how to construct your opening statement.

The bottom line: The primary cause of poor approach is poor pre-approach. This isn't true in every form of selling. But in most cases, unless we have some idea of our prospects' situations relative to what we're selling, we cannot set ourselves apart from the dozens of other salespeople calling them each week.

Think of what it means to our success to be different than the rest. Pre-approach is one way we demonstrate to prospects that we value their time and take their business seriously. In the end, respect opens the door to conversation and helps us learn more about how we can help our customers. From there, we're well on our way to building the foundation for a lasting business relationship that benefits both parties.

CHAPTER 3

Initial Communication
Gaining the Prospect's Attention

To succeed in sales we must overcome the inherent objections in the
mind of nearly every buyer: preoccupation, lack of interest, skepticism,
procrastination, and resistance to change. We actually begin to resolve
these objections early in the sales process by learning to see them
from a customer's point of view.

Assuming we've identified a new opportunity and spent sufficient
time on pre-approach, the next logical action in the sales process
is initiating contact with our prospects and opening the door to
further communications. Our goal is to gain favorable attention in
hopes of getting the first interview.

SHIFTING OUR FOCUS: FROM QUANTITY TO QUALITY

For most of us, getting good results from our initial communication is
one of the toughest parts of selling. We make countless phone calls. We
send numerous pieces of literature touting our new products and services. We even put our prospects on the mailing list for our company
newsletter. Yet, no matter what we do, we can't increase our response
rate. Why? Simply, we haven't done anything different to get attention.

Think about a recent phone call you made to a prospect. How did
you introduce yourself? What did you say after the introduction? What
was the person's reaction?

For many of us, regardless of what we sell, the answer to those questions is remarkably similar: "I said my name and my company name. I
spoke briefly about my product or service and asked if I could schedule
an appointment to visit. The prospect said she wasn't interested."

It's easy for us to give up at this point. Let's face it, unless we're selling an extremely popular product or service, it's often very challenging to get a prospect interested in what we have to say. This is especially true if we start our sales conversations or write letters in a way that sounds like every other salesperson out there.

This happens because we tend to put too much emphasis on the quantity of contacts we make, as opposed to the quality. We focus our energy on making a huge volume of calls and preparing nice-looking presentations, and then we hope that the sheer numbers will turn up someone who will buy. After all, sales is a numbers game, isn't it? That's what we've always been told. The more people we speak to, the more sales we'll make. Well, maybe and maybe not.

Sales will always be a numbers game to some extent. But as we'll come to understand as we study the buying and selling process, there are many things wrong with a strategy that's focused on volume alone. That's an old model of selling. In today's competitive sales environment, if we don't put the time and energy into making thoughtful contacts, we may not earn the opportunity to gain that first interview.

SHIFTING OUR FOCUS: FROM US TO THEM

Another reason why it's hard to get meetings is the tendency to emphasize our products and services too soon in the communication process. Before we have even asked questions, we're already offering solutions that may or may not fit a prospect's needs. Remember, pre-approach gives us enough information to make the initial contact. But it typically does not give us enough details to offer solutions.

Yet many of us fall into the trap of "selling" during our initial communication. That's why it's hard to stand out in the crowd. Prospects are so accustomed to this approach that every salesperson sounds alike to them. Then what happens? They turn down our request for a meeting.

In most cases, this represents a false turndown. We say "false" because, in reality, we haven't offered the customer-focused solution we would offer if we truly understood the prospect's situation.

Look at the scenario from the prospect's point of view. If she is a major decision-maker, we can bet she's always being contacted by people who are ready to offer her solutions in the first phone call or letter. So every day she goes to work, she knows she might be bombarded with salespeople wanting the one critical thing that is already in short supply—her time.

Understanding this perspective, it makes sense for us to do something different.

> *If you got in, ask yourself why and try to repeat the action. If you failed, ask yourself why and try to learn from the experience.*

THE CREDIBILITY STATEMENT: A KEY TO BEING DIFFERENT

If you look in the movie section of your local newspaper you'll see many advertisements. While they're promoting different movies, there's one thing most of these ads have in common: quotations from critics. "Two thumbs up!" reads one quotation. "A sure Oscar contender!" cries another. "Terrific performances!" screams another.

Every movie, even a bad one, has quotations from people saying how great it is. Why? What do these quotations give this movie? The answer: credibility. We see the quotations and we think to ourselves, "Other people have seen it and they loved it—maybe I will, too."

What impact would it have on us if the quotations were from the producer and director of the movie? Very little, because we expect them to say it's a good movie. After all, it's in their best interest to sell it.

In the same way, customers expect us to promote the benefits of our products and services. For that reason, the power of a third-party testimonial makes all the difference when it comes to building credibility for our companies and ourselves.

That's where the credibility statement comes in. The credibility statement takes the emphasis off us and puts it on the prospect by talking in terms of his interests. It also incorporates the experience of similar companies that have successfully used our products or services. Why does this work?

For one thing, the initial communication is no longer focused on our own opinion. Remember the movie quotations? What do you think is more effective? Telling a prospect what we think about our ability to provide solutions or what someone else has experienced?

The credibility statement is also effective because it's different from what most salespeople do. Think of it this way: How many salespeople call you and launch immediately into a presentation about their products and services? Most likely, every single one of them. And how many so-called personalized sales letters do you get in the mail that refer specifically to your wants and needs? Chances are, not very many.

Thinking of these experiences from our own point of view helps us understand why talking in terms of the other person's interests and using the experiences of our current customers will improve the odds that our initial communication will be successful.

BUILDING CREDIBILITY STATEMENTS

When we use a credibility statement, we suggest to the prospect that he might gain something by using our product or service. We then build credibility by letting him know that others like him have also benefited.

Where do we get the information to develop a credibility statement? From the experiences of our satisfied customers—and our pre-approach information. It's extremely difficult, if not impossible, to develop a credibility statement if we haven't done our homework.

The good news is, once we learn how to effectively use credibility statements in our initial communication, we can also use them in other parts of the sales process. Credibility statements can help us in working with gatekeepers and also can help us gain the prospect's attention during the first interview.

The more you use credibility statements, the simpler they become. While there is a structure to the statement, you'll eventually adapt it to a style and language that works best in your selling environment.

A good credibility statement in initial communication consists of four elements.

What we've done for other companies. Begin with benefits our company has provided other organizations relative to our prospect's business. We should avoid specific company names at this point unless we know for certain that the other person will respond favorably.

How we did it. Give an overview of how we, our company or our product or service is providing these benefits.

How we might be able to do it for the prospect. Suggest that similar benefits are possible for our prospect's company, but we need more information to make that determination. (Remember, we can't say a similar solution will work because we don't have enough information to make that claim.)

Commitment to follow-up. Conclude by moving to the logical next step (that is, asking for an appointment or asking permission to ask some questions). Simply, tell the prospect what you want.

Here's an example of an effective credibility statement we might use to begin a telephone conversation:

"There are a number of companies in Sydney that have increased their storage density by 50 percent. In fact, last year a company similar to yours increased its product storage in the same space and increased productivity of pallet moves per hour.

"They were able to accomplish this by reducing their aisle width and increasing the number of bays, which increased the number of pallets they could store.

"You might be able to achieve similar increases in storage density.

"May I schedule a meeting with you to determine whether we could provide you with the same results?"

As you can tell, an initial communication with a credibility statement is an entirely different approach from the one used by most salespeople—if it's done correctly. Here's a credibility statement that's not so effective.

"Roman and Company has been making power tools for thirty years. Our power roofing nailer has the lowest failure rate in the business. It could be the perfect tool for a remodeling contractor like you. Can I tell you more about this remarkable tool?"

Why doesn't this credibility statement work? One, it talks immediately about the salesperson's company. Two, it doesn't refer to similar companies that have had successes with Roman and Company. And

---

Electric Company, Inc.
Serving You For 30 Years

January 12, 2001

Ms. Margery Sams
Chief Operating Officer

Dear Ms. Sams:

Both the Orio and Hamilton hotels have reduced their energy
costs by up to 13% over one year as well as improving the
working environment for their employees.

Through computer modeling, they were able to create a hot
water utilization program that decreased hot water costs at their
downtown hotel in excess of 30%.

We may be able to realize similar results at Uptown Suites.

I will follow up with you on January 20 at 1:00 p.m.

Sincerely,

Gunther Heinz

Gunther Heinz
Electric Company

Figure 2: Credibility Statement

three, the final question gives the other person an opportunity to say,
"No."

To further understand the power of the last question, let's consider
a sales situation from your own perspective.

Say a financial advisor calls you. She has done effective pre-
approach and is aware that you're trying to save money toward a college
education for your child. If that person ends her credibility statement by
saying to you, "May I show you how you can invest your money with my

company's products?" she is making it easy for you to say, "No, I'm not interested."

But what if the advisor says, "Can I ask you a few questions to allow me to better understand your concerns about saving for your child's college education?" With that approach, it's a lot harder to turn her down.

The final question in both examples represents the same request: She wants to meet with you. The difference? The first example is spoken from her point of view. The second is from yours.

In this part of the Sales Advantage process, we'll discuss different methods for initiating communication, including tips on how to best use those methods. But keep in mind, no matter what approach you use, the credibility statement will most likely set you apart from virtually every other salesperson in the marketplace.

Methods of Initial Communication

- Telephone and voice mail
- Letters
- Brochures
- Samples
- Cards
- Media

Initial Communication: The Two-Step Approach

STEP 1: WRITTEN CORRESPONDENCE—FAMILIARIZE THE PROSPECT

While written communication is typically necessary at some point in the sales process, many salespeople don't like to voluntarily send prospects information before a phone call. Why? They say it gives people time to think up a good reason to decline their request for a meeting.

Sure that happens. But when it does, it's usually because the salesperson started "selling" too early or failed in some way to get the prospect's attention. That's why it's so important to write our initial correspondence in terms of the other person's interest.

Put yourself in the prospect's shoes. Pretend you're a human resources manager in a manufacturing operation. You receive a large packet of information in the mail from a professional recruiting firm highlighting their high-tech recruiting methods. The materials are accompanied by a standardized cover letter that begins, "To Whom It May Concern." What is your impression? Will you keep the information or throw it in the wastebasket?

On the other hand, what if the letter talks in terms of your interest? What if it's addressed to you by name and then talks specifically about how other organizations just like yours have enjoyed benefits from the recruiting firm's services? What if the letter then states it might be possible for your company to enjoy the same benefits?

Perhaps the introductory letter reads something like this:

"I noticed in the paper that you've been running employment ads for engineers. A company just like yours has increased its pool of highly qualified engineers by over 25 percent during the last two months in order to meet some demanding new projects.

"Our company has been able to help clients like Sturm & Associates and Greenbo Services streamline and accelerate their recruitment in this area.

"I believe we can help you achieve similar benefits in your recruiting efforts. We work with many engineers who are looking for employment and who possess the qualifications you've stated in your employment ads. By the way, it won't cost you anything.

"I'll call you on Thursday to see how this might work for you."

Now, if you are that human resources manager, are you more interested?

Keep in mind, while written communication is meant to create interest and build credibility, the primary goal is to sell an interview with the prospect—not the product or service itself.

An account manager selling mailing systems tells the story of how he established credibility via written communication and the two-step approach.

"My clients were largely nonprofit organizations at the time. I worked many of the major nonprofits, but I couldn't get into one of the biggest organizations. I was really frustrated about this, because I believed we could help them.

"So I decided to use the two-step approach, and wrote a letter to the decision-maker: 'I'm writing this letter because I can't seem to get through to you either by phone or in person. And what I have to tell you is that I have [an idea] for you I think you'll really like.' I then went on to build credibility by explaining how others had benefited from the system, how much easier it was to work, and how much it could potentially save him on a daily basis. Before I could call him, he called me.

"He said, 'Thanks for writing me that letter. I'm new here. I know you've called me several times but I get a lot of guys calling me and I just didn't know who you were. I've heard of your system. As a matter of fact one of our organizations back East says it's great. Why don't you come on out here and show it to me?'

"This turned out to be one of the biggest sales I ever made."

Bob Hanes, in selling Dale Carnegie Training programs in Indiana, also used the two-step approach quite frequently to build credibility before calling prospects. In one instance, by doing pre-approach, he found that the Detroit chapter of the United Auto Workers (UAW) did a significant amount of business with Dale Carnegie Training.

"As a result of seeing what was happening in Detroit, I decided it was time to get things started with the UAW personnel at the five General Motors plants in my territory. I made three telephone calls to the larger of the two UAW offices, attempting to set up an appointment with the president. He refused to talk with me on the telephone or to even schedule an appointment. He didn't know me, Dale Carnegie Training, or what we could do for his members. At that point, I quickly changed my strategy to the two-step approach, only I took it a couple steps further.

"Over a period of seven days, I sent him three different short notes about the benefits we were providing to a similar organization. I wrote these notes on plain white paper and sent them in plain white envelopes.

"As I recall, one note read: 'There might be a way to help your union members reduce some of their daily stress . . . is that important? The Detroit UAW/GM locals are doing this.'

"The second one read, 'There might be a way to help your members more confidently stand up to management . . . without striking. Would this be helpful? The Detroit UAW/GM locals are doing this.'

"The third one read, 'I know a proven way that might help your members get along even better with their spouses and children. Would this be helpful? The Detroit UAW/GM locals are doing this.'

"About three days after I sent the third note, I called the president's secretary and said, 'In the past seven days, I've sent three notes to your president about ways in which I feel I might be able to help your members. I would like to show him how this is being done by the UAW/GM locals in Detroit.' The secretary, who had opened the three envelopes and given the president each note, said, 'We were wondering if you were going to tell us what this was all about. He's curious to know what they are doing in Detroit.'

"The rest was easy. After seeing the president and getting his support, I put together thirteen UAW projects in the following twenty months."

Mr. Dale Carnegie himself often spoke of a letter he received from a potential employee. This woman was trying to sell her skills in response to an employment ad Mr. Carnegie had placed in the local paper.

"I wanted a private secretary, and I put an ad in the paper under a box number," said Mr. Carnegie. "I bet I got three hundred replies. Almost all of them began something like this: 'This is in reply to your ad in Sunday's *Times* under Box 299. I wish to apply for the position you offer . . .'

"But there was one letter that stood out. It went like this:

" 'Dear Sir: You will probably get two or three hundred letters in reply to your ad. You are a busy man. You haven't time to read all of them. So if you will just reach for your telephone right now and call 823-9512, I'll be glad to come over and open the letters and throw the worthless ones in the wastebasket and place the others on your desk for your attention. I have fifteen years' experience . . .'

"She then went on to tell about the important people she had worked for. The moment I got that letter, I felt like dancing on the table. I immediately picked up the telephone and told her to come over, but I was too late. Some other employer had grabbed her."

Why was that letter so effective? Because the applicant talked in terms of what mattered most to Mr. Carnegie.

Summary of Two-Step Approach

Step 1: Send written correspondence that builds credibility and interest.
Step 2: Follow up with a telephone call.

STEP 2: FOLLOW-UP PHONE CALL

Imagine that you're in the middle of preparing your sales forecast for the coming quarter. Your manager needs it by the end of the day. Yet, with everything else on your schedule, you didn't get started until this morning. But it's beginning to come together. You feel motivated and you think you have just enough time to get it finished.

All of a sudden, the phone rings. What's your reaction? Do you welcome the interruption? Or do you sigh and wish you had remembered to send all your calls to voice mail?

Of course, when it's our turn to make phone calls, we want other people to react differently. We want them to welcome our calls, despite the distractions in their own workplace. Unfortunately, our calls may not be welcome. And based on our own feelings about telephone interruptions, we can understand why.

Like it or not, the telephone is a great time-saving tool for the professional salesperson. However, between voice mail, automated attendants, and caller identification systems, doing business on the phone is more challenging than ever. It's getting harder to reach the people we're calling because it's easier for them to avoid us.

When we do get through, it's much more difficult to get the prospect's attention. On the telephone, our voice and words are the only things the customer experiences during the interaction. We don't have the advantage of facial expressions or body language. Therefore, we must be clear and concise, communicating in a way that makes us stand out over our competitors.

Fortunately, we can overcome these obstacles, as long as we plan our phone calls in the same way we would plan a face-to-face meeting. Again, it's all about using pre-approach information and developing a strategy that will make the best use of our time—and our prospect's time. We need to have a purpose for our call. We need to have a plan if we get the gatekeeper. We need to have a plan if we get voice mail. And so on. Think about it: Who do you think stands the best chance of talking with the customer? The salesperson who plans for initial communication, or the one who doesn't?

Telephone Selling Principles

On the telephone, your voice is all you can share with your customer. Practice good telephone skills and you will maximize your selling time. Remember:

- Get to the point. Listeners' attention spans are short on the phone.
- Smile—it will come through in your tone.
- Be courteous, but assertive.
- Put quality before quantity.
- Every "no" gets you closer to a yes.
- Be concise, clear, and persuasive. Let your voice be a shining example of enthusiasm, professionalism, and credibility.

Telephone Effectiveness: The Fundamentals

ATTITUDE

Al, an insurance salesman, used to make his initial phone calls sitting on top of his desk. He said it gave him a feeling of confidence, as if he was on "top of the world." Another salesperson actually had two desks in his office: one he sat at when he needed to do paperwork, and another he stood at whenever he made new-business development calls.

Those ideas may not be perfect for you, but you get the picture. Whatever keeps your attitude positive, within reason, do it. "I have something I say to myself before I initiate the call," said Larry Hann, a sales manager in Chantilly, Virginia. "I say, 'I'm an important person, you're an important person, and I'm calling for an important reason.' When I say those words and internalize the meaning, it influences my attitude, gives me courage and focus, and helps me sound the way I need to sound to a high-level person."

TONE OF VOICE

Confidence and friendliness are keys to making a good impression on the phone. This seems common sense. Yet we've all had times when we talk to people who lack energy and enthusiasm. How does that affect our feeling about that person or that company? Remember, success in sales doesn't really depend on who we know, it's who wants to know us that counts. We should make people want to know us immediately by using a friendly and confident tone of voice.

It's also a good idea to set the tone of the conversation with a polite request. For example, "Do you have about two minutes to talk with me?" A question like this, combined with a pleasant tone of voice, is courteous and professional. Thus, the prospect is more likely to be receptive to our conversation.

CLARITY AND BREVITY

If we've planned our credibility statement and a strategy for the phone call, we're well on our way to making our intentions clear in the initial phone communication. Many successful sales professionals prepare a script and then practice it into a tape recorder—or into their own voice mail—until it comes across as natural and unrehearsed.

USING THE PERSON'S NAME

Mr. Dale Carnegie said that a person's name is the sweetest and most important sound in any language. Not only do people like to hear it, but saying someone's name helps us remember it.

ENTHUSIASM

Enthusiasm is important throughout the sales process. It should come naturally from truly believing that the other person will benefit from what we have to offer. How can we expect someone else to be excited about our product if we aren't?

APPROPRIATE HUMOR

Appropriate humor does not mean, "Tell the great joke I saw on the Internet this morning." It means that if we are comfortable using relevant humor, we can use it to liven up our phone calls.

Michael Crom, executive vice president of Dale Carnegie and Associates, reports using humor on Friday afternoon sales calls when he was selling our training program.

"On Friday afternoons in San Diego I liked to call sales managers. I'd say, 'Hi, this is Michael Crom. I've been taking an informal poll of sales managers this afternoon. About half think that their salespeople are at the beach, and the other half think that they are on the golf course.' I always got a laugh. Then I would tell them the purpose of my call was to schedule time to share some ideas that would help them not care where their salespeople were on Friday afternoons. This was because the salespeople would have already met their objectives. This phone call got appointments!"

THE FUNDAMENTALS IN ACTION

Andrea Holden, in selling for the Publishing Division of the American Hospital Association, demonstrated a number of fundamental telephone skills when she got through to a hard-to-see prospect.

It all started when—as the top salesperson in her organization—Andrea was challenged by her boss to launch a new magazine in the highly competitive hospital/health care market by selling advertising to support the magazine's very existence.

"My boss gave me an expense account, a company car, a list of two thousand names, and a territory that covered twenty-one states and two Canadian provinces," recalls Andrea. "I was paid only on commissions, so I had to rely on phone skills in order to cover my territory efficiently and effectively."

As Andrea did her pre-approach work, she discovered that a large company known as Hill-Rom was an excellent prospect. "I called them and got the name of the person in charge of placing advertising. Then I called him once a week for two months and always got his voice mail. No matter what I tried, he never returned my call."

On a trip between Indianapolis, Indiana, and Cincinnati, Ohio, Andrea had an idea about how to make the telephone work for her. She knew she would pass through Batesville, Indiana, a small rural town and home of Hill-Rom. "I pulled off the expressway, found a pay phone, and, as always, got the prospect's secretary. I said, 'Hi, this is Andrea Holden with *Health Facilities Management* magazine and it's imperative that I speak with Mr. Collar right away.'"

This time, because her tone of voice expressed urgency and importance, the secretary put her through. When the prospect got on the phone, Andrea began talking in terms of his interest. "I have an idea for you. I'm on the expressway, I'm one exit away from your company, and I want to stop by and tell you how you can increase sales and enhance your corporate image by advertising in a new magazine that targets an audience of people who need your products. May I stop by and see you in ten minutes?"

The prospect began laughing. Not because Andrea had deliberately used humor, but because, as he said, "No one had ever called from the side of the expressway asking for a meeting." Impressed by her enthusiasm and curious about how his organization could benefit from working with Andrea, the prospect agreed to see her. When she got there, he proceeded to give her a tour of the facility and explained his organization to her.

What began as a stop off the highway resulted in the largest account for the new magazine. Over the years, Andrea and this customer maintained a strong business relationship that evolved into a friendship. And, while she applied several parts of the sales process in developing this relationship, it all started with a phone call from the side of the road.

Improve Your Telephone Efficiency

- Make an appointment to schedule appointments.
- Determine how many appointments you need per week.
- Batch calls.
- Use a tracking form.
- Complete a pre-approach form.

Telephone Barriers

GATEKEEPERS

The gatekeepers' job is to protect the person for whom they work. They have authority, albeit implied, to open or close the door to the organization. They not only get us in the organization, they can keep us in. And they can become a valuable ally in getting to know the personality of the decision-maker—and even the company as a whole.

The key is to make gatekeepers our allies. We shouldn't be annoyed when they want to know our business. That's their job. With that in mind, we must be prepared to convince gatekeepers that we can provide a valuable service.

In working with gatekeepers, there are two important things we should do, regardless of the selling situation:

Tell the truth. Our business is not strictly personal and rarely confidential, and usually not too important to anyone but us.

Be persistent. Persistence pays off for those who practice it.

The bottom line: As sales professionals, we should try to be cordial when we meet with anyone who has access to our prospects and customers.

Jyoti Verge, a sales professional in London, England, makes a habit of respecting gatekeepers and getting to know them as people first. This approach helps her build good business relationships in many companies. In one instance in particular, a gatekeeper named Rebecca not only helped get Jyoti in the door, she was a valuable partner in moving the business relationship forward successfully.

"When I went to my first meeting at a potentially large account, the person I was supposed to meet could not keep our appointment. But I had waited for him in the lobby of his office for quite a while before I found that out. During that time, I started talking to his personal assistant, Rebecca. Once we started chatting, we found we had a lot in common and developed great rapport.

"As our relationship evolved over the next few weeks, I learned a lot about the organization from Rebecca's point of view. I found out she managed all the personal assistants in the company and she offered to get information from them to help out with my pre-approach on the company's needs.

"Once I had the background they gave me—along with information from the Internet and the company's annual reports, and so forth—I started sharing some ideas with Rebecca. She became excited and immediately found time on the decision-maker's calendar for a twenty-minute meeting. Before the meeting, I called Rebecca and gave her an overview of my agenda and the things I planned to discuss with her boss. I asked for her opinion and input because I really had learned to value her insight.

"Not only did Rebecca help me get on her boss's calendar, she made a point to introduce me to others who would be involved in the decision-making process. In the end, I not only gained commitment for one project, I developed a long-term relationship with this company and great friendship with Rebecca. In fact, we probably would've become friends with or without the business relationship, because I was truly interested in Rebecca as a person. You just never know where it will lead."

WHEN THE GATEKEEPER ANSWERS: WHAT TO SAY

Success in working with gatekeepers is like any other action in the sales process: We must have a plan. Using our pre-approach information, we should know exactly what we are going to say or do to improve the odds of talking to the prospect.

Remember, gatekeepers are there to screen out people who don't bring value to the company. For that reason, there are typically three things the gatekeeper wants to know: who we are, what company we represent and, sometimes, why we're calling. Why not anticipate those questions by answering them for the gatekeeper? In essence, we can make it easier for gatekeepers to do their jobs.

First, identify yourself and your company. Your tone should be friendly, but purposeful. You should say your name clearly and slowly, exuding confidence. As you can see, simply by doing that, you've eliminated two of the three questions.

Now for the third question: What's it in reference to? Fortunately, there are a few tools available for answering that question as well. You can:

Use a referral. As we'll discuss later in this chapter, using the name of someone the prospect knows and respects greatly enhances your chance to speak with the prospect directly. If you're going to use a name, however, you must be certain that the prospect knows and respects the person.

Use a redirected referral. Here's how it works. Simply place a call to the president's office. In almost every case, you will be redirected to another person. This gives you the opportunity to say, "Could you please transfer me to that person?" And once transferred, say something like, "Hi, this is Alan Adell from Phelps Distributing. I was referred to Carol Divers through Mr. Coreel's [president's] office." Then continue with your introduction.

Refer to previous correspondence. This is when the two-step method becomes valuable. "Please tell Mr. Chin that I'm calling in reference to the e-mail he received yesterday." When referring to previous correspondence, avoid using words like "brochure," "literature," "information," or "letter." Instead, try "correspondence," "writing," "fax," or "e-mail."

Should you ask them if they've read your correspondence? Our advice is no. Here's why. What if the conversation goes this way?

"Hi, this is Paul Williams from SCR Technologies. I'm following up on an e-mail that I sent to you yesterday. Did you get a chance to read it?"

"No," he responds. "I have about two hundred e-mails waiting to be read. Give me at least a week."

Although it's not impossible to recover from that response, it's difficult.

If you prepare an opening like the one we've discussed, you take a big step in ensuring that your communication with gatekeepers will be successful. Remember, your script doesn't have to be identical to the examples in this chapter, but it should be well prepared and thoughtful. If you make the gatekeeper's job easier by communicating well, the gatekeeper is more likely to make your job easier.

VOICE MAIL: THE ELECTRONIC GATEKEEPER

While secretaries and receptionists are still screening calls, more often than not, they're putting us through—to voice mail, that is. It's easier than ever for people to screen our calls now that voice mail is such a prevalent tool in the workplace.

Instead of seeing voice mail as a barrier, however, see it as an opportunity to talk directly to the prospect—something we don't get with a human gatekeeper.

Surprisingly, when we poll our training course participants, a large number of them claim to hang up on voice mails rather than leave messages. It's hard to understand why. What is the chance someone will call us back if we don't leave a message? Zero, right? On the other hand, if we do leave a message, we automatically increase our odds that we will get a return phone call, and, ideally, a meeting. If we've called fifteen times and never left a message, as far as that prospect is concerned, we haven't called.

Why is it our tendency to avoid leaving messages? Usually it's because we feel as if we're becoming an annoyance. It's okay to feel that way, but it's not okay to let that fear hold us back. Every successful salesperson has felt that way at some point in his or her career. But the difference between successful salespeople and average ones is that the top performers don't let it get in their way. We can't make a living in sales if we aren't willing to be persistent. Remember, inventor Thomas Edison had eleven thousand documented failures before he got the light bulb to work. Where would we be if he had stopped at ten thousand?

Fortunately, we don't need nearly as many attempts to be successful with voice mail. Remember, leaving voice mail messages is just like any other sales activity we don't really like to do. Our attitude makes the biggest difference. If we see voice mail as an opportunity to speak with the prospect, rather than as a barrier between us, we're halfway there.

Here are a few tips to help voice mail work for you:

Always leave a message. As we just mentioned, this is the opposite of what everyone wants to do, but it's the only way other people know we're trying to reach them.

Leave pertinent information and do it concisely. You don't want to say too much about your product and service. However, you do want to give the prospect important information he needs to a) understand the purpose of the call and b) return the call. In some selling scenarios, primarily business-to-consumer, every part of the sales process occurs via voice mail. In these cases, voice mail selling is actually practical.

Always leave your phone number as the first and last thing you say. You should say your name and number slowly and clearly. This will encourage the other person to write it down and call back. Not only that, the prospect may miss it the first time, so you save him from having to review the message again.

Retain control of the outcome. In your message, you can advise the prospect that you'll call back the following day at a specific time. You may leave a similar message several times until you make contact. But the point is, it keeps you in control. Of course, when you say you'll call back, you have to keep your word. A good contact management system is valuable for this kind of follow-up.

Press 0, and ask for the prospect. If she then picks up the phone, the first question you should ask after introducing yourself is, "Is this a good time for you to talk for two minutes?" Participants in our training program who use this approach regularly tell us that for every one person who is annoyed at being paged or interrupted, they talk to ten who are interested. Now that's making the numbers work in our favor!

These ideas can help move a voice mail message into a more meaningful conversation. The key, regardless of the selling situation, is to leave a voice mail message that gets the prospect interested. To do that, you need to do or say something that gains attention.

Once You Get Through: Getting the Prospect's Attention

We never get a second chance to make a first impression. And the same goes for getting attention. If we don't get prospects interested in the first thirty seconds, we probably won't get a second chance.

So how do we do get attention? How can we make prospects see us as different from every other salesperson who calls? There are two ways:

> *Use a credibility statement.* As discussed earlier in the chapter, credibility statements are your secret weapon against the competition. Practice credibility statements every time you have an opportunity, and soon, they will become second nature. Based on your pre-approach information, develop credibility statements that will fit different scenarios. Then, you have them ready and available to adapt to individual customer communications. Remember, very few salespeople take the time to use this tool. If you use it, you will have the edge over most salespeople in the marketplace who don't.

> *Use an attention getter.* Another method of gaining attention is simply by using attention getters—phrases or actions that help get our prospects' minds off what they are doing and on what we are saying.

Attention getters are typically used early in the sales process. We can use them to set appointments, during telephone interviews, or at any point in the presentation when we feel the other person's attention is wavering or lost. They provide us with the opportunity to plan and execute a fresh and interesting approach that's different from those used by other salespeople.

Building Attention Getters

While attention getters run the gamut from using words to taking action, they must be relevant, specific, and meaningful to the prospect.

That's why attention getters in the sales process are somewhat like our wardrobe. Just as we wouldn't wear all of our clothes at one time, we won't use all of the attention getters at once. Certain ones work better with certain prospects, just as some of our clothes are more appropriate for certain occasions.

Here are some of the most common attention getters.

COMPLIMENT

Mr. Carnegie always said, "Everybody likes a compliment." Well, don't we all? Unfortunately, compliments also can work against us, because they are often overused among sales professionals. So why do we bring them up? Because compliments are still a viable way to get someone's attention—if they're used correctly. It all comes back to pre-approach.

Think of it this way: Most potential buyers are tired of hearing salespeople comment on their families, new facilities, or nice offices. Yet those empty compliments are what most salespeople use. That's not to say we wouldn't compliment people on those things if we sincerely mean it. But remember, those statements don't set us apart from anyone else.

On the other hand, if we use our pre-approach information, we can compliment our prospect on something that's meaningful and relevant.

For example, "Maria, I wanted to let you know that I really respect what you've done in the community. I read in the newspaper last week that your department raised ten thousand dollars for the local animal shelter." Or, "Luiz, I'm impressed at the business results you've been able to attain since taking over this department. Our mutual friend Maria told me that your bottom line has improved by 25 percent."

If we keep our eyes and ears open and do pre-approach, paying meaningful compliments can become second nature.

ASK A QUESTION BEARING ON A NEED

This is a straightforward, no-nonsense way to begin our initial communication, both on the phone and in writing. But we can't ask just any question. We should ask questions that are relevant to the person's general needs. For example, we could ask something like, "If there were a way for you to increase the productivity of your associates without incurring major costs, you'd want to know about it, wouldn't you?" Again, we can use our pre-approach information to develop relevant questions.

REFERRAL

If you remember our discussion about working with gatekeepers, you'll recall that using referrals is probably the most effective way to get someone's attention. Research shows consistently that referrals will strengthen our direct communication with prospects more than any other method. Beginning our conversation with, "Hi, Mary Fakhoury suggested I call you. My name is. . . ." is much more effective than starting with our own name. However, we need to make sure the prospect and the referral have a good relationship before we use this method.

EDUCATE

This attention getter requires us to be a traveling news-gathering bureau. We must actively read trade papers, magazines, books, and newspapers. We should be looking for news items and market information that will be useful to our prospects, including news we hear from other customers (as long as it isn't gossip).

When we can approach people with timely attention getters, we are suddenly perceived as being more than just salespeople. But the information must be relevant. If we've done an effective job at pre-approach, we should be acquainted enough with our prospect's business to know what news might be interesting to that person.

STARTLING STATEMENT

If we do or say something out of the ordinary, we increase the odds that our prospect will want to see us.

In *The 5 Great Rules of Selling*, author Percy Whiting tells a story about a New York salesperson who was successful at getting appointments with very prominent businesspeople. He explained this astounding track record by the fact that he always "startled" his prospects by asking for an appointment at an odd time.

Instead of suggesting an 11:00 A.M. meeting, for instance, he would specify 10:50 A.M. Of course the busy executive might have another appointment at eleven, but probably wouldn't have anything scheduled at 10:50. What's more, the salesperson's request also implied that he valued the prospect's time and would make the interview as concise as possible.

We can also make a startling statement without saying a word. Sometimes, unique actions get attention.

Take sales professional Frank McGrath from San Diego, for example. In selling radio time, he was faced with a buyer who was deemed impossible to see. He sent the prospect a one-hundred-dollar check to endorse to the prospect's favorite charity. This earned him favorable attention and a major account.

Likewise, Bill Hermann found it difficult to get a meeting with the managing director of a large computer company in San Diego, California. But Bill didn't give up. He instead tried a creative approach. He bought a fresh hot apple pie from a local bakery. Bill attached a letter that stated: "Who cuts your slice of the pie? I have some ideas that I would like to discuss with you about how to enlarge your slice of pie." Next, he delivered the pie, telling the manager's secretary that this was a perishable gift. Two hours later Bill easily scheduled the appointment.

When Kevin Fannon sold high-end computer networking systems for a New York–based company, he also used a pie as part of his two-step approach. In Kevin's case, he needed to re-establish a business relationship that had been damaged by his predecessor.

"When I joined the company, I was told this particular account would be my largest customer. Unfortunately, because of a recent turn of events, the relationship had been damaged. So instead of being one of the company's biggest accounts, the customer stopped doing business with us entirely," said Kevin.

"No matter what I did or who I called, I couldn't get anyone to talk to me. Even when some doors began to open at one level of the organization, the owners of the company were still resistant to re-establishing a relationship. I talked to my sales trainer to get ideas. He told me how a pie had been used in other situations. Being new in sales, I was open to any idea that might get the customer's attention.

"Of course, the pie alone wouldn't do it. I wrote a letter along with the pie, apologizing for our company's mishandling of the account. I also accepted responsibility for the situation and stated that the pie represented 'humble pie.'

"A few hours after receiving the package," said Kevin, "the president's assistant contacted me to coordinate a meeting that would help re-establish relations with the customer. I heard that the president forwarded our marketing materials to his staff, but he kept the pie."

Kevin's letter and humble pie opened the door with the decision-makers and the two companies eventually began doing business again. Even though Kevin is now an account manager for another computer networking distributor, he believes the personal relationship he established with this customer will enable him to continue a mutually beneficial business relationship.

Mike Lowe also needed a creative approach for a hard-to-see client. Mike knew he had a good idea for the customer if he could just talk to him. But for three months, the prospect was unreachable.

After trying more traditional approaches, Mike decided to send the man one shoe, gift-wrapped in a shoebox. When he followed up with a call in a few days, he explained that he just wanted to get a foot in the door. The prospect laughed and said he never saw anything like that before. Mike got the appointment and an opportunity to bid on some work. He won the bid, and the company has been a steady client ever since.

Remember, no matter what method we choose to gain favorable attention, the goal is to gain that all-important first interview with the prospect. By using tools such as credibility statements and attention getters, and focusing on the prospect, we greatly increase the odds that we will stand out from the crowd. In turn, we have a better chance of helping the prospect and creating a long-term business relationship that truly is customer-focused.

CHAPTER 4

The Interview
Building Trust

> All things being equal, most people will buy strictly on the best price. The salesperson's job is to help the customer see that things are un-equal. We do this by asking the right questions at the right time and presenting the right solutions in the right way.

We've identified the opportunity. We've done pre-approach. And our initial communication got the prospect's attention. At this point, we are exactly where we want to be: in direct contact with our potential customer.

Remember, the first three elements in the sales process are focused on improving the odds that the prospect will spend time with us. But now that we've been successful at scheduling a meeting, we need to improve the odds that the time together is pleasant and productive for everyone.

Contrary to common practice, we should not attempt to sell a specific solution during the first interview. Why? Because most sales-people do.

Unfortunately, many of us find it challenging to change that mindset. In most cases, we feel so fortunate to get a few minutes with people that we try too hard to impress them. We feel rushed. We feel compelled to share as much information as possible about our products and services in hopes that the prospect likes what he hears and wants to spend more time with us. And even though we think we've come prepared to ask questions and learn more about his situation, the questions typically represent surface-level information. As a result, we never dig deep enough to get valuable information that may give us an advantage over our competitors in the sales process.

For those reasons, among others, talking in detail about our products and services at the first meeting is not the best approach. That's not to say it's impossible to gain a buying commitment when we talk about our companies and ourselves. In some selling situations, we can. But in many of today's sophisticated selling applications, top sales performers have a different approach: They build rapport and gather information in a way that places the focus on the customer.

Building Rapport

When was the last time you made a major purchase from someone you didn't like? Chances are, it doesn't happen very often. The same thing is true about our prospects. Granted that someone likes us doesn't guarantee a sale. But if our prospect doesn't like us, there's little chance of developing a strong business relationship. That's why it's so important to build rapport with our customers quickly and consistently throughout the sales process.

What is rapport? It's simply a combination of good interpersonal skills, effective listening, credibility, and professionalism. It is a process that builds confidence and establishes a relationship between a potential customer and a sales representative. When we have good rapport, the atmosphere becomes friendlier and more relaxed. Trust develops. The prospect is more inclined to answer our questions and to share information more freely. This is very important as we gather information to develop the right solution. In turn, a strong rapport usually means that people will be more open to the ideas, suggestions, and solutions we present.

Building rapport is something we begin at the first interaction with a prospect and continue throughout our entire relationship. It doesn't matter whether that relationship lasts thirty minutes or thirty years, because our ability to build rapport makes a big difference in virtually any type of selling environment. In long sales cycles with large-ticket items, rapport is the key to lasting business relationships. In transaction-based selling, the rapport we build with customers not only affects the current sale, it often leads to referrals for future business.

Based on what we've learned from our training course participants, we believe that in 90 percent of all sales calls, the fate of the meeting is determined in the first two minutes. Why? At this point, the prospect is still preoccupied with other things. A meeting she attended. A phone call she just finished. A report that's due to her manager by the end of the day. Employee evaluations she must complete. The list goes on.

With that understanding, make it a priority to start building rapport immediately. Before you go into each meeting, ask yourself these questions: What starts to build trust and puts a person at ease? What makes my prospects say, "This person listens and is capable, and I like him," or, "I believe she can help me solve my problems"? Taking time to reflect on these questions will make a difference in how you approach each meeting.

Let's face it: There are few companies that have a product that sells itself, where customers break down the door to get it. In all other cases, we need rapport.

Interview Guidelines

- Project confidence. Look as if you have a message of importance for your customer and act accordingly.
- Always pay attention to your personal appearance.
- Prepare attention getters. Don't depend on inspiration.
- Avoid using "I just happened by" for a face-to-face meeting.
- When meeting with more than one person, talk with everyone.
- Use creative pleasantries.
- When using humor, be sure it is at your own expense.
- Don't overdo talking about a customer's hobby.

Interview Fundamentals: Drawing on Human Relations Principles

There's nothing magical about building rapport—it's just an extension of our philosophy of sincerely trying to see things from the other person's point of view. This philosophy is really the backbone of the Sales Advantage approach to selling.

You'll notice that quite frequently in this text we use analogies that relate to your own experiences, or we ask you to step into the customer's shoes. We do this for a reason. If we learn to see situations from other people's perspective, we become much more effective as sales-people.

Brian Kopf, a sales representative in Chicago, Illinois, talks about the first time he approached a customer from that person's point of view versus his own.

"I was meeting with a local manufacturing company that makes molds for the glass industry. They thought they had an idea about what they needed when I went into the meeting. But instead of finding out their budget and asking general questions like I usually did, I put my-self in their shoes. I made an effort to learn more about them. I started by asking them about specific challenges they were currently having. When they'd answer one question, I'd probe deeper and ask another. We ended up taking a tour of their shop floor to see the types of machines they were using. Because I did not accept the fact that they 'knew' what they needed and really tried to see things from their point of view, I was able to come out of the meeting with a much better understanding of their business. I was able to implement an entirely different solution for them, one that was much more effective for their situation.

"In my daily activities, I am not only a salesperson, I also see myself as a consultant," said Brian. "If I can't see things from their point of view, I won't be able to implement an optimal solution for them."

When Chris McCloskey ran her own graphic design business for four years, learning to see things from her customers' point of view increased her business 234 percent in just one year. "When I first started freelancing, I would take a layout in to my clients for their review and approval. While they liked my work, they often had a lot of questions about why things were laid out in a particular way. Their questions indicated to me that my design was not what they had in mind. As a result I would spend countless additional hours redesigning pieces to fit what they were looking for.

"Once I realized the importance of understanding the customer's point of view, I learned how to do a better job of asking questions and listening before I proposed a design. I used many of the tools from the Sales Advantage. But the key was really seeing things from their point of view."

Seeing things from the other person's point of view is a valuable tool in any corner of the world. Gualtiero Berti, marketing manager for Siemens Italy, was having trouble getting a meeting with top management of a potential client. Every time he asked for a meeting, they declined because they were doing business with one of his competitors. What did he do? He decided to see things from the end user's point of view, instead of management's perspective.

"When I couldn't get a meeting with senior management, I thought about who in the company could derive the greatest advantage from using my product. I decided it was the maintenance person. That is the person who gets up in the middle of the night when the machines break down. So I decided to go to the maintenance person, and he was able to test our products. The result: We reduced maintenance problems almost immediately. The maintenance person realized he would no longer have to get up at night to fix the machines.

"He began purchasing a few parts at a time, which he could do without management approval. Eventually, after several years, there were so many Siemens parts in the plant that management started to see the value. They were very happy with the way things were running—all because we made the effort to understand the maintenance person's point of view. Today, we have dramatically increased the amount of business we get from this customer."

For Ian Kennedy, managing director for Wolfson Maintenance in England, seeing things from the other person's point of view has made a huge impact in how he approaches customer relationships.

"We were having major problems with the computer systems that we were supplying to the Royal Navy. The problems escalated to the point where I got a call from the Ministry of Defence (MOD) project manager, who, to put it mildly, was very direct in his speaking. Generally, our company was having difficult times and our previous reaction had been to try to smooth things over and provide short-term fixes. However, I was in the middle of my sales training at the time, so I tried a different approach.

"I weathered the storm of complaints and suggested that, in order to really get to the bottom of the problem, I would personally visit every warship that reported problems (there were ten of them) and actually go to sea with them to understand the issues firsthand. The MOD project officer agreed and, to my surprise, also agreed to pay for me to do this.

"When I got to the ships, I found that the problems were a combination of software problems, a lack of training and support for ship staff, and the fact that their needs were different in many areas from what we had been asked to provide.

"The result was that the navy commissioned us to perform more training and support and to develop the systems further to meet the newly understood needs of the users.

"Now, the navy is our largest customer and we have completed over $5 million of business with them. Just by seeing things from the customer's point of view, we turned what was almost the end of our business into a sales opportunity."

Seeing things from the other person's point of view is just one of thirty human relations principles Mr. Carnegie wrote about in his book, *How to Win Friends and Influence People*. Many of these principles tie closely to the sales process. Why? They help build an atmosphere of trust.

BECOME GENUINELY INTERESTED IN THE OTHER PEOPLE

Too often, we see people only as job titles—potential buyers of our products and services. We refer to people as the "Vice President of Marketing," or the "Senior Engineering Manager." We often make the mistake of being interested in the needs of the person who has the title, rather than the real person behind the job. When we remind ourselves that there is a human being behind the title, there's often a dramatic impact on the amount of rapport we can generate.

It helps to forget about what this potential sale is going to mean to our organization and us. Toss away thoughts of commissions. The other person's interest in our offerings will die at exactly the time when our interest in commissions begins. It will be written all over our face. Instead, demonstrate a genuine interest in getting to know the people you meet.

Beat Muller of Safenwil, Switzerland, sells automobiles for Seat,

Chrysler, Jeep, and Renault. He relates a unique selling situation in which his genuine interest in a customer's child built rapport and ultimately gained commitment.

"I was just saying goodbye to a client at an auto show when I noticed a small girl. She was standing right in front of me and was inspecting my tie. Being used to children, I immediately bent down to her level and held out my hand. 'Hello. I'm Beat,' I said, 'What's your name?'

" 'Eveline,' was her reply. 'You have a really nice tie.' Then she held my tie in both hands and studied it carefully. Her parents stood nearby and watched.

"After a short conversation with Eveline I stood up and greeted her parents. But Eveline felt comfortable talking and continued to bombard me with questions. Her parents just watched and listened. Then I began to include the adults in the conversation.

"The family visited our dealership after the show. During the negotiations with her father at our second meeting, Eveline played with the toys in our play area. As a farewell present, I gave her a small toy car. As the customer left, he said he would contact me again, after he looked around at my competitors' products.

"After four weeks he called me and required an urgent appointment. We met the same day. Of course Eveline came, too. Before we'd even said hello, she informed me that she'd rather have the red Seat Toledo.

"One particular thing struck me about this sale: Had I ignored Eveline and her many questions and just focused on her parents, I would probably not have been successful. The trust that grew between us occurred because I took the six-year-old seriously and I was genuinely interested in her questions. I'm sure there were other factors involved, but the rapport we developed played a big role in building the customer relationship."

Using our pre-approach information in the interview also demonstrates a genuine interest in our prospects and their companies.

Dr. Earl Taylor, a Dale Carnegie Training sponsor from Greensboro, North Carolina, had an opportunity to meet with the chief executive officer of a top Internet-related company in New York City.

"The company was interested in one of our products. It was

arranged for me to fly to New York where I was to meet with the CEO to discuss a program that would involve his key team members from around the world," says Earl.

"I began to research everything I possibly could about the company. I looked up background on the industry. I was seeking information on their competitors, sales volume, market share, company history, you name it. Gene Viesta, a member of our sales team in New York, found two speeches on the Internet that the CEO had given. He shared those with me.

"In one of the speeches, the CEO made a reference about the number of calls he gets from his investment bankers, financial advisors, and others trying to get his financial business. He made the statement that he doesn't talk to any of these people because he has the best financial advisor in the world: his wife.

"Do you think I found a way to work that into the presentation? Absolutely. I wanted to show him that I was genuinely interested in him and his company. One method for accomplishing this was to demonstrate that I had done my homework in preparation for the meeting. That's a tangible benefit of good pre-approach and it goes a long way in building rapport with other people."

Earl's first impression at that important meeting was a good one. He earned the prospect's trust, gained commitment, and established a continuing business relationship between the two companies.

Stop/Look/Listen

When first meeting a prospect:

Stop thinking about yourself, other issues and your presentation. Focus exclusively on the other person.

Look at the other person. Get a vivid impression of physical appearance, demeanor, and mannerisms. Create a mental image of this individual.

Listen to the person's name. Listen carefully for the correct pronunciation of the name. If necessary, ask for the spelling. Do not proceed with the conversation until you know the person's name and can accurately pronounce it.

BEGIN IN A FRIENDLY WAY

The way we introduce ourselves and greet the other person ultimately sets the tone for the meeting. This is more than a handshake. It's a way of projecting to people, "I'm pleased to be here, you are important to me." Frequently, we are so focused on our personal agenda we miss the person's name and needs. This means we're listening to respond, rather than listening to understand. This might be the difference between gaining trust and losing it.

Even if the meeting is intended to discuss a difficult situation with a customer, we can't let our negative emotions control our attitude. We don't have to be happy about the meeting. But we should be pleased that the customer is giving us a chance to keep the business and resolve the issues.

SMILE

Practicing the human relations principle of smiling does not mean that we sit across the desk in a business environment and wear a childish grin or foolish expression. It merely suggests that we are pleased to have the opportunity to help another person, and that attitude should show on our face.

With the business world becoming even more global, smiling is also a practical tool to help overcome language barriers between people from different countries.

Raymundo Acosta S., president of Acosta Deportes, a sporting goods company in Mexico, recalls a time early in his sales career when a smile alone earned a customer relationship.

"At the time, the Summer Olympics were being held in Mexico City.

I was working in a sporting goods shop downtown and there were many tourists looking for souvenirs. A German couple approached me. They did not speak Spanish, and I did not speak German. But I smiled at them. I think by my smile, they could tell I would be helpful.

"We were able to communicate by pointing at different things in the store and using body language. It turned out they were looking for a T-shirt with the Mexican flag imprinted on it. I helped them find the T-shirt and I could tell they were very grateful. They even came back to the store later and brought me a souvenir from Germany as a way to say, 'thank you.' That experience made a lasting impression on me and I will always remember what a difference a smile can make."

For some of us, the action of smiling seems obvious; it's hard to understand why Mr. Carnegie would develop an entire human relations principle around the benefits of it. The reason? Smiling doesn't come naturally for everyone. In sales situations, no matter how we feel, we need to smile. As Mr. Carnegie said, "Try out the smiling habit. You have nothing to lose."

MAKE THE OTHER PERSON FEEL IMPORTANT, AND DO IT SINCERELY

Mr. Carnegie also shared these words of wisdom: "One of the surest ways of making a friend and influencing the opinion of another is to give consideration to [his or her] opinion, let [him or her] sustain a feeling of importance." In other words, if we want to convince people that what we have to offer is important, we have to make them feel more important, too.

If we develop our skills in the human relations principles and truly learn to see things from the other person's point of view, we will naturally make them feel important. But we have to be sincere about it.

During a sales training course in Chicago, Illinois, a participant shared this story:

"When I joined my company, I inherited an existing customer account that I called upon at least every other week. The individual involved was a plant manager who was quite proud of his industry knowledge.

"Of course, I was equally proud of my sales career and my industry knowledge and was eager to make my own impression on the plant manager. Unfortunately, our initial conversations didn't go very well. I often contradicted everything he said. For two years, I would stop by the plant and the pattern was always the same. The plant manager and I would constantly banter about the industry. We never made a connection and, suffice it to say, I personally didn't make any sales with this customer, even though my company had a history of doing business with him. Eventually, the plant manager called my boss and said, 'I don't care if that guy ever sets foot in my plant again.'

"I was hurt, and I chose to simply move on to other opportunities. But after I learned about the human relations principles, I decided to give it another try. After three years of no contact, I got the courage to go back in there and see him.

"The manager was surprised to see me. As we began our conversation, I smiled and made every effort to start on a positive note. I could see that the plant manager still held his beliefs about the industry rather close. But instead of arguing with him, I began to ask the manager questions about his point of view. As I listened, I began to see this person as someone who had a long history in the industry, and he was delighted to be heard. It was clear to me that my sincere interest in his opinion made him feel important.

"I didn't ask for business that day. I thanked the plant manager for his time and told him I had gained much from our meeting. The next week, the plant manager called and placed his first order with me—one that was bigger than he'd ever given the previous salesperson at my company."

TALK IN TERMS OF THE OTHER PERSON'S INTERESTS

Think of the last time you had a conversation with someone you considered a "bore." What made that person unpleasant to be with? Most likely, it was that he or she talked at length about his or her own experiences. Of course, people who talk about themselves frequently don't mean to monopolize the conversation. But that doesn't change the fact that they aren't much fun to be around.

Building Rapport: Words From the Other Side of the Desk

Here's what some customers in the paperboard packaging industry had to say about building rapport. And there's a good bet they speak for any type of customer, in any type of business.

Prompt return of phone calls. We can be quite forgiving about other things if you are easy to reach and prompt in returning our calls.

Technical knowledge. Understand your own products and services and also our company and our requirements. We expect you to do your homework before you call on us.

Strong customer service. We want it to be easy to make an order, easy to check out order status, and move up or delay shipment.

Occasional progress reports when appropriate. If we call to check on something or ask about a new item, give us an update.

Respond to our emergency needs. When you get us out of a jam, we remember you for a long, long time.

Deliver as promised. When you don't deliver as promised, we remember you for a long, long time. When you see that you can't deliver on time, call and let us know.

Don't jam price increases down our throats. Work with us when prices are moving upward, and if the price increases, tell us.

Excerpted from "Customers Make Wish List for Service," an article in *Paperboard Packaging Magazine*, April 1999, by David Ehlert.

In selling situations, talking in terms of the other person's interest is the foundation for effective information gathering. When we ask questions and focus the conversation on the interests of the prospect, chances are he or she will naturally develop an interest in us. (We'll apply this human relations concept in the information-gathering section of this chapter.)

Jim and Chris McCann founded 1-800 Flowers.com in 1986. The

business has changed and grown dramatically since then. Along the way, 1-800 Flowers.com invested heavily in automation and became a full-fledged gifting company. Even though they are proud of their progress, they don't often talk about it when they're talking with individual customers.

"We're often asked to speak to business audiences," said Jim. "And businesspeople will often ask about our computer system. The truth of the matter is we love to talk about our computers. We've spent millions and millions of dollars on them, and on the analysis of our system. But if we talk to our direct customers, that's a different story. The customer ordering gifts doesn't really care about the computer system. At the end of the day it's still a one-on-one relationship. After the customer leaves the store or hangs up the telephone, he needs to feel that the gifts got delivered the way we said they would. The customer wants to know we've done our job."

Dr. Brett Ireland, a chiropractor in Palmerston North, New Zealand, applied this human relations principle when he wanted to expand his business. To accomplish his goal, he needed to acquire the large building next to his current offices. The property was priced much higher than he'd anticipated, and he couldn't offer the amount of money the seller was asking. Brett realized that if the seller made the decision purely on what he could offer, he might be rejected and would not get the chance to expand his practice.

"Before I understood how important it was to see things from the other person's point of view and talk in terms of his interests, my normal action would have been to put together an offer per the real estate agent's requirements and hope for the best. Instead, I decided to apply the human relations principles in a very real and practical way. I sat down and wrote out all the possible options I could think of that would benefit the owner of the space, while not costing me money. I then contacted the owner directly and made an appointment to see him.

"Initially he seemed reluctant to discuss the sale without the real estate agent being present, but I asked if I could have just a few minutes of his time. I explained that I thought my offer would be comparatively low but wondered if there were other benefits to him that I could include in the offer. I then started on my list. Much of what I had thought of was of no benefit to him, but some things had very tangible benefits to both of us. The meeting lasted about thirty minutes. In that time I was conscious not to refer to any of my wants or needs, but rather always asked what I could do to help him."

The supplier, David S. Neal, was impressed. "As Brett stated, I was initially reluctant to discuss the real estate deal with him, but his assurances that he did not want to discuss the cost swayed me to give him some time," he said. "I was struck by his honesty, and recognized that he was looking for ways to enhance his offer and make it more attractive without it costing him any more in financial terms. Two of his suggestions actually solved some perplexing problems that I had lost considerable sleep over. The most important of these was a delayed settlement, which gave us time to find another building without moving to a temporary location."

Today, both parties are pleased. "I was impressed with Brett's strategies and the lateral thinking that had gone into his proposal," said Neal. "It created a win-win situation that had far-reaching benefits for my organization."

Adds Brett: "The end result was an offer that had a number of additional clauses that cost me no more and, in fact, helped me and gave a number of tangible benefits to the supplier. It also established a good relationship between us and the sale was a very amicable one. It was a win-win deal.

"It has also highlighted to me how often we get so wrapped up in what we want that we become blinded to the other people's needs and therefore reduce our ability to communicate effectively. I now find that it helps me to sit down and honestly try and see the issue from the other person's perspective. That way, we can both walk away happy."

LET THE OTHER PERSON DO A GREAT DEAL OF THE TALKING

It's often said that we're given two ears and one mouth for a good reason: We should listen at least twice as much as we talk.

Lloyd Zastrow, district sales manager for Incoe Corporation, a manufacturing company in Troy, Michigan, recalls one of many meetings in which letting his prospect do the talking built immediate rapport. In this case, it also helped him discover things he had in common with his customer.

"When I called on the vice president of Mold Makers, Inc., in Fort Worth, Texas, we sat down in his office and I immediately found common ground (we were both from the Midwest originally). Also, during the conversation, I learned that we enjoyed the outdoors and hunting. I listened intensely, with interest, as he talked about his wife and daughters and how they, too, liked to hunt. What I thought would be a short meeting went on for over an hour. I am confident that by listening to the prospect and really looking for the common ground, I gained his trust and respect during our very first meeting."

Mary McCarthy, a sales representative with GSI Lumonics, a Boston-based Laser Positioning company, says that letting her customers do most of the talking makes a big difference in her ability to offer the right solutions to customers. In one case, it even helped her identify an opportunity to gain a large amount of business away from a competitor.

"The customer was a huge multi-billion-dollar pharmaceutical company, and the challenge was convincing the prospect, who was already satisfied with our competitor, to consider our product.

"When I called the buyers, I sat back and let them do a great deal of the talking. I listened intently and encouraged them to talk about themselves, and then I talked in terms of their interest. Based on this dialogue, I was able to determine what specific component of our product offering would appeal to them.

"I then suggested a meeting to see a demonstration of this product line based on the needs they communicated to me. We had a meeting and, at that meeting, I presented a solution to their specific problem, rather than a 'this-is-our-stuff' demonstration."

The result?

"We are now doing business with this company. It's one of the highest-profile accounts in my territory. And the relationship with this customer is a new caliber of customer for my company and its product. As a result, I'm able to approach other similar customers about providing them solutions as well."

PLEASANTRIES

When we meet someone, whether it's the first time or the fiftieth, it's human nature and expected practice to say, "Good morning," "How are you," "It's good to see you," and so forth.

These pleasantries represent an expected form of common courtesy that does not relate to the sale, but merely establishes a point of common ground from which the conversation can be launched. Simply, these pleasantries are indicative of a well-mannered and gracious individual.

In most cases we don't want to spend more than two or three minutes with pleasantries during an interview. However, it's a good idea to follow the customer's lead. We always want to make sure we're taking as much time as necessary to put that person at ease.

Pleasantries are not viewed the same in all parts of the world. For example, in some countries, we wouldn't use a person's first name until we had asked permission. In others, using the title Mr. or Mrs. would seem too formal. In some business environments, it's not even appropriate to conduct a business conversation unless we've spent significant time on pleasantries. In others, too many pleasantries would be viewed as detracting from the business purpose of the meeting.

If you are responsible for handling international accounts, you should use pre-approach to determine the appropriate role of pleasantries in your prospect's country.

Another word on pleasantries: Don't always use the obvious ones. For example, it's a good bet that almost every salesperson before us has commented on the weather or on some current news event in the community. For that reason, pleasantries are most effective when they are unique and, if possible, relevant. This is a good time to check our pre-approach information before the first meeting. Unfortunately, depending on the sales environment, we may not have had time to do pre-approach. And sometimes it's not possible to find good information. In these cases, how do we set ourselves apart with pleasantries?

Again, we need to be creative.

Jay Broska, account executive for a packaging equipment company, relies on his company's unique shirt to begin some of his sales conversations. He wears it when he calls on customers in the plant setting. "The logo on that shirt is so eye-catching and curious, the prospect's eyes typically go straight to it. Picking up on that, I make casual conversation about it, and we usually have some laughs. It's a good way to break the ice and get the sales meeting started."

Cheryl Blalock, territory manager for a legal software firm, found a unique way to start her meetings during the busy holiday season. "During the end of the year, everyone's busy with the holidays and with year-end activities at the office. I knew that almost everyone I would meet would likely be pressed for time and under a lot of pressure.

"At the beginning of the meetings, I would start by asking the prospect a simple question like, 'How's your day been going?' More often than not, they would respond by telling me about some of their frustrations. With that, I would reply that I had a great holiday poem I'd love to share with them at the end of our meeting. Invariably, they'd want to see it right way. The poem was humorous, so we'd both share a laugh. It changed the whole atmosphere in the room and they became much more comfortable talking with me."

Getting the Sale Started

Part of building rapport is moving our customers logically toward a conversation about their needs. Depending on the situation, we will use one or more of these three techniques to move from pleasantries into the sales discussion: 1) attention getters; 2) credibility statements; and 3) why talk statements.

> The first 10 words are more important than your next 10,000.
> —Elmer Wheeler, *Sentences That Sell*

SALES STARTER 1: ATTENTION GETTERS

As we discovered in the last chapter, attention getters can be used at any time during the sales process, but are most often used near the beginning of our conversation. Remember, attention getters typically fall into these categories: compliment, ask a question, referral, educate, and startle.

SALES STARTER 2: CREDIBILITY STATEMENTS

During the interview, credibility statements can easily be adapted to start the sales discussion. The first three steps in developing our statement remain the same. The primary difference in the interview is the question we will use in the last step. Obviously, since we are already talking with the prospect, we won't need to establish parameters for follow-up. Therefore, the final question of our credibility statement simply asks for permission to proceed with the interview or with the questioning process. For example, "May I ask you a few questions to determine your specific needs?" or "Do you mind if I proceed by asking a few questions?" Both of these examples, among others, represent courteous and appropriate ways to move into the sales discussion.

Now we have seen that there are a variety of times we can use a credibility statement. Some options are summarized in the graphic below.

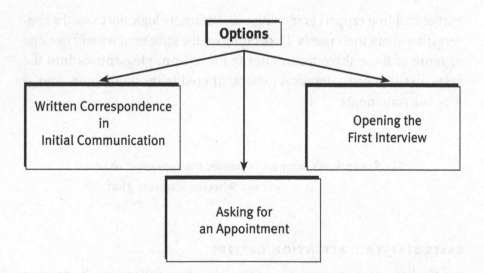

Figure 3: Credibility Statement Options

SALES STARTER 3: WHY TALK STATEMENTS

Another alternative we can use to make the transition from pleasantries to our sales conversation is the why talk statement. Simply, this statement speaks in terms of the other person's interest and reminds them why we're meeting. After all, it's probably been a few days, if not a couple of weeks, since we scheduled the appointment. Any chance that something else has gone through the prospect's mind since then? Absolutely. That's why we owe it to him to show respect for his time by clearly and concisely stating the purpose of our conversation.

What does it do for us? Overall, developing a why talk statement helps us think about the prospect's point of view and forces us to focus on the specific discussion we want to have with the prospect—before we have that discussion. When we get to the meeting, we'll be better equipped to ensure that we both have the same objectives in mind.

We can use a why talk statement either in person or on the telephone. Regardless, it must include three vital components:

A specific customer benefit related directly to the meeting itself —not just "why talk," but why the other person benefits from having the meeting. In some cases, this relates to the credibility statement from our initial communication. If we mentioned that we want to talk to the prospect about something we've done for another company, he will expect us to talk about it.

An overview or agenda of the meeting itself. This can be done verbally, or it might involve a written agenda that we present to the customer. Be sure to ask the customer if there's anything he would like to add to the agenda.

A question requesting permission to proceed to the first point on the agenda. This simply shows courtesy and demonstrates respect for the other person's time. This is the same type of question we would use to make the transition from a credibility statement into the interview.

Although it appears simplistic, the why talk statement can be a powerful tool for the professional salesperson. It shows the prospect that we are prepared to talk about his issues, not ours.

Here's an example:

"Our purpose today is to help you identify ways to save money on your printing costs while improving the quality of your brochures. After our discussion, I'm confident you'll have discovered specific cost savings opportunities even if you don't buy from us right now. The agenda I suggest we cover today would be:

- Examine your current printing systems.
- Determine what you would like to improve about your printing.
- Look at some possible solutions to some of the challenges you are experiencing.
- See if there's a good fit between what we do and what you are trying to accomplish.

"Does that make sense to you? Is there anything else you would add?

"May I ask you some questions to get a better understanding of your current situation?"

Here's another one:

"Today we will be reviewing the needs of the people in your organization who would be using the new phone system, to ensure the system would meet their needs. I suggest our meeting cover the following points:

- First, I'd like to know what challenges you are facing in changing the phone system.
- Next, let's bring two of your employees into our meeting and ask them about their needs.
- Then, let's see how that ties into what management is looking for.
- Finally, let's determine the criteria for your buying decision so that we can provide you with an accurate proposal. How does that sound?

"May I ask you a few questions to get us started?"

Why talk statements work well in virtually any environment. Sandy Monk, program manager for the U.S. Army, used many of the Sales Advantage tools in nontraditional selling situations. In one instance, she recalls how the why talk statement helped her start a difficult conversation on a positive note.

"A recent reorganization added a new service line to my area. I was excited to inherit three very competent professionals to deliver the services, but less than enthused to take on a particular secretary who had been underperforming for years. My experience and intuition told me that she could not meet the challenges of my program and my personnel regulations indicated I could not simply dismiss her.

"Simultaneously, another secretary in the organization, with exceptional skills and attitude, expressed a desire to transfer from a position where she felt constrained. My ideal solution was to swap the secretaries. So, not only was I confronted with a delicate personnel situation, I had to 'sell' my solution to everybody involved.

"To build rapport with the other program manager, I composed a why talk statement describing the benefits of the secretary swap. I sent it via e-mail. I knew this particular manager would feel more comfortable responding at his own pace with a written introduction rather than a phone call. In a subsequent spontaneous encounter, the manager indicated his interest in my proposition and gave me permission to proceed with my agenda by arranging a meeting with him and his executive secretary.

"At our face-to-face meeting, I was tempted to jump in and describe my proposition to swap secretaries. However, I used the meeting to gather information and gauge their interest. I asked questions and let them talk. I determined that their primary interest was maintaining equilibrium within their administrative staff, while their buying criteria were a secretary who worked well with intense supervision and good attendance." (Buying criteria and primary interest are covered later in this chapter.)

"I finally proposed my solution, based on what they had said, and framed it in terms of meeting their needs. At the end of the meeting, I still did not have commitment. Although I wanted to leave with a commitment, I suggested that they interview the secretary I wanted to transfer before they made their decision.

"She interviewed successfully and they asked her to join the other program. The secretary I wanted then joined my program. Everybody felt good about the decision.

"In thinking back, had I approached this meeting any other way, I might not have even had the opportunity to present my solution. While I know that using many selling principles in this situation helped me succeed, it was the why talk statement that opened the door for conversation."

Sharon Biernat, sales manager at International Promotional Ideas in Chicago, Illinois, took her why talk agenda to another level by combining it with an attention getter.

"In my industry, we have a Golden Pyramid award. This award measures the end result of promotional item use, such as increased sales or improved attendance in the workplace. I entered that contest and won two industry awards.

"One day, I got an idea. On the agenda, I not only put down all of the points we were going to cover, I added the Golden Pyramid award. During a break in conversation, my prospect asked me, 'Hey, what's this Golden Pyramid award?' So I had an opportunity to explain it. It really impressed him that the award measured actual results of my company's effectiveness in recommending promotional products. He was so impressed that I walked away with a commitment to enter one of our promotional products for this award—and an order. That's unusual with a large company like this, because the sales cycle is usually longer. Today, I add the Golden Pyramid award to every new prospect's agenda."

Information Gathering

The rapport we build from the moment we meet people is essential to establishing a foundation for trust. The information-gathering portion of the meeting is where we ultimately earn their trust. This is important, because trust makes our prospects and customers more comfortable in sharing valuable information we need to help develop a unique solution that truly satisfies their needs and wants.

If we know how to ask good questions and listen carefully to the answers, we'll learn things our competitors won't learn. Prospects will tell us exactly what products and services we can sell, how we must present them, and, ultimately, how to appeal to the Dominant Buying Motive that leads to the commitment.

Unfortunately, many of us approach information gathering in a way that never develops a high level of trust. We set out to get budgetary numbers, product or service specifications, and due dates. Then, we wonder why we're competing on price. While price is sometimes a legitimate issue, it can often be an indication that we didn't establish trust. We didn't dig deep enough during the questioning process to find out what's truly important to the customer.

Food for thought:
Each time we write "not interested" on a sales report, we should stop and think: Was the prospect really not interested or did we fail to interest the prospect?

To understand the role that trust plays in our relationships with our customers, think about your best friend. If he or she asks questions about personal issues, you're usually inclined to answer those questions openly and honestly. On the other hand, if a stranger asks the same questions, you aren't as likely to share your feelings.

Consider this: Say you're sick and you go to the doctor. You walk into her office and sit down. After a few minutes, the doctor walks in, smiles, and gives you a firm handshake. After exchanging a few pleasantries and then talking about her successful experiences in treating patients, she writes a prescription and sends you on your way.

How confident are you that the medicine she prescribed is exactly what you need? How much do you trust her diagnosis?

Fortunately, you'd never encounter that kind of situation at the doctor's office. But that's how some salespeople approach their interviews. Instead of effectively questioning the prospect before presenting a solution, many of us are tempted to "write a prescription" right away.

We want to offer solutions before learning exactly what our customers need and want.

What happens if we do something different from what most salespeople do? What will it mean to our sales career if customers trust us more than any other salesperson? To most of us, it would make our jobs very rewarding. Would price still be an issue as frequently as it is now? Probably not.

If we develop a strategy for gathering information, we can offer solutions to customers knowing that we're giving the right answer to the right person at the right time for the right reason. We no longer sell just hoping that our solution is the right one. We know it is.

Getting the Answers: What Do You Need to Know?

What we learn in the information-gathering portion of the interview not only helps us develop unique solutions, it prepares us for negotiations and helps us minimize—or even avoid—objections. Simply, it gives us a picture of the customer's world as he sees it. Sales professionals who set themselves apart in the marketplace know how to sell in the customer's world.

Before we decide what questions to ask, we must determine exactly what we need to know from our customers. That information typically falls into four key categories.

1. THE PRIMARY INTEREST (WHAT THEY WANT)

This information tells us exactly what the product must provide—for example, accurate and timely reports, dependable transportation, or lower rejection rates. In turn, we can identify which product or service we will be presenting as our solution.

Keep in mind, the primary interest is not the product itself, it is always the product of the product. The common mistake many salespeople make is to assume that customers want a product or service, when, in fact, customers want what our products and services can do for them.

For example, we don't really want a laptop computer. We want the flexibility that a laptop provides. If we're purchasing contact management software for our computer, our primary interest is not defined as

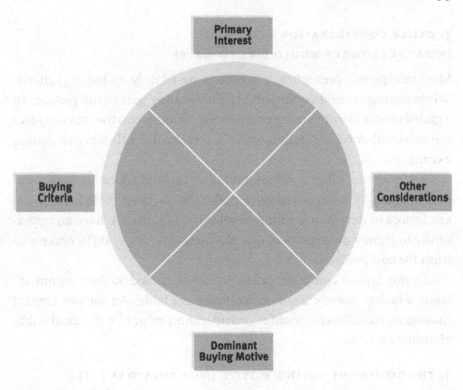

Figure 4: Interest Areas

the software itself, it is the ability to easily maintain a customer database and ultimately increase sales with a reliable follow-up system.

2. THE BUYING CRITERIA (REQUIREMENTS OF THE SALE)

These are the specific aspects of the product or service that must be included in our solution. This includes requirements such as size, color, speed, warranty, or availability. Unless we meet the buying criteria, the sale cannot proceed.

Again, if we consider the laptop computer example, our buying criteria might include price, weight, and modem speed. As for the software, our criteria might include the availability of technical support, or alarms to remind us of appointments or product updates.

The buying criteria we get from our customers become the facts that we will share about our products or services in the solution presentation.

3. OTHER CONSIDERATIONS
(WHAT CUSTOMERS WOULD LIKE TO HAVE)

Most salespeople present their solutions based only on buying criteria. While buying criteria are important, they're only part of the picture. In a global economy with strong competition, finding creative ways to meet the subtle other considerations will often make the difference in getting a commitment.

For example, other considerations can include special service, local parts availability, or technical service after the warranty period. These are key factors in developing a unique solution, because we have an opportunity to show how aspects of our products or services differentiate us from the competition.

In our laptop computer scenario, other considerations might include whether there's a service contract available. As for the contact management software, another consideration might be the availability of online updates.

4. THE DOMINANT BUYING MOTIVE (WHY THEY WANT IT)

The Dominant Buying Motive is the compelling emotional reason that our customer will buy. By understanding the emotional reward that results from a successful purchase, we can identify benefits that will have the most impact in the decision-making process.

Sounds easy, right? Not exactly. Most of us think we know why our customers want to buy. Yet, in reality, the "why" we've uncovered may have nothing to do with emotion.

Consider the laptop computer example. Why does a person want one? A logical answer would be, "So she has flexibility when taking her work on the road." Is that the Dominant Buying Motive? Not at all. In fact, that's the primary interest. Remember, the primary interest (what the customer wants) is not the product; it is what the product will do for the customer.

The Dominant Buying Motive, on the other hand, is the emotional reason the customer wants to make a good decision. For example, maybe she wants to get more work done while she's traveling so she has more time to spend with her family at home. Remember, flexibility to take work on the road is not emotional, it's logical. But feeling good about having more time to spend with family members—that's an emotional link.

Even though most people find themselves purchasing products and services for logical reasons, there is usually an emotional reason they eventually make the purchase. If we learn to appeal to that emotion in our solution, we will be different from other salespeople. And our customers will notice.

In Depth: The Dominant Buying Motive— The Emotional Reason People Buy

Almost everything we have ever bought, even impulse items, we've bought because of some compelling, emotional reason. Our primary interest pushes us toward the buying decision. But the ultimate decision to buy is primarily driven by our emotions.

For that reason, the Dominant Buying Motive is as critical to the sales process as the engine is to a car. Similar to the way an engine helps to put a car in motion, uncovering a primary emotional motive improves the chances of a business relationship moving forward.

The amazing thing is that most people who are selling today, and even selling somewhat successfully, do not understand this concept. Therefore, they don't know how to use it to help their customers.

Granted, it's possible to gain commitment without uncovering the Dominant Buying Motive. In those situations, however, the customer usually has recognized his own emotional reason for buying.

No matter what the product or situation, we can generally classify buying motives into five categories. To illustrate these categories, let's consider a common scenario for most of us: buying a house. Why do we make the decision to commit to an incredible amount of money to own a home? For most people it's the largest single debt they'll ever face in their life. Even if you haven't been through it yet, chances are you will. Or at least you know many people who have.

In this case, let's say we live in an apartment and we decide it's time to get a house. Why would we leave an apartment? After all, someone else maintains it for you, there's a wonderful swimming pool, and our monthly payment is only one-third of what we'd put into a house. Why

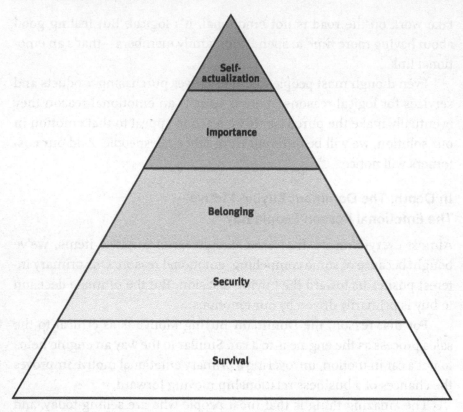

Figure 5: Dominant Buying Motives

would we give up all that for a place that is totally ours to maintain and carries a large debt, not to mention other financial obligations such as insurance and taxes, and all the new "things" that make our house a home? When we look at it realistically, it's not a logical thing to do.

But we don't buy on logic. We make an emotional decision that we justify by using logic. We might have said: "We can write off the interest on our taxes. We'll be building equity. We're enhancing our net worth. Long term, if we stay in the apartment, we're not using our money wisely." All of these are logical reasons to support our decision.

But the truth of the matter is, we typically buy a house for an emotional reason.

Maybe we have to buy it because we have no other place to sleep. This is survival. Or, maybe we want the security of owning our own home. There's also the possibility that we buy it for a sense of belonging, so our family can feel like part of a community. Buying a house may also provide us with a feeling of importance, because our family and peers can look at us with admiration and say, "Wow, what a house, you've really made it." Or finally, we may have just been searching for self-actualization, because when we buy our dream house, it feels good to have made the right choice.

Whichever one of those motives was most compelling, that was our Dominant Buying Motive—the emotional reason that caused us to make the decision to move from an apartment to a house.

We even have a Dominant Buying Motive when we make such quick decisions as where to eat lunch. We're hungry and we have the money to buy food, so we're a qualified prospect. But our Dominant Buying Motive of survival might lead us to the salad bar instead of the dessert bar.

Mary Sue Stallings sells financial products for Lexington State Bank in Lexington, North Carolina. She is one of many sales professionals who appreciates what the Dominant Buying Motive means to her customer relationships.

"I attended a retirement dinner for one of our long-time bank customers. He and his associate were successful entrepreneurs and had built their own business from the ground up. Following a period of growth and prosperity, they continued to expand and increased the success of the multi-million-dollar business. Eventually, an out-of-state company that wanted to buy their company approached them. Our customer agreed to stay with the new company as a consultant during the transition. Shortly thereafter, he decided to retire.

"I made an appointment with the customer to talk about his plans and goals and to establish an investment plan for his proceeds. As I asked him questions, I also learned about plans he had for his family. I recognized that this man had a strong love for his family and wanted to make sure he provided for them. It became clear that the emotional reason for any business decision he would make with our bank was that it would have to give him peace of mind that his family was well protected in the future.

"Once I identified the Dominant Buying Motive, I asked questions aimed at that motive so I could further identify what solutions I might be able to offer this customer. As we continued to talk, I suggested that perhaps he might want to consider starting another company. Not too long after that meeting, he called me and wanted Lexington State Bank to help him finance his new business venture. Not only did we lend him the money, he also trusted us to invest a sizable amount of his own money."

Had Mary Sue not identified the customer's Dominant Buying Motive, the solution of starting another company might have never been presented. Why? Because the conversation would have likely remained focused on the bank's products, not the customer's unique circumstances. By understanding the emotions behind the customer's decision, she was able to offer him a solution that went beyond the scope of simply investing his money. Mary Sue identified his motive and helped him achieve an important goal.

THE QUESTIONING PROCESS:
THE KEY TO SOLUTION DEVELOPMENT

When it comes to asking questions, we all have good intentions. But do we really get below the surface level and ask questions that help us determine the primary interest and the Dominant Buying Motive?

For many of us, the answer is no. That doesn't mean we go to meetings unprepared to gather information. It just means we haven't prepared in the right way.

Think about it: How many sales conversations begin with questions like, "What is your budget? What kind of equipment do you want? How many projects are you looking at?" And the list goes on. Granted, these are issues that have to be addressed at some point in the process. But if we start there, or stop there, what are we doing that is different from what other salespeople do? What are we learning from the prospect that's different from what the competition knows?

Remember, even if people are buying the same basic products and services, they are usually buying them for different logical and emotional reasons. If we learn to ask the right questions and listen to learn, the customer will tell us each and every time exactly what it is he wants to buy and why he wants to buy it. From that information, we can develop our solution presentation in a way that demonstrates our interest, insight, and ability to talk in the other person's language.

Greg Jacobson, from American Power Conversion in Washington, D.C., sees firsthand the connection between effective questioning and solution development.

"In one particular situation, my customer was the U.S. Postal Service. I am in the power protection business, which ultimately means that we sell battery backup systems and surge suppression for data centers and the networking equipment within. We were up against two competitors who had arguably as good a solution as we did. I fortunately knew this going into it and planned accordingly.

"I learned that when all other things are equal, people buy from people they like or people who care about their concerns. So I had to find a way to make them realize that I cared about their requirements and could address them one by one.

"By asking question after question about the specific challenges that they faced, where they wanted to go and what was preventing them from getting there, I was able to get to the heart of the matter. I eventually learned that, outside of the generic need for power protection in their data center, they really wanted power protection to be an active part of the network operations. By this, I mean that they wanted to interface some of their common software solutions with our hardware.

"This was definitely something we could do. I was able to illustrate how it could work. What I soon realized was that the competition never even got around to learning about this concern. Fortunately, by questioning the customers, I got them to open up and give me information that they didn't give my competitors. Who do you think they were going to buy from at that point? All other things being equal, they bought from the person who got into their world and was able to address their specific concerns. As an aside, that was my single largest sale for the year and has yielded quite a bit of return business."

Elisabeth Leleu, part owner of Sonatex Laminating Canada, Inc., describes how asking the right questions made her better prepared to send the right product samples to a customer. "I was on the phone with the garment department of CCM, our number-one customer. The person I spoke with was looking for a fabric to be used in a football shirt. If I had made a note of this general request only, I would have wasted the customer's time and mine.

"Instead, I started to ask more specific questions regarding things such as how they were going to use the fabric and what type of durability they needed. It turned out that the fabric CCM was looking for was for shoulder pads and elbow pads. Having mentioned padding, I could come up with a fabric solution that provides protection and higher durability. So when I sent product samples to the customer, I was able to send the right samples, instead of wasting the customer's time looking at fabrics that wouldn't be appropriate."

Do these salespeople have an advantage over their competitors? Absolutely. Top sales performers know how to gather information effectively and use it to develop unique solutions that truly satisfy the customers' needs and wants.

STARTING OFF RIGHT

Before we begin the questioning process, it's important to use a why talk statement or credibility statement.

Once we have established credibility, we immediately need to focus the conversation on the customer. Remember, everyone has different issues and buying motives. So when it comes to the information-gathering process, it really pays to take the time and prepare some discussion-starting questions that are specific to that particular person.

Our pre-approach information is critical in this scenario. Let's say we're trying to sell radio advertising and our prospect—the owner of a new gym—doesn't advertise. We happen to know that another new gym only a few miles away is selling three times as many memberships per month than our prospect's gym, because their rates are 15 percent less expensive. We also happen to know, however, that our prospect's gym is really a better value for the money because of what's included in its memberships. For that reason, we believe radio advertising would be a great way for the prospect to communicate the value of his product to his target audience.

Armed with our pre-approach knowledge, we could phrase one of our opening questions in this way: "Would you please tell me how your sales representatives are dealing with the challenge of the other gym down the street that's offering memberships at 15 percent less than yours?"

Clearly, this question is more effective than simply asking, "Why don't you tell me some of the challenges you're facing?" Why? Because it's relevant to the prospect and it demonstrates that we are familiar with the issues in his world.

When we get into the other person's world, our questions naturally become more thought-provoking. If the prospect looks at us and says, "Hey, that's a great question. I never thought of that before," that's a good sign that our discussion is on track.

Salespeople who do a good job of asking questions are able to find out important points that their competitors won't discover: They know what keeps their prospect awake at night. They understand her frustrations. And they know exactly what opportunities she is not taking advantage of because she doesn't know they exist. What happens then? These top performers are no longer viewed as salespeople. They're viewed as trusted resources who have the customer's best interests at heart.

QUESTIONING PROCESS FLOW:
AS IS, SHOULD BE, BARRIERS, PAYOUT

If we understand that the purpose of questioning is to uncover the primary interest, buying criteria, other considerations, and—most important—the Dominant Buying Motive, then what types of questions should we ask?

Simply, we want to ask questions that evoke answers about the prospect's current situation, where she wants to be in the future, what's standing in the way of her ideal situation, and what the payoff is when she gets there. This model of questioning is called "As Is, Should Be, Barriers, Payout."

As Is questions provide insight into the customer's current situation. We might discover that our customer lacks timely reporting from her current supplier. Or we might discover that something like transportation is an issue.

Answers to the As Is questions will help us determine which of our products and services meet the prospect's needs. Without a clear under-

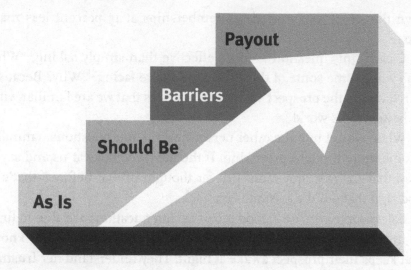

Figure 6: Questioning Process

standing of the strengths and weaknesses of the current situation, we don't have any foundation upon which to build a solution.

Once we've asked questions to determine the current situation, we then need to know where the prospect wants to be in the future. Essentially, Should Be questions represent a verbal depiction of how people see themselves or their organization when things are running at optimum.

We also need to ask Barriers questions to learn what influences are keeping the customer from achieving her Should Be situation. Sometimes, it can be as simple as budget. Other times, it's more complicated, such as having to retool an entire plant. Barriers can include budgets, tariffs, duties, language differences, geography, compatibility, and even shipping costs.

Sometimes, barriers can also be objections. How do we know the difference? In most cases, but not all, barriers are things that are somewhat out of our control and may have nothing to do with our products and services. Since we can't control tariffs, they are most likely barriers. Budget issues, on the other hand, could represent both a barrier and an objection. We have to judge each situation individually. If we're not sure, asking more questions can help clarify the issue.

Finally, Payout questions uncover the emotional reward our customer receives when she reaches the ideal situation.

As you've probably guessed, the answer to the Payout question ties directly to the Dominant Buying Motive. Does the customer get a bonus for saving the company money? Does she get less pressure from her boss regarding missed shipments? Does she ease her workload so she can spend more time with her family? Does she feel happy about doing something good for the company? All of these are payouts. Remember, the answer to these questions is not "higher productivity"—that's the answer to the Should Be question. The answer to the Payout question is how the customer benefits from increasing productivity. Simply, what's in it for her?

QUESTIONS HELP BUYERS SEE THEIR NEEDS MORE CLEARLY

When we become skilled at the "As Is, Should Be, Barriers, Payout" model, we'll often uncover a selling gap: the difference between a customer's current situation and where he would ideally like to be. As professional salespeople, being able to recognize the selling gap helps us be more effective in working with our customers. Why? We might be able to help our customers see the situation more clearly. They may even convince themselves that they need a change in the status quo.

The gap between the As Is and Should Be situation is more obvious with some people than others. Consider a plant manager who had to shut down a production line because a piece of equipment was too old and quit operating. His selling gap is pretty obvious. His current situation is lost production time. His desired situation is to be up and running so he can meet customer demands.

In other cases, the selling gap is harder to identify, or even nonexistent in the mind of the buyer. Take, for example, a vice president of human resources who has been outsourcing her payroll to the same provider for ten years. She's satisfied with its performance. Her current situation doesn't necessarily motivate change. In fact, it's likely that getting a new payroll provider isn't even on her list of things to do. She does not see a gap.

Both scenarios represent common selling challenges. While the plant manager's current and desired situations are fairly obvious, he could be considering several companies to provide the piece of equipment. Thus, the salesperson has to find ways to convince the plant manager that his company is the right choice.

In the case of the human resources director, it's the salesperson's job to actually unearth a selling gap. How? By using the questioning model. As the customer talks through the As Is, Should Be, Barriers, and Payout answers, there's a possibility that she may talk herself into the idea that things could be better. In essence, she lowers her own opinion of her current situation and raises her own expectations of a payroll provider.

Either way, we are better equipped to provide a solution. Knowing where our customers are versus where they want to be is the first step in helping them achieve their goals.

IN ACTION: THE "AS IS, SHOULD BE, BARRIERS, PAYOUT" MODEL

George Haas, a sales professional for Contractors Sales Company in Albany, New York, relates a story of how the questioning model helped him develop a unique solution for one of his customers.

George knew that his customer could solve a lot of his production problems if he would order new equipment instead of the used equipment he'd been ordering for more than three decades.

"The challenge was to convince the father and sons, owners and operators of the business, that this new machine would produce a better-quality product faster and more reliably than the old unit. They operated a rock quarry and hot-mix asphalt business. The crusher, which is the piece of equipment I sell, is a critical item in the success of the business because it produces all of the final specification stone. It must consistently produce thousands of tons of specification material a year for them to be successful.

"By applying the questioning process, I determined that their As Is situation was that the current unit in use was functional, but would not produce material that would meet specifications. Parts were still available, but something had to be done with the process overall for them to continue to make products they could sell.

"Their Should Be situation was to produce quality product without constant attention on operation or repair. In fact, during my conversations with this customer, their old unit broke down and a friend loaned them a unit to complete the construction season. Even so, they were still giving consideration to fixing up the old one.

"The Barrier to their Should Be situation was downtime. Each time production stopped, the plant felt a negative impact on everything from stone sales to commercial customers to hot-mix production on the other side of the operation.

"At this point, I was able to determine that the Payout, or Dominant Buying Motive, was survival. The long-term success of their business would be in jeopardy if they couldn't reduce the production downtime."

George sold this piece of equipment, his first-ever new-equipment sale, by appealing directly to the Dominant Buying Motive of business survival. He also addressed the customer's Barriers, or other considerations, by demonstrating his company's ability to respond in the event of problems with the new piece of equipment. By doing this, he provided his customers the bridge from As Is to Should Be.

Robert Kuthrell, investment specialist for Charles Schwab in Westmont, Illinois, also sees the value of using the questioning model to identify important customer issues. In one instance, he was able to keep a customer who had threatened to take her business elsewhere.

"I received a disgruntled call from my regional vice president, indicating that he had just spoken with one of our valued customers who was planning to transfer her $3.7-million account to another firm.

"I immediately called this customer to find out why she wanted to terminate her relationship with Schwab. By asking questions to clarify the real reason, I learned that she was pleased with many of the services she received but was disappointed with her recent investment performance. I used the 'As Is, Should Be, Barriers, Payout' model to identify her specific source of displeasure. I learned that she was looking for more personal guidance, so we both agreed to meet and discuss her situation further.

"In assessing her overall situation, she expressed both a need and a desire to delegate the day-to-day investment responsibility to a professional. As it turned out, that was the main reason she was leaving Schwab. She went on to explain that, before her husband passed away, he managed their investments using a professional money manager and felt that was the key to his success.

"Through a series of probing questions, I was able to better understand the customer's current situation (lack of investment expertise); the 'Should Be' situation (a trusting relationship that allowed her to delegate the day-to-day decision making); the 'Barriers' confronting her (the need for personal guidance) and the Dominant Buying Motive (peace of mind knowing that her investments were being managed by a trusted professional).

"By drilling down on the customer's interest and focusing on her needs and circumstances, I was equipped with enough vital information to recommend a workable, win-win solution: I advised her that Schwab had a nationally approved referral network of fee-based money managers and that I would be happy to assist her with the prescreening and interview process.

"I met with her several times over the next few weeks. She eventually agreed to work with a manager from a short list we developed together based on her overall investing needs. In the end, this customer canceled her outgoing transfer of accounts and established a very close professional relationship with a money manager in her neighborhood."

Liz Dooley, a sales professional in Baltimore, Maryland, recalls how the questioning model helped her communicate with purchasing managers who were often her first point of contact in selling uniform programs to major corporate clients.

"In one situation, I was working with a trucking company. I met with the purchasing manager regarding their uniform program. In the past, I had been intimidated by aggressive purchasing agents. But on this appointment, I was determined to use the questioning model and minimize the information I shared about my company's products and services.

"So I planned out my questioning flow. I wrote out all of my As Is, Should Be, Barrier, and Payout questions. What normally was a short meeting lasted for over an hour. I asked lots of questions and she talked. I walked away with five pages of notes and I knew the emotional reason why she would make the buying commitment.

"As a result, I was able to put together a targeted and thorough proposal that really tied back to her specific needs. She immediately passed the proposal through the chain of command and I had the opportunity to present my solution to the next level of management. I don't think I could have generated the same results had I not used the questioning model and really focused on listening to the purchasing agent's answers."

Building Trust Through Effective Listening

The secret of influencing people lies not so much in being a good talker as in being a good listener. Most people, in trying to win others to their way of thinking, do too much talking themselves. Let the other people talk themselves out. They know more about their business or problems than you do. So ask them questions. Let them tell you a few things.

—Dale Carnegie

Asking effective questions is just one part of the information-gathering equation. As Liz Dooley's example illustrates, listening and understanding the answers is another.

When we ask participants to tell us their biggest takeaways from our training program, overwhelmingly, they tell us: "I learned to listen."

Contrary to popular belief, selling is not a game for people who have the "gift of gab." Think about Sherlock Holmes, Columbo, Fox Mulder from *The X-Files*, or any famous investigator. Can you imagine how these people would solve murder mysteries and other perplexing situations if they did all the talking?

For that matter, leaders in any business become successful because they know how to listen. According to *Looking Out, Looking In*, a textbook written by Ronald B. Adler and Neil Towne, a study that examined the link between listening and career success revealed that better listeners rose to higher levels in their organizations. The ability to listen well was also linked to persuasive skills, showing that good listeners are good speakers.

The sales profession is no exception. If we look at truly successful salespeople, we'll find their listening skills are superior to most.

The Dale Carnegie and Associates book *The Leader in You* says: "People everywhere love to be listened to, and they almost always respond to others who listen to them. Listening is one of the best techniques we have for showing respect to someone else. It's an indication that we consider them important human beings. It's our way of saying, "What you think and do and believe is important to me."

LEVELS OF LISTENING

Needless to say, we can all recall times in which we listened intently to what someone had to say. On the other hand, we've also been in situations where we've pretended to listen because our mind was not focused on the conversation.

Both scenarios are just normal patterns in our listening skills. In fact, in our Leadership Training for Managers course, we identify four basic levels of listening. Our goal as salespeople is to reach the top level possible: listening for understanding.

Level 1: We ignore. As professionals, we don't intentionally ignore people we're meeting with. The idea in this level of listening is this: We should recognize that we may not be paying as much attention to our customers as we should. On the other hand, our ability to ignore can sometimes even help us be better listeners. We need to be able to ignore distractions, such as ringing telephones, overly talkative coworkers, or other interruptions that interfere with our concentration.

Level 2: We pretend to listen. Sometimes, we just act as if we're listening. In a sales situation, pretending to listen can be dangerous. Our customers most likely will recognize our inattention during the meeting. And if they don't see it during the meeting, we can almost bet they'll notice when we present the solution. If we don't listen well, we risk not being able to offer a solution that meets their unique needs.

Level 3: We listen to respond. Most salespeople fall into this category. As soon as the customer says something, we want to offer a solution. Learning how to listen to our customers means we stop thinking ahead of them and start thinking real time. In most selling situations, it means that, even if we think of a solution during our conversation with the customer, we don't interrupt. We avoid the tendency to "jump in" the second we hear a way in which we might help. Later in this chapter, we'll offer a suggestion on how to overcome this tendency. We can all be more effective if we resist the temptation to respond and let the customer talk. After all, the more the customer talks, the more information we can gather.

Level 4: We listen for understanding. Clearly, this is the highest level of listening possible. When we listen to understand, we are listening authentically as opposed to listening automatically. We eliminate distractions. We don't pretend to hear what the customer is saying; we really hear it. And we aren't trying to offer solutions before the customer is finished speaking.

TIPS FOR BETTER LISTENING

Just as with any skill, listening takes practice. Here are a few things to look for as you hone your listening skills.

Stay focused. If we all agree that listening is an important skill, why is it so hard for most of us? Aside from preoccupation and distractions, listening is difficult for a physiological reason. According to Adler and Towne, although we're capable of understanding speech at rates of up to 600 words per minute, the average person speaks between 100 and 150 words per minute. Thus, we have a lot of spare time to occupy our minds with while someone else is talking.

Effective listeners use this spare time to better understand the speaker's ideas, rather than letting their attention wander. Try this exercise: For the next sixty seconds, center your attention on one of your key customers. Think about that customer and nothing else. Time yourself, and the second you think of anything else, stop the clock. Even if you are thinking of the customer and some other idea at the same time, stop the clock. How did you do?

If you're like most of us, you only went several seconds. Does this point out some form of an inadequacy on our part? Not really, it just reminds us that concentration is an area that needs constant work.

Receive words and emotions. Words often represent only part of the message. We often disguise our real emotions behind the words we say. If someone says, "How are you?" our typical response is usually, "Fine, thanks," even if things aren't going well.

As you'll see when we discuss the customer evaluation and negotiation elements, we need to be adept at reading the customer's emotions behind the words—or the nonverbal cues. These cues can provide us with buying signals, warning signals, and other important information we need to understand and respond to our customer's hidden issues.

Don't interrupt. Our mind is thinking faster than the other person is talking. So there's a natural tendency to offer our comments, even if the customer isn't finished speaking. Or if the customer says something that relates directly to what our product or service can do, it's hard to resist the temptation to offer a solution right away. Most of us would agree that interruptions disturb the communication process and represent one of the most difficult listening challenges.

As Dale Carnegie himself said, "If you disagree with them, you may be tempted to interrupt. But don't. It's dangerous. They won't pay attention to you while they still have a lot of ideas of theirs crying for expression. So listen patiently and with an open mind."

A suggestion: Instead of interrupting with a comment, write it down on a notepad. At the end of the conversation, you can do one of two things: If you sell products with a short sales cycle, you can immediately begin talking through your solution based on the notes you wrote. If you're selling higher-value items with long sales cycles, you can use these notes to work with your internal team in developing a unique solution.

Either way, you get the thought out of your head, onto paper, and can immediately resume focusing on what the other person is saying. Of course, before you take notes, it's always a good idea to ask for permission.

Resist filtering. Filtering is a natural process that's based on our individual past experiences, education, culture, gender, religion, and other factors. Filtering tends to make us focus on points of strong agreement or disagreement. When we filter we're missing part of the picture. We should not judge people based on who they are or on our own beliefs about a subject. When we do, we're filtering the information to only hear the things we want to hear. Think of what happens when two people, with strong, differing opinions on the same subject, are discussing their views. Each person is so convinced that his point of view is the right one that neither is receptive to alternatives.

We've heard such conversations. Maybe we've even been part of one. The point is, when we meet with our customers, it's no time to choose sides.

Summarize the message. When customers have shared a lot of information with us, we should respond with a brief summary to be sure we heard correctly. This forces us to listen for understanding, rather than listening just for the sake of taking notes.

For example, we can say something like, "So, Charles, if I understand what you're saying, you feel frustrated that you have to work late on Fridays because your current freight carrier is always behind schedule?" This demonstrates to Charles that we're attempting to understand his situation fully. And Charles's response to that question helps us determine if we really know what he's saying.

LISTENING THAT BUILDS RELATIONSHIPS

For Jim Tenuto, former Merrill Lynch vice president and now owner of Renaissance Executive Forums in San Diego, California, effective listening was the key to the one of the biggest sales of his career.

"There's a very large corporation here in town that's privately held," he said. "The owner is one of the four hundred richest people in the country. Naturally I wanted our office to get some of her investing business. When we telephoned her office we were told that a certain executive in her firm handled all of her personal investments and all of the corporation's investments as well. So we placed a call to this executive, who was the assistant treasurer at the time. The first sentence out of his mouth was not encouraging: 'I'm trying to get rid of brokers, not add them. Why should I even agree to see you?'

"We said, 'because we're from Merrill Lynch and we have outstanding research to offer.' He agreed and we got an appointment with him. At our first meeting he came right to the point: What would we do if he gave us $2 million?

"After we asked questions to establish his investment objectives, we suggested a strategy. He asked us to write our remarks up as a proposal. My partner and I worked on the proposal as we were driving back from La Jolla to our office in Rancho Bernardo. We put in all the numbers, typed it up, and sent it over by courier that day.

"The next day the assistant treasurer called us up and asked us to invest that $2 million for him. He said it was the first time anyone had ever listened to him. And it was the first time anyone had ever been willing to commit anything to paper. That account grew to around $25 million."

Tom Saunders, merchant banker with Saunders, Karp, and Company, is in the business of advising big corporations about how to invest large sums of money. His number-one technique: listening to customers. "It all goes back to listening," he said. "What was really on his mind? Why had he said no? What was the real reason behind it?

"I've had a twenty-five-year relationship with AT&T, which has been just extraordinary. I think it's all basically been due to listening. I can give you the best-looking brochure. I can throw up all the slides. But still I've got to find out what's in there that's interesting to that person. What's on this person's mind? What does he think about? How does he look at things?"

Lisa Foster, with Cole's Printery in Barbados, has been able to quantify the difference effective listening makes in her sales calls. "The ability to listen to my clients has helped me better advise them with more confidence. During my first year of really working on my listening skills, my sales increased 155 percent and I won the company's sales incentive award."

Effective questioning supported by good listening can often uncover different and even bigger opportunities.

Susan Cucullo, account executive for H. A. McLean Travel, Inc., in Woodbridge, Ontario, Canada, found that effective listening actually helped her company discover a niche for one of their products.

"We provide corporate travel services to many large companies. By doing better questioning and listening, I discovered that many companies I visit do not have a proper billing arrangement when purchasing air travel. Many travelers are using their own personal credit cards to expense their travel, which affects their personal credit line. Once I started uncovering this trend with my prospects, I was able to sell a product that we have which no other agency had offered: BTA, or Business Travel Account.

"Because I learned to listen, I uncovered a need that our agency could fill. Now, I am able to offer new prospects and existing customers a unique product that other agencies don't seem to offer."

Susan is proud of what she's been able to accomplish just by honing her fundamental questioning and listening skills. "I've learned to not offer a solution to customers until I know exactly what it is they're looking for. This not only results in better relationships, it's actually helped my company sell to a niche in the marketplace."

Clearly, a strong combination of listening skills, effective questioning, and good rapport is what we need to be successful in our first meeting with a potential customer. But it doesn't stop there. We must always use and refine these skills each time we interact with customers. If we're effective in this important part of the sales process, we are able to build a level of trust that's essential to any successful business relationship. Without a doubt, our customers will notice the difference. And so will we when it comes to reaching our potential as professional salespeople.

CHAPTER 5

Opportunity Analysis
Determining Prospect Potential

A successful salesperson who takes the time to see everyone who is willing to talk will not be successful for long.

In a perfect world, every information-gathering meeting would result in a qualified prospect. Of course, we all know that's not the case. That's why we have to gather information in the first place. Not only do we uncover buying motives to help us develop solutions, we get the basic information we need to determine if and when we will pursue doing business with the prospect's organization.

Opportunity analysis is critical to our sales planning. Why? Because it helps us allocate our time more efficiently. It also helps us focus our efforts on the people who are most likely to have genuine needs for our products and services.

Unfortunately, many salespeople make the mistake of pursuing almost every prospect with the same tenacity. When that happens, their efforts often become diluted. Instead of having a good number of productive conversations with quality prospects, they're having surface-level conversations with anyone who seems interested in buying "someday."

Even if a company is using a product or service similar to ours, we still may discover that no opportunity exists within this organization. Or we may find out that the opportunity has requirements beyond our willingness or capacity to deliver.

For Tom Stundis, sales representative at Marr Scaffolding in South Boston, Massachusetts, analyzing opportunities caused him to actually refuse an order from a customer who was anxious to buy from him.

"My sales visits with this one particular customer initially were very brief. I would bring product literature, ask a lot of questions, and offer to help in any way I could. Soon, I began to understand his needs and problems and I saw an opportunity to fill one. This was a small order but I followed through on that order like it was the biggest one we had. As time passed, the small orders continued to come and I followed through on every one.

"Approximately seven months after my initial visit, the owner called me about a significantly larger purchase. As I provided the product information and quotation, I sensed he was rushing into his decision. He wanted to purchase the unit that day. I could have easily completed the order and gotten a huge deposit. But against what the traditional sales mentality might suggest, I actually refused to take the order that day.

"Upon further discussion, I found my customer was going away for a week. I suggested using that time to have his mechanic meet with me at our office to get a hands-on demonstration of the unit he was interested in. This would also provide the mechanic with an opportunity to meet our service manager and see our shop in action. The owner liked the idea.

"I had some anxious moments the next few days. I thought I might have analyzed myself right out of a big opportunity. I received a lot of pressure from my coworkers that I should have closed the deal that day. However, I stuck to the game plan. The sale eventually went through. I followed up with a safety training session for his staff and they each received certification for the proper use of the unit.

"When the unit was delivered, I encouraged the owner to be there. On that day, he told me he had never felt so good about a purchase.

"My relationship continues to grow with this customer. He uses us exclusively to move and service his equipment. When his needs involve a rental, price is never an issue. He has helped me sell several other units to other customers through his honest and unbiased referrals, of which I'm sure the story of me refusing to take the order is a highlight."

Tom's decision required a lot of courage. Yet his story is a great illustration of how analyzing our opportunities not only helps us, but can also help our customers make good decisions.

In general, when we approach opportunity analysis, we can be most effective by separating our opportunities into four distinct categories.

Now. The prospect has a clearly defined need that must be addressed immediately.

Example: A manufacturing process requiring a constant supply of goods or services that you can provide.

Near Future (less than six months). A situation exists or will exist that must be addressed in the next several months. It is not an immediate need. However, it's one that is specific and predictable.

Example: A corporation invites bids beginning on a certain date in the future; a company's new budget won't begin for six months; a company is currently operating under a contract that won't expire for three months.

Distant Future (more than six months). A situation exists or will exist that must be addressed but does not represent an immediate need. However, as with "near future" prospects, the need is specific and predictable.

Example: An office equipped with computer and communication technology that operates with limited capacity in an environment that is experiencing rapid growth. The company is being compelled to outsource an increasing volume of its computer and communication needs.

Never. There is no opportunity for the application of our product or service at this time, nor is there likely to be any opportunity in the future. We don't want to waste the person's time regarding any future business and we need to move on and focus on better opportunities.

Example: A vertically integrated company has a business segment that provides a product or service similar to ours as an internal supplier.

Besides placing our prospects in categories of urgency, we can also determine whether the people to whom we're speaking represent qualified prospects. This is somewhat different from the qualification of prospects we do in pre-approach. In pre-approach, we're simply trying to determine if we should call on a person, and if so, how we should approach the conversation. In opportunity analysis, we have already met with the prospect. Our main goal now is to determine where we go next in the sales process.

To make this determination, we can ask ourselves some key questions about our prospects: Is their need or want great enough to justify the cost? Do they have access to the necessary resources? Are we talking to the decision-maker? Can this become a profitable business relationship for both parties?

If we don't think we're talking to the decision-maker, then we need to go back and acquire more information to find out who will be making the decision. If we don't think this is a profitable relationship for both companies, then we may need to rethink pursuing the business altogether. On the other hand, if the answer to all these questions is yes, we know we can proceed with confidence to present the solution when the timing is right.

Marco Carrara, a partner with Andersen Consulting Italia (now Accenture), talks about how his organization has adopted a company-wide strategy around opportunity analysis.

"Until several years ago, our way of approaching the market was this: All opportunities are pursued. We accepted all clients. The partners made sales and decisions at their own discretion.

"Then, we changed our strategy. Our company decided to pursue a few large opportunities as a team, rather than many small opportunities as individual partners. We set parameters for the types of opportunities we wanted to pursue. But we knew that in order to adopt this strategy, we would need a way to analyze each opportunity to determine if it fit the parameters.

"We created four different categories: 1) Is the client deserving of an analysis? 2) To what extent can the client benefit from work by Andersen? 3) What is the probability of getting the work? and 4) What is the probability of having the ability to do good work?

"From there, prospects are assigned a score in each category. Based on the total number of points, we determine whether to pursue doing business with that prospect.

"Within a few years after we began using this approach, our portfolio of clients dramatically changed. Once we began analyzing each opportunity systematically, the number of clients declined by approximately one-half while our average client size multiplied three to four times worldwide. Our staff has grown, but not our number of clients. That says a lot about the power of opportunity analysis."

As Marco's story illustrates, having a system to analyze opportunities after we gather information ensures that we are pursuing the types of prospects with whom we want to do business. While Andersen's categories are different from those illustrated in the Sales Advantage, they are effective in helping the organization accomplish some important sales goals.

The point is, a system of opportunity analysis ensures that we're planning our sales strategy and not just selling on instinct. Sales professionals who manage their prospects accordingly are usually better able to meet and respond to customer needs and typically gain more commitments. Think of it this way: we try hard to value our customers' time. Why not value our own time just as much?

Qualify Your Prospects

Is your prospect qualified? The answers to these questions will help you decide.

- Is the need or want great enough to justify the cost?
- Does the prospect have access to the necessary resources?
- Is this person a decision-maker?
- Can this become a profitable business relationship for both companies?

CHAPTER 6

Solution Development
Giving Customers
What They Want

Selling, to be a great art, must involve a genuine interest in the other person's needs. Otherwise, it is only a subtle, civilized way of pointing a gun and forcing someone into a temporary surrender.

—H. A. OVERSTREET

W hen it comes to providing solutions for our customers, we need to make sure that we're standing out in the crowd of salespeople who are competing for the same business. How do we accomplish that objective? By giving customers solutions that address their specific wants and needs, as well as their emotional reasons for making the buying decision.

"Of course," we say. "We do that. We pride ourselves in providing good solutions. We are problem solvers." To an extent, most salespeople are problem solvers or at least intend to be. Yet we need to ask ourselves if we are really providing the best solutions possible. Are we really analyzing our customers' needs to the extent they need to be analyzed?

Two purchasing agents were talking about a new product. One said, "I want to know more about it." The other said, "Ask the salesperson." "Oh," said the first one, "I don't want to know that much about it!"

As we've already learned, our success in developing unique solutions is tied directly to how well we ask questions and listen to understand the answers. Have we determined the primary interest? Do we know the buying criteria? Do we understand the barriers standing in the way of the customer's Should Be situation? Are we aware of the other considerations? Have we uncovered the Dominant Buying Motive?

If we can answer yes to all of those questions, we probably have an edge over our competitors. Why? Remember, most salespeople provide solutions at the features and benefits level. If we can develop solutions that demonstrate the application of the product in the customer's environment, while also appealing to the emotional reason for buying, we increase the odds that our solution is exactly what the customer needs and wants.

In reality, there are many times when the customer himself may not know what he needs. That's why a thorough job of information gathering on our behalf is so important—and so critical in building a trusting relationship with the customer.

For example, consider John Sullivan's firm, Testing Machines, Inc., which manufactures testing equipment for the papermaking industry. When he begins to develop solutions, he learns that, sometimes, a client's diagnosis doesn't tell the whole story. So when a client places an order with him, he makes it a point to ask questions and get more information about the client's needs.

"I had a client who called and wanted to order a specific piece of equipment," recalls John. "But after asking some specific questions, I determined that they needed an entirely different solution. We could have simply taken the order for the equipment the client requested, but it wouldn't have solved his problem. And, ultimately, the customer wouldn't have been happy. It's critical to apply the right solution to the problem and guide the customer to that solution. That builds trust. And that is what creates customers. If we simply take orders, then we don't have customers."

A sales professional from a telecommunications company relates a similar story. "One day we had a repeat customer who said he needed to add more equipment for his system. So I went in and I quoted him a price. It was expensive. But while I was there, I noticed that his equipment had not been kept up-to-date. He had been performing some of the maintenance work himself to save money. So I said, 'Let's spend a few of your dollars and clean up your existing equipment.' He agreed and our technicians went in and spent four hours on maintenance.

"When they'd completed the cleanup it turned out he didn't have to buy any new equipment after all. Once cleaned and maintained, the customer's existing equipment could handle the volume quite easily. Not long thereafter we got a nice letter from him saying, 'I can't believe it. You could have taken advantage of me and sold me a lot of equipment I didn't really need. But you didn't!'

"Because we had been honest and approached his situation as unique, he trusted us. Now, this customer will not make a move in telecommunications without talking to me first. I've sold him far more than what that original contract was worth. And he's recommended us to several other clients."

Each of these sales professionals shared stories that demonstrate the value we bring to the customer and the trust we can develop when we truly take time to analyze the situation and develop a unique solution.

With that in mind, we need to step back and take an honest look at ourselves.

Have we gathered the information we need to provide a unique solution? If not, we need to go back and ask more questions.

Are we providing solutions too soon before we really understand the customer's situation? Remember our discussion about listening with the intent to respond. That's what many of us are inclined to do. Before we've finished the interview, in all the enthusiasm for making the sale, we've already told the customer how our product or service addresses their problems. Sometimes, these solutions will work. But more often than not, they do not truly satisfy the customer's wants and needs.

Molly Geiger, sales representative with Standard Register in Chicago, Illinois, learned this lesson firsthand.

"Even though I know better, I still sometimes make the mistake of assuming that I already know what the customer needs," says Molly. "I went into this one particular appointment thinking I knew the answer the customer was looking for. I hadn't asked many questions prior to the appointment so I made some assumptions. During my presentation, they stopped me and said my solution was not what they wanted.

"At that point, I stopped my presentation and took a step back. I started asking questions about their specific situation, things that were relevant to them. I realized what I needed to do and wished I had asked the questions first. It's so important to get the facts before presenting a solution to the customer. I wasted my time and, more importantly, I wasted theirs.

"Luckily, they let me schedule another appointment so I could present a more suitable solution that would fit their needs. But it could've easily gone the other way. I learned a valuable lesson that day and I don't plan on anything like that happening again."

Eddie Azizian, territory manager with Western Pacific Distributors in Hayward, California, shares an example of how solution development ties strongly to our ability to gather information effectively and offer solutions at the right time.

"Far too many times, we as salespeople jump right into the solution or selling stage before doing fact finding or gaining interest through effective questioning," says Eddie.

"As an example, I met with a local franchisee from a major chain of fast food restaurants. He surely could have purchased his food service equipment directly from the manufacturer rather than our wholesaler distributorship. But, by listening more than speaking and finding out what my prospect really wanted, I was able to earn his respect. I put myself in his shoes and let him do a great deal of the talking. I didn't tell him what he needed. I let him tell me what he needed, which was the local value-added service he couldn't get by ordering straight from the manufacturer. We could provide that service for him.

"As a result, I obtained a purchase order for a substantial amount of money and have earned a customer that will reorder from us, not directly from the manufacturer."

In Eddie's situation, if he had approached the customer by talking in general terms about his company's equipment, the results could have been much different. Why? Because the customer could purchase the equipment anywhere. What he wanted was local service. When Eddie asked relevant questions and really listened to the answers, the customer told him what he needed.

Ignazio Manca, marketing manager for Onama S.p.A. in Milan, Italy, also notices how seeing things from the customer's viewpoint makes a difference in developing solutions.

"When I questioned the customer about a new dining facility he wanted to build, he told me what his ideal situation was," says Ignazio. "His main concern was an efficient operation, attention to details, and a beautiful environment. During the sales process, I learned that other companies had focused more on selling him on the quality of food. Food was important to him, but it was not the focus of the client's thinking.

"I began to think of the situation from the client's point of view and imagined the things that would please the client. As part of the solution I developed, I brought him to see a modern facility we had built, with the characteristics the client was looking for. He was fascinated with the environment, orderly personnel, and attractive signage. We never talked about the quality of the food. Without any doubts or hesitations, the client signed the contract.

"To me, the message here was to give up your own idea of what you think the solution should be and think about what the customer is really asking for."

If we sell items with shorter buying cycles—such as cellular phones in a retail environment—the customer's needs and wants could be pretty straightforward. If that's the case, we are expected to offer solutions right away. But in most cases, especially on large-ticket items with long buying cycles, we need to take more time. We need to gather as much information as possible, combine it with our product knowledge, and create a solution that exceeds the customer's expectations.

Create Unique Solutions

Depending on your industry, you need to create ways to increase the value of your products and services:

- Service: Provide an additional service that exceeds customer's expectations without commensurate cost.
- Delivery: Identify methods that will put the product or service in place consistently on a timely basis.
- Installation: Get the product online with no disruption to normal operations.
- Financing/credit: Provide customers with terms that meet or exceed those of their most favored suppliers.
- Technical support: Do whatever is necessary to ensure minimum downtime and maximum productivity.
- Training: Offer sufficient training to ensure that the organization optimizes the benefits available through the product or service.
- Other: If you can think of other ways to make your solution unique, you stand an even better chance of standing out from your competitors.

DEVELOPING A SOLUTION—ONE PIECE AT A TIME

At this point, have we earned the right to tell the prospect what she needs? Absolutely—if we've done a good job of gathering information. When we follow the questioning model, it will point us directly to the primary interest, buying criteria, other considerations, and Dominant Buying Motive.

Keep in mind, when we develop our solution, we should do so in a way that overcomes any doubts our prospect has about our product or service. We're answering questions such as, "What is it? What will it do for me? Who says so besides you? Is it worth it?" Each and every solution we develop must answer these questions that are weighing on the customer's mind.

Regardless of whether we discuss our solution during the initial meeting or at a later time, we need to develop it in a way that builds cred-

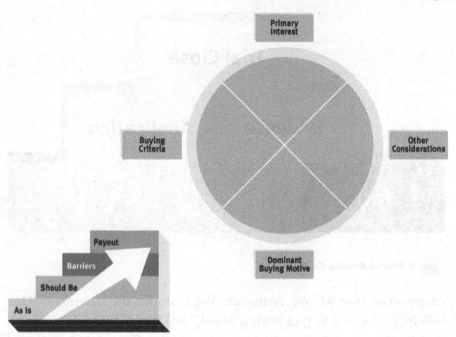

Figure 7: Questioning Uncovers Needs

ibility and makes the customer want to do business with us. The solution building blocks will help ensure that every solution we develop is unique to each customer's specific situation. How? By breaking the solution process into six distinct pieces: facts, bridges, benefits, application, evidence, and trial closes. If we follow this logical process of solution development, we force ourselves to address each person's wants and needs individually.

Remember, most salespeople don't develop solutions that go beyond facts and benefits. By practicing the building blocks and applying them consistently, we ultimately improve the odds that our solutions are more meaningful than any of our competitors'.

BUILDING BLOCK 1: FACTS (WHAT IT IS)

Every solution we develop should contain a number of indisputable facts that provide the customer with general information about our company, its products, and its services. These are specific and true statements describing some aspect of our product and service that the

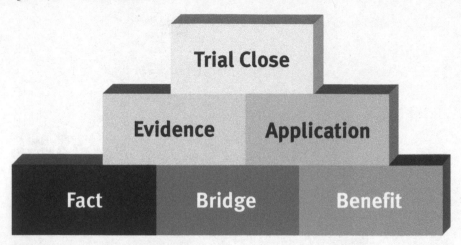

Figure 8: Solution Building Blocks

customer accepts without hesitation. For example, the statement, "Our building is located at 3712 Spring Street," is a fact. "We stock parts and supplies for every Tech product we sell"—that's a fact.

Many salespeople have a tendency to use claims or generalities, mistaking them for facts. A claim may sound like a fact, but it is usually perceived by the customer to be our own opinion. For example, "The gears in our robot arm are the highest quality in the industry." This is probably a claim in the mind of the buyer. The statement may be true, but the phrase "highest quality" doesn't sound convincing. Saying, "The gears have the highest success rate in the industry," is better, but still a generality. The buyer may still feel it's a claim. Instead, we might say, "According to an independent review, our gears last 22 percent longer than the industry average." Doesn't that sound convincing? When we are more specific in our facts, customers have more confidence in our solutions.

BUILDING BLOCK 2: THE BRIDGE

The bridge is a transitional phrase that links the fact and the benefit to create a conversational and cohesive statement. We can use almost any conjunction as a bridge. Bridges include words such as, "thus," "therefore," "which means," "so," "which provides," and "you'll like this because." An example would be: "We have a certified technician on staff, which means . . ."

BUILDING BLOCK 3: BENEFIT (WHAT IT DOES)

Presenting facts without benefits is like eating a hamburger without the meat. After all, we don't want that burger because of the bun. We want it because of what's inside. Just like a hamburger, facts and benefits combined are what the customer wants to see in our solution.

Benefits apply to anyone who buys a product or service—they are not specific to individual customer applications. Benefits are essential because they provide a clear picture of what each fact means to the customer. For example: "We stock parts and supplies for every Tech product we sell, which means everything you need to keep your equipment working is available when you need it." This is a benefit, because everyone who buys a tech product will benefit from in-house stocking of parts and supplies.

Occasionally, the benefit from a fact about a product is so obvious that we don't need to mention it. But always keep in mind that people don't buy things, they buy benefits—what things will do.

A good rule with respect to product knowledge is, "Know much—talk little." In other words, we must know as much as possible about our products and services. But in our solution, we should only offer the information that's relevant to the customer's needs, wants, and motives.

Fortunately, most companies do a good job of boosting product knowledge through training. But sometimes, it pays to take initiative to get more knowledgeable about our products and services, especially when we're selling at the application level.

Product Knowledge and Solution Development

- Read industry and trade magazines.
- Search the Internet and web pages.
- Read the books and manuals provided by your company.
- Ask your boss and other salespeople about specific applications.
- Spend a day or two with your application engineers or users.
- Get information from prospects and customers.
- Visit factories, plants, and home offices after your initial product training.

BUILDING BLOCK 4: APPLICATION
(WHAT IT DOES FOR EACH SPECIFIC CUSTOMER)

It's crucial to know how to communicate the application of our products and services. Remember, when communicating general facts and benefits to a customer, we're communicating at the same level as most salespeople. We are simply telling customers what our products and services will do for everyone.

When we add the application, we begin to involve the customer by talking in his language. How? Because the application portion of our solution is specific and unique to each customer, it clearly shows how he personally benefits from our products and services. The application can also reference the Dominant Buying Motive—the emotional reason why the customer wants what we have to offer.

Take, for example, the statement we've used in previous building blocks. "We stock parts and supplies for every Tech product we sell, which means everything you need to keep your equipment working is available when you need it." Now, we add the application: "So you can get parts within one hour, instead of sending out your systems for repair or waiting for out-of-town service and delivery. Your staff will be much happier because their downtime will be minimal, and you will have fewer complaints from them."

Clearly, when we get to the application level, we start talking about how our product or service works for the customer. We move into their world and become a strategic partner. The customer is then thinking, "Hey, you understand."

BUILDING BLOCK 5: EVIDENCE

We must have the ability to support the elements of our solution in a way that's memorable and powerful. Therefore, as we develop our solution, we need to find ways to include evidence that validates the information we present to our customers.

Evidence is a great tool to help overcome a person's doubts, and it's one of the easiest ways to enhance the impact of our solutions. Yet we have found over the years that gathering evidence is one of the most neglected activities of sales professionals. Everyone knows they should

Demonstrations

Examples

Facts

Exhibits

Analogies

Testimonials

Statistics

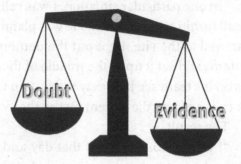

Figure 9: Evidence *defeats* Doubt

do it, but very few people really take the time to do it well. Again, wouldn't you rather be one of those salespeople who has evidence in your toolbox? We like to say "Evidence *defeats* Doubt."

Demonstrations. Illustrating a key point of our solution by using a demonstration, especially with the product or service itself, is a powerful addition to any presentation. As Percy Whiting said in *The 5 Great Rules of Selling*: "A good product doesn't need arguments; it needs demonstrations. A simple demonstration is more convincing than 10,000 words. It will sell more in a minute than gab will sell in a week."

Why are demonstrations so effective in interesting customers? Because they typically require the customer to get involved. While an exhibit is something a customer can see and touch, a demonstration brings the exhibit into action. The customer sees firsthand how the solution will affect her company.

Kevin Kinney, who sold telephone systems in Boston, Massachusetts, saw firsthand the impact of demonstrations in his closing ratio. When he didn't use a demonstration, 25 to 30 percent of his prospects became customers. When he did start incorporating demonstrations into his solutions, his closing ratio more than doubled to 80 percent.

"I discovered the power of this tool almost by accident. We had a demonstration kit that, on the outside, looked something like a big suit-case. I really didn't like using it because it took a lot of time to set up and it was rather cumbersome to carry around. But I started to notice that almost every time I brought it out, I gained commitment.

"In one particular situation, I was calling on the decision-maker of a small furniture store chain. He was planning to open a new store. When I arrived at the site, I got out the demonstration kit for our telephone systems and set it up in the middle of the room. Then I let him and others on his team see how easy the system was to operate. I let them transfer calls and use the system just as they would on an everyday basis."

The result?

"I gained commitment that day and the customer asked for three more phone systems to be installed at their headquarters and at other stores."

An interesting note about Kevin's story: This particular prospect had already decided to go with another provider prior to Kevin's demonstration. "I had to use a lot of other selling tools to get back in the door, but the demonstration is what drove the buying decision. And the fact that the purchase came that same afternoon is also pretty exciting. Because in this business, it's rare that buying decisions come on the same day as the presentation."

You might be thinking, "I sell an intangible product. Demonstrations won't work for me." That's a logical thought. But that's the very reason we would want to use demonstrations. Instead of showing specification sheets or brochures, for example, we could use videos or PowerPoint presentations to get the customer involved.

Paul McGrath of Sydney, Australia, found a creative way to demonstrate radio advertising.

"It's difficult to demonstrate in the radio business. The best we could often do was show some statistics and talk about ratings. My company took it a step further, though. We would actually produce a unique ad for each customer and then edit the tape to sound as if it was actually on the air. Then we would play the tape for the customer and let them keep it. Most customers would play it over and over again.

"We ended up increasing sales significantly with this technique because it appealed to the customer's emotions. We turned the intangible into a tangible, just by making a little extra effort on the front end of the sale."

Examples. Anytime our product or service exceeds customer expectations, we have a success story we can use as an example. When this happens, we need to add it to our evidence file.

What if we can't think of anything? We can ask other salespeople in our organization to share examples of successes they've observed. We can ask our sales manager or any of the executives of our company—right up to the company president if that's realistic—for stories they know about. When we find a customer who is exceptionally enthusiastic about our product or service, we should ask why.

When using examples as evidence, keep these guidelines in mind:

Tell the truth. In other words, we shouldn't invent success stories. The best reason for not using invented examples is this: They sound invented.

Talk about the product or service, not ourselves. The best examples are usually the ones that happened to us. We can tell them better. But we must be sure that we are not the hero of the examples. We don't share success stories to glorify ourselves. We share them to glorify the products and services we have to offer.

Make the success stories move. Examples should have a plot, action, and most of all, a happy ending. We should say something positive that happened to someone using our product or service.

Examples must be relevant. The example must reinforce a point that is meaningful to the customer's situation. For example, a travel agent talking to a young honeymoon couple looking for a romantic cruise probably won't find it too effective to share a success story about how she planned a trip to Europe for a large group of senior citizens. That example won't be relevant to her prospects.

Facts. Not only can we use facts in developing our solutions, we can also use other supporting facts to provide evidence. Are we using facts upon facts? Yes we are. Let's go back to the previous example of the gears in the robot arm. After citing a fact and benefit, we might add the many reasons (facts) that the gears in this robot arm last 22 percent longer. For example, the evidence could be, "They're made of stainless steel. The lubricant is sealed in. Each piece is individually tested for cracks, strengths, and size." These additional facts support our key fact that the gear is durable. Using additional facts often enhances our credibility.

We can also turn facts into understatements and use those as evidence. An understatement sounds something like this: "This new automated system won't run all by itself, but you can run it with one operator instead of six."

Why would we ever understate anything about our products and services? Here are some of the reasons:

> **It keeps us from exaggerating.**
>
> **It keeps our talk from sounding like "high-pressure" selling.**
>
> **It favorably impresses our customer.**
>
> **It is convincing.**

For example, if we say, "This new voice-activated phone system will save your secretary more than an hour a day," we leave room for doubt.

If we use understatements, suddenly our credibility is enhanced. "I believe this machine will save your secretary at least an hour a day. The reason I believe it is that the office manager at Unity Federal told me yesterday that these machines are saving their secretaries nearly two hours a day."

A financial services representative in the banking industry found an understatement to be the piece of evidence that "solidified" one particular customer account. He used it when proposing one of his bank's cash management products as a solution for a potential customer.

"I said to the customer, 'I am not sure if our program can help you grow your business by the 28 percent average we've seen on our portfolio. But I am convinced that you could grow by 10 percent.' "

Clearly, an understatement can be effective and credible. Should we try to understate all facts about our products? Of course not. If we use too many understatements, we lose the impact. A solution full of understatements would be no understatement at all.

Exhibits. Exhibits are something the customer can see and touch. While a demonstration is an active form of evidence, exhibits do not require the customer to get involved.

An auto show in a large convention center is a good example of an exhibit. We can see the cars up close, sit in them, touch them, and so forth, but we can't drive them. Think back to Kevin Kinney's story about phone systems. If Kevin had not let his prospects physically use the phone systems, he would have merely had an exhibit.

In some sales situations where demonstrations are not possible, exhibits are highly effective. Gayle Herlong found that to be true when she sold heating and air-conditioning systems.

Gayle was about to make a presentation to a hospital administrator who made it clear that she did not know much about the heating and air-conditioning systems in her facility. Not only that, the administrator had also indicated she was not interested in learning more about such systems.

How would Gayle get a prospect like this interested in her solution?

She decided to go for an exhibit. First, she took some Polaroid photos of the hospital's existing heat and air-conditioning systems, especially those on the rooftop that the administrator admitted she had never actually seen. As Gayle took a photo of the intake fan, she noticed a huge air handler that was full of lint and dirt. She reached in and grabbed several handfuls of the gray, sticky, gummy dirt and stuffed them in a brown paper bag.

At the appropriate moment in the presentation, Gayle showed the administrator photos of the rooftop equipment, and then took out a big handful of dirt from the paper bag. "This is the dirt that was stuck to the intake fan of your air-handling unit," she said. "What effect do you think it will have if some of this dirt is sucked into your hospital air system?"

The administrator seemed relieved when Gayle refrained from handing her the dirt, but instead, put the dirt back in the bag and left it in the center of the conference table for the rest of the meeting. This clever demonstration was a reminder that the administrator was not getting the service from her equipment that she thought she was.

Against all odds, Gayle walked off with the sale.

Paul McGrath of Sydney, Australia, relates a story of a salesperson he knew who sold corporate jets. Obviously, this salesperson couldn't bring an actual jet into the meeting. So what did he do? He brought in a small model jet with the name of the prospect's company painted on the side.

As a sales professional for Cintas Uniforms, Liz Dooley used a similar idea to reach a key decision-maker.

"Working with an office supply company, I was not in touch with the decision-maker. I was talking with a secondary decision-maker. Because of that, I couldn't get commitment. Everything had to be reviewed by her boss.

"I needed a way to get her off the fence and get a decision about whether they were going to use the program. So I actually created their uniform. I had a sample of the shirt and pants made up with their logo. Then I just stopped by her office. When she walked up to the reception area to see me, she got really excited when she saw the shirts. She said, 'Larry has to see this.'

"She walked me right back to the president's office. By the end of the week I had a contract for a uniform program."

Analogies. An analogy supports our solution by helping the customer compare the familiar to the unfamiliar. Salespeople who are skilled at using analogies can take virtually any commonplace item or scenario and relate it to the solution they present to their customers.

For example, "Our technical staff is a lot like the electricity in your house. You don't always need the lights on, but when you do, the electricity is there. The same goes for us. When you need our technical staff, we'll be there, twenty-four hours a day. Getting hold of us is as easy as turning on the light."

Notice how this statement takes the familiar (electricity) and relates it to something that is unfamiliar or unproven to the customer (our technical staff). By drawing this comparison, we enhance the customer's understanding of how our solution meets his or her needs.

Analogies are often effective when we sell complicated products, especially with buyers who may not understand the technical facts and benefits. User buyers are an example. For instance, if we are selling a software system to an accounts payable staff, they don't really want to understand how the software is configured. They just want to know that they'll be able to learn it easily and use it efficiently. In a scenario like this, we could say, "Learning to use this software is like learning to drive a car. It seems complicated at first, but then it becomes second nature."

Testimonials. There's a saying that goes, "A whisper by a satisfied user is louder than a shout by a self-interested salesperson." In our sales training, we frequently ask our participants, "How many of you carry with you any form of testimonial letters to support the success of your products and services?" Rarely do more than 20 percent raise their hands. Yet, what better evidence can we provide than a statement by a satisfied customer?

Like examples, testimonials are a type of evidence we gather as the result of exceeding customer expectations. Typically, testimonials acknowledge our company's capabilities, in spoken or written form, from someone who has used our products or services successfully. Testimonials differ from examples in that they are usually provided directly from the customer, rather than secondhand through our own language.

When it comes to testimonials, we don't necessarily need extraordinary facts or statements. Sometimes, just good and specific applications are best. The more specific the testimonial is, the more convincing it is as evidence. It also adds more credibility if the testimonial is written on an original copy on the customer's letterhead.

To find testimonials, we can go to satisfied users and ask for them. To make it easier for our customers, we can ask the customer what he or she is willing to say and write the testimonial letter ourselves. Then, we ask the customer to approve it, print it on his or her own stationery, and sign it.

Of course, some customers will want to write the letter themselves, so we won't want to prevent them from doing so. Whatever the case, the key is to minimize the inconvenience to our customers and be sure to work within their individual comfort levels.

If you're new to selling or are just trying to add to your current testimonial file, ask your sales manager and other salespeople if they have letters in their files you might be able to use.

We can also develop a list of telephone testimonials. These are very effective in supporting the facts we plan to use in developing our solution.

For example, if we say, "A number of grocers in nearby towns have found this to be a fast-moving item," we are leaving room for doubt. If, instead, we say, "Here is a list of grocers in this county who have stocked this item and found that it moves quickly. Please feel free to call anyone on this list," we have just made our presentation more convincing.

Statistics. Accurate and documented statistics are always helpful in supporting our facts and benefits. They are especially effective when we're dealing with numbers-oriented customers.

We should be careful not to confuse facts and statistics. While a numerical fact might relate to a specific piece of our solution, statistics usually represent a comparison of other numerical information. This includes percentages, ranges, and averages.

For example, a fact might be that our company has 1,512 users of our software product who say we have exceeded their expectations. This fact alone might be meaningless to the customer unless we use a statistic: An independent agency conducted a recent survey that indicates 92 percent of our customers say we exceeded their expectations.

Another key with statistics is to keep them relevant. It's not really effective to tell a person that 98 percent of our customers who lease will eventually buy the product when leasing isn't one of her considerations.

Remember: Fools can figure and figures can fool. So we shouldn't build our whole presentation around statistics.

Building an evidence book. Have you ever met or interviewed a writer, designer, or someone else in the creative communications business? If you have, you've probably noticed they often carry a portfolio of their work. And what about architects? If they're called to bid on a project, it's pretty certain they'll walk into their meeting with designs and drawings from past projects. This is the "evidence book" they present to prospective clients. And just as these professionals have adopted this system of proof, so can salespeople.

An evidence book is extremely helpful when we're looking for ways to support the solution we've developed. In most cases, we won't share the whole evidence book. But, as we work to develop unique solutions, we will determine which pieces of evidence are most relevant to the customer's primary interests and Dominant Buying Motive. Having an evidence book filled with a variety of proof provides us an invaluable support tool that enhances our credibility in the customer's eyes.

An evidence book is a compilation of the different types of evidence we've covered in the previous pages. It:

- Provides information about our company
- Shows how our products and services have satisfied customers
- Demonstrates the applications customers are making of our products and services

Ms. Lu Li Fung created an evidence book as a requirement of Sales Advantage training. She did it because she had to, but quickly found out what a powerful selling tool it is.

Ms. Lu runs a teashop in Nantou, Taiwan, a famous tea-producing region of the country. One day after she finished her evidence book, a customer and his friend came to her store to buy some tea. They asked her for a recommendation. Since Ms. Lu needed to practice her sales presentation for her class, she asked the customer if he had time to listen. The customer said he did, so Ms. Lu gave a six-minute presentation, complete with evidence book and flip charts.

The customer was so impressed that he gave a business card to Ms. Lu. "I have never seen anything like this. My company is looking for a supplier for our tea drink products. We already have ten bidders, but I think we will make an exception and let you be the eleventh bidder. Please come to my company, bring your evidence book, and do that presentation for my boss and the purchasing committee." It turned out that her customer just happened to be the purchasing manager of one of the largest food and beverage companies in Taiwan (Tai-shan Industries).

Ms. Lu went to Tai-shan's headquarters and did two presentations. Her presentation was so well received that Tai-shan informed Ms. Lu that they would do business with her on a test basis. She asked them to clarify just exactly how much tea they would be ordering for the test. The customer said "Two thousand kilograms." She was shocked, because her entire annual sales previously had been two thousand kilograms.

Ms. Lu went home and began preparing for this order. After this test order, Tai-shan was very satisfied, so it gave her a second order of twenty thousand kilograms of tea. She had to form a new company and hire many people just to take care of this order. Finally, Tai-shan decided to use Ms. Lu permanently as the major supplier of their tea beverage products. They gave her an order for one hundred thousand kilograms of tea.

She is now one of the most successful tea merchants in Nantou. Many tea farmers line up outside her company each morning to sell her their tea. And it all started with good timing and a solution presentation that contained an evidence book.

Granted, this situation is unique because Ms. Lu didn't have to go through earlier parts of the selling process. But if we think about it, there's always a possibility that our biggest customer may turn out to be that person who simply crosses our path at the right time. And when that happens, we need to be ready. An evidence book is one tool we have to help prepare us for that important moment.

At Dale Carnegie and Associates, one of our sales teams in San Diego created a photo evidence book. They visited graduates and took their pictures with a Polaroid. Then they asked the graduate to sign their own business card and then write on it the number-one benefit of taking Dale Carnegie Training. Clients loved this, and the people who were considering training enjoyed looking at these books for people they knew or for people who had similar jobs.

While evidence books have traditionally been printed materials, the evolution of technology allows us to create electronic evidence books. Today, with laptop computers, it's possible to take our evidence book to a more advanced level. We can show our company's Internet site. We can use video or audio clips of satisfied customers. We can even share video clips of our products or services being used.

No matter what evidence you decide to use, remember that proof is personal. In other words, choose the right type of evidence for each customer. Facts and statistics don't impress everyone. Some people prefer exhibits or demonstrations. Make it a point to know your customer well enough to know what type of evidence will be most effective.

Radio advertising is a good example. Just by showing the right statistics, almost any major radio station can offer evidence that it is the number-one station in a particular market segment. Unfortunately, these statistics aren't meaningful for everyone. The point is, don't fall into the habit of using the same evidence for every customer.

BUILDING BLOCK 6: TRIAL CLOSE

As we're developing our solution, we should identify points in the upcoming presentation where it would make sense to get the customer's feedback. This is when we want to use a trial close.

Think back to the example we've been using about the in-town technicians. Here's how the trial close would work in that scenario.

Fact. We stock parts and supplies for every Tech product we sell . . .

Bridge. Which means . . .

Benefit. . . . Everything you need to keep your equipment working is available when you need it.

Application. So you can get parts within one hour, instead of sending out your systems for repair or waiting for out-of-town service and delivery. Your staff will be much happier because their downtime will be minimal, and you will have fewer complaints from them.

Trial close. Getting maintenance or replacement parts for your equipment, without having much downtime, is important to you, isn't it?

If the customer answers, "Yes," then we're on the right track. But if we sense some disagreement, we now have a chance to clarify the issue immediately.

We don't want to wait until we've presented our entire solution to assess the customer's reaction. We may have to revise our solution based on their answer to the trial close. Or we may find, since our last meeting, some of the issues may have changed.

By having checkpoints throughout our solution, we can go back and address the issues that need more clarification, or we can avoid taking the customer's time on things that are no longer barriers to gaining commitment.

There's another reason that using trial closes is a good idea. If we have done our homework and we are presenting our unique solution effectively, we begin to build an atmosphere of agreement that our solution meets the customer's needs. If she's agreeing along the way that our solution is on track, it's more likely she'll be agreeable when we ask for commitment.

CHAPTER 7

Solution Presentation
Sharing Our Recommendations

Many salespeople are so intent on telling what the product is that they forget to tell what it does.

—PERCY H. WHITING

Can you think of a time when you were really not in the market for a product or service, but the salesperson's presentation was so compelling, you had to think twice? Or maybe it was the other way around. Maybe you were interested in making a purchase, but the salesperson did not communicate very well. In that case, you may have walked away confused, not knowing whether you should go forward with the buying decision.

Most of us have experienced both of these scenarios at some point in our lives. That's why it's important for us to realize that selling is not just a people business, it's also a communication business. Even if our solution is exactly what the customer needs and wants, our ability to communicate our ideas effectively will likely increase the odds that we gain commitment.

We must have the ability to express our solutions in a compelling and persuasive way. Even if communication isn't our strong point, most of us can learn to share solutions with our customers in a way that captures their attention and keeps them interested.

How to Be a Powerful Communicator

Whether we're sharing a solution in person or on the telephone, communication fundamentals written by Dale Carnegie can dramatically improve the positive impact of our presentation.

BE EXCITED ABOUT YOUR TOPIC AND EAGER TO SHARE YOUR IDEAS

This gets back to the whole issue of enthusiasm. If you have trouble being excited about your product, you might want to try an idea Percy Whiting shared in *The 5 Great Rules of Selling:* Spend some quality time selling yourself on your product or service. "Think over its values. Realize them. Burn them into your mind. Consider what your product will do for [your customers], the money it will make for them, or possibly the fun they will have using it. Say these things over to yourself. Think them in your heart . . . light the flame of your enthusiasm." When you've sold yourself, the excitement in your presentation will come naturally.

BE ANIMATED WITH YOUR VOICE AND GESTURES

Dale Carnegie once said, "We should be natural in the sense that we express our ideas and express them with spirit." In other words, it doesn't matter what we say if we're standing somewhat rigidly in front of our audience or talking in a monotone on the telephone. If we look or sound bored, our listeners will be as well.

Think about popular contemporary speakers, such as Zig Ziglar. What makes his presentation style so compelling? It's the way he uses his voice and body language to engage the audience.

Danger Words

There are many words we're tempted to use in our presentations that we often think add credibility. But in most cases, they are simply trite and overused. If you include one of these words in your presentation, make sure you can back it up with facts and evidence.

- Best
- Largest
- Quality (or highest quality)
- Fastest
- Quickest

Hint: Any adjective that ends in "est" is probably a danger word.

SPEAK DIRECTLY TO YOUR LISTENERS

This rule is not so much about eye contact as it is about talking in terms of the customers' interests and seeing things from their point of view.

The good news is, if we have succeeded in using the Sales Advantage tools, the presentation of our solution should automatically address the issues that are important to our customers. But it's not unusual for new issues to arise as we begin to present our solution.

As a loan officer for Lexington State Bank in Winston-Salem, North Carolina, Linda Maynard sensed apprehension in a room full of people to whom she was making her presentation.

"This customer was a huge cash management prospect for me," said Linda. "I had to appear before their executive committee to present one of our products as a solution for their cash management needs. When I began presenting my solution, I immediately felt their apprehension toward a new product and a new banker. I sensed they needed to be reassured that my bank and I could handle their business.

"Even though I hadn't planned on it, I gave them a very brief history of my cash management experience. As it turned out, the treasurer knew and respected a lot of the people I worked with at my previous bank. With that knowledge, my credibility was enhanced. He quickly became receptive to my presentation.

"As I closed my presentation to the group, I offered to assist any of them with personal banking needs they might have. For me, the 'icing on the cake' from this meeting was the fact that one of the officers of the company inquired about doing her personal banking with us. Before the end of the day, I had her checking account business, a safe deposit box rented, a credit line established, and an ATM card in the system.

"Needless to say, in a couple of days, we had the new cash management account up and running for this customer's business. His company earned approximately ten thousand dollars in interest income they had never earned before due to the absence of a cash management program. Now, we also provide them with additional services such as corporate credit cards."

Had Linda just presented the solution as she had intended, she might not have achieved the level of rapport she developed in that particular meeting. Instead, she knew the audience was interested in her professional background, and she responded accordingly. "Had I not been tuned in to their mood, I would've missed a very important opportunity to build trust. And I might have missed the opportunity to do business with them."

When we present our solution, we should also be sure to talk in the customer's language.

How do we do that? For instance, if a customer told us specifically that our product or service would boost productivity (what he wants), which will potentially earn his department recognition in the company (why he wants it), we'd want to use that same language in our solution presentation. It shows that we listened to the customer and understood his needs.

Here's another example. Say we're selling a new computer system, and our prospect mentions that Kerri and John (his direct reports) have been very frustrated because the current system crashes at least twice a day.

When we present our solution, we could find ways to incorporate specific details of his situation. "I can only imagine how frustrated your team must be when the system crashes twice a day. I think Kerri and John will be quite pleased when they see that our system is much more reliable."

Of course, we would need facts and evidence to back up that statement. But that we have made a statement specifically about elements in the other person's world demonstrates our good listening skills.

Put yourself in that customer's shoes. Wouldn't you be more inclined to do business with a salesperson who talked in terms of your interest than with one who simply gave you a presentation on features and benefits? Remember, anytime we can demonstrate our ability to understand the customer's world and speak his language, we increase our credibility in his eyes.

Scott Jamieson, president of Hendricksen, The Care of Trees, tells how he and his company organized a successful sales presentation by using the solution building blocks to develop a presentation that talked in terms of the customer's interest.

The challenge? "After twenty years of having our contract renewed without having to rebid, our customer—a city just outside Chicago, Illinois—required us to go through a bidding process and make a presentation to the City Council.

"I prepared an evidence book that included several letters of praise about our company from residents in the city, news articles highlighting our community service and our commitment to giving back to the community. The most useful thread throughout the presentation was that of presenting our unique benefits specific to the city—things I knew were important to them and no other tree care company could ever claim.

"With each benefit I attached the application—'What it means to the city'—to really drive home the point of how we provided value to the city.

"We nearly got a standing ovation for our presentation. More important, we were awarded the contract for another six years. We later heard a comment from a council member that our presentation was outstanding and really showed that we understood the city's needs and wants.

"Several weeks later one of our board members, who is a marketing professor at Northwestern University, was speaking at an event. During her speech, she mentioned that she was on our board. When she said the name of our company, a voice from the audience nearly shouted what a great company we are. That voice was from one of the council members who had been at our presentation."

BE CONCISE AND GET TO THE POINT

While this is important in all types of presentations, it's probably most important when we're presenting our solutions on the telephone. After all, we can't use visuals to get attention and we don't have the benefit of interacting with the customer to use demonstrations or exhibits.

In any presentation, we shouldn't give any more facts than our customers need. Remember, the story of creation is told in the book of Genesis in 400 words. The Ten Commandments contain only 297 words. Abraham Lincoln's famous Gettysburg Address is just 266 words in length. And the United States Declaration of Independence required just 1,321 words to set up a new concept of freedom. A good rule of thumb is this: When we hear ourselves say, "To make a long story short," it is generally too late.

Commonsense Guide to Clarity

- Have your subject clear in your own mind. About half the fuzzy selling efforts today are due to fuzzy thinking.
- Use short, familiar words. Remember this: Out of the 266 words in Abraham Lincoln's Gettysburg Address, more than 185 have only one syllable. It's still quite a memorable message.
- Don't talk too fast. Think ahead of your customers, but talk behind them. Pause often.
- Don't expect customers to understand complicated jargon. This is especially important in technical sales. Granted, it's likely that some of your listeners might understand, but will everyone? On the other hand, be careful not to "dumb it down" too much, to the point where you insult your customers.

REMEMBER THE POWER OF EVIDENCE

Say we're listening to a presentation for the best new fitness machine ever offered. It's guaranteed to make us fit and trim with very little effort each day. If the salesperson launches into a lengthy verbal description of the equipment, we might think he has something to offer. But we aren't necessarily convinced that it's the best fitness machine ever.

What happens if that same salesperson shares stories about famous people who own this piece of equipment? What's more, he shares with us testimonials from people like us who have sold every other piece of fitness equipment they own just to use this magic machine. Now, what kind of impression do we have?

Without a doubt, evidence makes a big difference in the impact of our presentations. A sales professional in Santa Clara, California, found this tool to be the key in gaining a large order. In fact, by using evidence, he was able to prove that his product was far superior to his competitor's.

In selling insulated wiring to computer manufacturers, this salesperson discovered that one of his top accounts had given a large order to a competitor because of a big price difference. The salesperson knew something wasn't right, so he got some of the competitor's wiring and had it analyzed by his research and development department. What did he find? Unlike his company's product, the competitor's wiring wasn't fireproof.

The salesperson then set an appointment with his customer. During the presentation, he almost appeared to be selling the competitive product because both products had the same characteristics and the competitor's wiring was indeed less expensive.

Then, he said to the decision-makers, "As you can see, both products meet your specifications and my product is more expensive. They are alike in many ways, except for one important thing." With this, he lit a lighter and held the flame under the competitor's wiring. The insulation began smoldering and ultimately caught fire. His audience was astonished. The salesperson then held the flame under his company's wiring, as he reminded the customers that his product was fireproof.

He concluded by asking, "Gentleman, which wiring do you want inside your computers?" The customers subsequently canceled their order with the competitor. They also thanked the salesperson for his research, which potentially saved their company hundreds of thousands of dollars.

Clearly, by bringing the facts to life with a demonstration, this sales professional powerfully persuaded the customer that his product was superior. What if he hadn't used evidence? Would the outcome have been as successful? Remember, when it comes to presenting our solutions, actions often speak louder than words.

SUMMARIZE FREQUENTLY

There's a story about a sales representative who waited too long to summarize his point. He turned to the customer and said, "Do you follow me?"

"I have so far," the man answered, "but I'll say frankly, Mr. Peek, if I thought I could find my way back, I'd quit right here."

In other words, if the customer isn't following our solution presentation, it's probably our fault. And the sooner we know, the better.

We can use summaries in conjunction with our trial close questions. But we have to be careful not to get too repetitive. Use unique summaries and trial closes to ensure that the customer understands. Summaries, just like trial closes, are a good way to test the level of interest in the solution we're presenting.

IF POSSIBLE, GET THE CUSTOMER INVOLVED IN AN INTERACTIVE WAY

It all goes back to demonstrations. This is easier for some of us than others, especially if we're conducting the presentation in person. But if we can include something to get the customer involved in the solution presentation, it can greatly enhance the power of what we say.

Interactivity works particularly well when we have a product the customer can see or feel. For example, say we're selling computer software. It certainly makes sense that our customers would be more engaged in our presentation if we brought some samples for them to try. Even if we're not presenting in person, we could send the customer a sample program and then discuss it on the telephone.

While products are more conducive to interaction, it is possible to involve the audience when selling services, too. What if we are selling a logistics management service and we want to prove a point that no customer is ever put on hold for more than thirty seconds? Letting our customers place a few calls would validate in their minds that our claim is true.

CHECK, DOUBLE-CHECK, AND TRIPLE-CHECK THE FACILITY, AUDIOVISUAL EQUIPMENT, AND LOGISTICAL FACTORS

It's always a good idea to determine what tools we need, if any, before the day of the meeting. Then, we can check with our customer beforehand to see if those tools are available. We can also ask for permission to arrive early and get acclimated to the presentation environment. Most customers will be very gracious about answering our questions and allowing us to arrive early to prepare. In fact, they will often appreciate the care we're putting into the presentation.

Jarrad McCarthy, sales representative with Endagraph, a full-service graphics company in Export, Pennsylvania, discovered an added benefit of showing up early at a customer's site. "I had a meeting with Ladbrokes Racing Corporation to sell the customer interior graphics for his gaming restaurants. The meeting was with Ladbrokes' architects and vice president. I got there early and met the architects, who were early also. I sold my ideas to the architects before the customer ever showed up. When the customer arrived, the architects were so excited about the ideas they virtually presented them for me. I didn't even have to do my formal presentation. They repeated everything to my customer I had explained to them."

Presentation Options

Chances are, unless your typical sales presentation is fairly repeatable and predictable, you'll use different methods for different customers. Time constraints, physical location, and customer availability will influence your decision in selecting the most appropriate and most effective presentation alternative.

Stand-up Presentations

ADVANTAGES

- Allows the sales professional's personality to influence the decision
- Encourages question and answer sessions
- Presents an opportunity to share additional information
- Can change the presentation if additional issues arise

DISADVANTAGES

- Allows the sales professional's personality to influence the decision
- Provides a basis for comparison in presentation styles between competitors
- Offers an advantage to strong presenters from the competition
- May not be interactive

Telephone

ADVANTAGES

- Time-expedient
- Minimal out-of-pocket expense
- Flexible

DISADVANTAGES

- No personal interaction
- Difficult to read the customer's reactions
- Minimal time allotted
- Can eliminate demonstrations and exhibits

Proposals

ADVANTAGES

- Eliminates being misquoted
- Objective data is clearly presented
- Allows consideration over a longer period
- Easily shared with others

DISADVANTAGES

- Allows consideration over a longer period
- Provides specific information beyond our span of control
- Diminishes personal interaction

Conversational

ADVANTAGES

- Allows the sales professional's personality to influence the decision
- Is typically more of a dialogue than a structured presentation
- Allows more latitude and less formality
- Typically interactive

DISADVANTAGES

- Typically happens very quickly
- Is influenced heavily by one person's opinion
- Requires good listening, retention, and concentration from the customer

Team

ADVANTAGES

- More diverse personalities
- Greater knowledge base

- Diverse presentation styles
- Comprehensive coverage of key issues
- Typically organized more thoroughly

DISADVANTAGES

- Too many presentation styles
- Too much information
- Personal relationships are less likely to be formed
- Typically longer in length

Technical

ADVANTAGES

- Demonstrates our organizational expertise
- Assures the accuracy of our presentation
- Allows a broader spectrum of questions
- Shows the technological base of our organization

DISADVANTAGES

- Can move the presentation into a discussion involving too much of the "how" rather than the "what" of our products/services
- Can become dry for the nontechnical buyer
- Can overwhelm the buyer with information

Turn Up the Impact: Use Showmanship

The word "showmanship" usually conjures up visions of old-fashioned selling. You know, the door-to-door vacuum cleaner salesman who interrupts our dinner and then, using as much animation and drama as possible, pours a huge amount of dirt on our carpet. From there, he proceeds to clean it up. He uses our vacuum and then he uses his vacuum. Then he shows us how much better his product is than the one we're currently using and how much cleaner our house will be with little effort.

Granted, the vacuum cleaner salesman in this story is using showmanship. But we need to change that negative image we have in our minds. Sure, the word showmanship is a little "old-fashioned," but the concept is alive and well and working for successful salespeople all over the world.

Showmanship is nothing more than adding an element of drama to your demonstrations. Dale Carnegie once said, "The truth has to be made vivid, interesting, dramatic. You have to use showmanship. The movies do it. The radio does it. And you will have to do it if you want attention."

Once we learn and, most important, feel comfortable with showmanship, it's a tremendous sales tool that can create a lasting and positive impression on our customers, especially in today's competitive marketplace. Remember, we don't necessarily use all the sales tools we have in the box. But the more tools we know how to use, the more chances we have of beating our competitors.

Adding showmanship to our selling efforts is often most effective when presenting the solution. However, it's appropriate in any selling situation where a dramatic or unusual demonstration would enhance the customer's understanding of the product or service.

Sometimes, it's effective to use showmanship during the presentation or after we've submitted our proposal.

Russ Pearce is a partner of Selling Solutions in the United Kingdom, a business development consulting firm specializing in marketing, sales, design, and training. He found that adding a little creativity after his presentation helped him gain commitment with a customer who appeared to be hesitating in making his decision.

"We made a proposal to the customer, a photographer. Despite a number of meetings and follow-up, he was not making a decision in our favor. Our biggest fear was that the work would go to another, more established firm.

"All three firms bidding on the job had provided quotations, presentations, and portfolios. But it occurred to me that the photographer's real need was for creativity, and that was the one thing that none of the organizations had demonstrated. I was suddenly struck by the clarity of the situation and, therefore, felt very confident in doing something a bit 'off the wall.'

"So I decided to order a pizza, but not just any pizza. I bought a large one with cheese, pineapple, and a sweet corn base, so that it was completely yellow. Then, I had the message, 'It ain't what you do, it's the way you do it,' written in peppers and mushrooms. Since I didn't know whether the customer was vegetarian, I took no chances.

"I personally delivered the pizza and was then told I had the contract. I think the customer was drawn to the fact that I actually demonstrated creativity instead of just claiming to offer it. I don't even think of this as showmanship, necessarily. I just think of it as congruency and integrity. The lesson for me was, simply, 'Be what you claim.' "

Since Russ's business is built around creativity, the message on the pizza was appropriate for his situation. Having a pizza delivered may not be right for your industry, but something else might. The key is to be open to the possibilities of what you can do to make your company stand out from the rest.

Guidelines for Showmanship

Showmanship is typically entertaining, but its sole purpose is not to entertain. To ensure that our actions are appropriate, it helps to remember these guidelines:

- It must be relevant to the customer relationship.
- It must be in good taste.
- We must feel comfortable with it.
- Our customer must react positively.
- The action should be memorable.

Getting Comfortable with Showmanship

As with most things that take us out of our comfort zone, using drama requires courage, along with some practice. To get started, it helps to understand the ways in which we can incorporate these techniques into our selling efforts.

DO SOMETHING UNEXPECTED OR DRAMATICALLY DIFFERENT

Jeff Leonard knows why doing something unexpected makes a big impact. He recalls getting up the courage to use showmanship when his company was bidding on a large project in Greensboro, North Carolina. "As I was driving to one of the contractors' offices, I decided I wanted to do something out of the ordinary—and I decided to use the bed of my pickup truck to do it.

"Reason being, while most of my truck is in good shape, the bed of my truck is completely dented and banged up from one end to the other. But it got this way by helping my customers. If they call me and say that they need just one joint of pipe, or anything else, at their job site, then I immediately load it up with a forklift and take it to them. The result of my added service is a scratched and dented truck bed.

"By the time I arrived at the prospect's office, I had concluded that my truck was something to be proud of. These people were going to remember me for some time to come. That was my goal.

"I found their office, walked into the lobby, and greeted the receptionist. I said, 'Hello, I'm Jeff Leonard with Foltz Concrete Pipe Company. I do not have an appointment, but it is very important that I speak to Sam right away.' She seemed as if she would be willing to help me. My large smile and a handful of note pads (with our company logo on it) prompted her to ask, 'What is the subject of your visit with Sam?'

"I said, 'I'm glad you asked. I need for him to come out to the parking lot immediately. I must show him my truck. That's all I can say at this time.' I now have a very serious look on my face and she paged Sam quickly on the intercom system.

"After a minute or two, Sam came through the door. I quickly grabbed his hand and shook it vigorously. I then asked him, 'Could you come out to the parking lot for a minute or two? There is something I must show you.' Extremely puzzled, he said, 'What is it? What do you want to show me?' I said, 'It's my truck. I must show you my truck.'

"He followed me to the parking lot. I continued to promise that I would only take up a minute of his valuable time. I told him that I knew that he was very busy working the Greensboro project estimates, but that this truck was critical to the Greensboro project.

"We arrived at the truck and I said, 'Well, what do you think? Is she a beauty or what?'

"He replied, 'Yes, it's a pretty truck. But why did you want to show it to me?' I asked him to come over and look into the bed of the truck. I slammed down the tailgate real hard and said, 'Do you see all the scratches, dents, bumps, bangs, and destruction in the back of this truck? It came from hauling pipe and many other storm drainage items out to my customers' jobs when they forgot something or didn't order enough. I took it out to the jobs and unloaded it for them so that they could keep their men busy on the job site. I just wanted to show you what I'll do for you. I just wanted to show you that I'll beat and bang up my truck to save your company some time and some money. I just wanted to show you my truck because I'm so proud of it. Well, I gotta go! Thanks for your time!'

"He said, 'Hey, wait, don't go yet. Have you got a few of your business cards?' I said, 'Sure, here you go.' I gave him my card, some company hats, and more note pads. I said, 'Look Sam, I told you that I wasn't here to take up much of your time and I'm not. Just call me if I can help you.'

"I opened the door with my efforts that day. I stretched myself mentally and emotionally in that unusual display. It was kind of scary but it was also fun. The interesting part of that sales call is that I never talked about concrete pipe. I only talked about my truck."

As a side note, Jeff Leonard's sales career with Foltz Pipe was so successful that he is now the president and CEO of the company.

USE ACTION AND MAKE SOMETHING HAPPEN

R. G. Sanderson, a retail salesman for General Foods in Enid, Oklahoma, shared a story in which showmanship helped him gain a record number of sales in a slow territory, at a slow time of year.

"One day, my immediate supervisor told me that the district sales manager would soon be out to work with me for a day. I learned that I was supposed to make a drive on Certo, which is used in making jams and jellies.

"The product managers in New York had not bothered to consider that, in northern Oklahoma, March is not the month for making jams. It is the month for shoveling snow.

"That week, when I noticed a grocery store throwing some black-colored, fully ripe bananas into the trash, I started trying to find a way that these bananas could be used in making a jam. When I looked into our Certo recipe booklet, I found a recipe for pineapple-banana jam. I made up some of the jam and found it to be rather tasty. Then I got an idea. Here's what I did.

"I would walk into a grocery store, go up to the banana stalk, pick up several black, fully ripe bananas, and ask the grocer what he was going to do with them. He usually answered, 'Throw 'em away.' Then I would ask, 'Aren't you throwing away your profit?'

"He, of course, would admit it. I would then say, 'If you had a merchandising plan that would not only sell those black bananas for you but also sell Certo, sugar, paraffin and jelly glasses, you would like to try it, wouldn't you?' The answer was always, 'Yes.' By the time the district manager came out to work with me, I had made up jam for the grocer to taste.

"What were the results? When my boss came out, I was ready. He worked with me in a snow-covered country territory on a day the temperature was around fifteen degrees Fahrenheit. In spite of the snow and cold, we sold every account we called on that day. For my two weeks' assignment on this product, I sold more than all the people in my sales group put together. And when the first promotion from the retail ranks was made from the Oklahoma City District, I got it!"

Even though small grocery stores are becoming more scarce today, the ideas behind R. G.'s use of showmanship are powerful. He did more than try to push Certo. He did more than simply show the grocers the jam recipe. He took action. He made his ideas come to life in a dramatic way. That's the idea behind showmanship.

USE A STRIKING EXHIBIT OR DEMONSTRATION

Heinz Meier of Lostor, Switzerland—owner of Auto Meier AG, Strengelbach and Zofingen—used a memorable demonstration in trying to overcome some problems he faced during a partial business renovation.

"When I was rebuilding my garage in the dealership, the fire department officials laid down plans for an emergency exit that was not a very practical solution in my eyes. The exit led from between the shelves in the spare parts store in the cellar, over an outside staircase, and ended exactly in the middle of our covered exhibition area. Because the steps down to the cellar were unprotected, the authorities ordered us to erect solid steel railings around the steps, which completely destroyed the look of our car showroom.

"Instead of erecting the railings, I fitted a flat metal grid over the hole, which didn't spoil the attractiveness of our facility.

"The day arrived when the authorities came to carry out their inspection. They didn't accept the metal grid. They believed, in case of a fire, people would be trapped under the grid and not be able to escape. They said the grid had to be taken away and replaced with the intrusive railings.

"I didn't agree. So I grabbed the three inspectors by the hand and took them into the cellar. When we reached the back of the cellar, I explained to the three amazed men that I was now going to simulate the escape from a fire with them. Not giving them time to think or say anything, I cried out at the top of my voice, "Fire! Fire!" I took the first man by the hand and ran quickly in the direction of the emergency exit and, therefore, to the controversial steps. All three followed me instinctively, as if there really were a fire. When we got to the steps, I pushed with all my weight under the metal grid, which flew across the floor above, and within seconds all four of us were standing outside.

"The three officials, before so stubborn, now looked at each other in amazement. The boss just nodded at me and you could tell by looking at him that he was very impressed. He just said, 'You win. You've persuaded us that your solution with the metal grid is absolutely practical. You'll get the necessary approval.'

"I am still convinced that simply by talking about my solution I would never have achieved my goal. My showmanship won the case for me and showed that sometimes actions really do speak louder than words."

TURN A DEMONSTRATION INTO A CONTEST

A salesperson in the plastic molding business wanted to prove that his product was superior to the others in his industry. What did he do? He brought the moldings into his meetings and stood on them. Then, he would get his customers involved. He would make a contest out of it, challenging them to break the molding by standing on it and jumping up and down. Of course, the molding never broke, and the salesperson proved his point.

Is there any element of your product or service that could become a contest? If so, you have an opportunity to try some showmanship and do something fun with your customers.

AROUSE CURIOSITY DRAMATICALLY

Showmanship does not necessarily call for elaborate equipment. For example, consider the vending machine salesperson who uses a large piece of paper to make his point at the opening of his solution presentation. In speaking to the customer, he unfolds a heavy piece of paper, spreads it out on the floor, and opens with the phrase: "If I could show you how that space could make you some money, you'd be interested, wouldn't you?"

As we can tell from the examples in this chapter, showmanship doesn't have to be difficult or "corny." By getting showmanship-conscious, we can be on the lookout for ways in which we can put relevant drama into our solution presentations.

Regardless of how we deliver our presentation or what tools we use, we need to remember two important things:

> *Make the presentation relevant to the customer.* If our presentation is simply in the form of a proposal, we need to make sure that we've asked enough questions to make the proposal unique to the customer. Simply addressing the requirements on a Request for Proposal (RFP) doesn't guarantee that we know all the customer's issues. We should still ask questions and find ways to add an element of personalization to each proposal we develop. In addition, if we have a standard PowerPoint or overhead presentation, we should find ways to personalize it for each customer. Maybe we can add the company's name at the top. Maybe we can use a couple of slides to present customer-specific objectives. Whatever the case, we shouldn't miss this opportunity to show our customers how much we appreciate their individual situation.

Put yourself into the presentation. Our job is not to narrate. It's to involve and highlight. In other words, if we use PowerPoint visuals as evidence, we should only use them as supporting pieces. They should not be the focus point of our solution presentation. If we show a video, we should describe how the key points in the video relate to the customer's situation. If we decide to use a demonstration, we should make sure it's something we're comfortable with, rather than something we don't like doing. In other words, customers are buying us as much as they are buying our products. Any time we can add a personal approach, we improve the odds that our presentation is relevant to the customer.

CHAPTER 8

Customer Evaluation
Moving Toward Commitment

The salesperson's job: to persuade people to want what they already need.

—E. ST. ELMO LEWIS

At this point, we've presented our solution. For the most part, we feel a huge sense of accomplishment. Now, we can catch our breath, sit back, and wait for the customer's decision, right? Not exactly.

Unfortunately, selling isn't that easy. If it were, then everyone would want to sell. It's very rare, especially in long sales cycles, for someone to commit to a purchase immediately after we present the solution.

On some occasions, especially when large capital expenditures are involved, customers may need to consult a buying committee or analyze how the solution will work within existing budget constraints.

On the other hand, there are also many times when budgets and committee reviews are not the real issues. It's those times we need to address as professional salespeople. The "I need to think it over" response often represents a stall in the sale and it can harm our chances of ever gaining commitment.

Why do customers intentionally stall? Many times, it's because we haven't given them a sense of urgency to buy. While we may have successfully shown them how our product or service fits their application, we haven't necessarily motivated them to commitment.

There are two reasons why this happens: 1) We fail to read, we misread, or we misinterpret the customer's buying or warning signals. Consequently, we don't respond to them. 2) We misunderstand or don't appeal strongly enough to the Dominant Buying Motive.

Buying and Warning Signals

Throughout the sales presentation, our prospects are constantly evaluating our words and actions. They respond to everything we present to them, verbally, physically, or emotionally. These responses are cues that we can view as buying or warning signals. As sales professionals, we must possess the ability to recognize these signals, accurately interpret them, and respond accordingly.

A big part of success in selling is being constantly aware of what our customers are thinking. Buying and warning signals are important checkpoints in the sales process to help ensure that our thinking is aligned with theirs.

BUYING SIGNALS

In most sales discussions, a time comes when our customers are ready to commit. This time may be a short second or a long month. In any case, we can look for buying signals—anything the customer says or does that indicates that he or she has a more favorable position regarding buying our products and services.

To best understand buying signals, it helps to think about our own behavior when we feel positive about a purchase. Do we physically relax around the salesperson? Does our voice exude excitement? Do we talk faster? Do we move faster? Chances are, our customers do the same things.

There are two types of buying signals: nonverbal and verbal. While it's important to recognize both types of buying signals, skillful salespeople become extremely adept at reading their customers' nonverbal cues. Why? People who are not open in their verbal communication style can tell us a lot by their actions. By looking for shifts in our customers' bodies and expressions, we learn when to stop our solution presentation and ask for feedback that may be critical in moving the relationship forward.

For many of us, the nonverbal cues are the most difficult to read. And sometimes they mislead us. After all, at times—out of common courtesy—people pretend to be interested in a product or service even if they lack the emotional motivation to buy.

In most cases, however, it's hard for anyone to disguise their true feelings behind their actions. For that reason, we need to learn what people do that may indicate an interest in buying.

Buying Signals

- Relax—and especially if they open their hands
- Lean toward you
- Assume a more pleasant expression
- Show agreement with your solutions by nodding
- Step back to admire your product
- Make minor decisions that support the major buying decision
- Have an unusual sparkle in their eyes
- Do something that indicates they already own the product

When Jeannette R. Liller was a military recruiter, she frequently relied on nonverbal buying signals, such as the ones mentioned above, to determine whether candidates were sold on the idea of joining. One particular candidate stands out in her mind.

"I met with a young man named Ed Johnson and I knew where I was every step of the way just by watching his reaction. He was sitting on the edge of his chair almost the whole time. When I said that we could pay for his college education, he nodded his head up and down and got a big smile on his face. He was very excited about it. When I told him the next step was taking the physical and gave him options of when to take it, he immediately decided when he wanted to take it. While he didn't come out and specifically say, 'I'm going to join,' I could tell he was serious about it."

Jeannette's story demonstrates some very obvious nonverbal buying signals. But our customers sometimes give us nonverbal cues that aren't so easy to interpret, for example:

- Re-examining a product sample
- Picking up the proposal or purchase order
- Shifting or moving their eyes
- Reaching for paperwork
- Picking up the literature and reading it

With these types of nonverbal cues, there's always a danger they may not be buying signals. For example, a customer may pick up our product sample because she doesn't like the way it looks. Or she might pick up the literature and put it in her filing cabinet as a cue she's no longer interested in the conversation. If you're uncertain about whether a nonverbal cue is a buying signal, you may want to ask some questions to clarify the customer's position. We'll cover these types of questions later in this chapter.

Verbal buying signals, on the other hand, are often much easier to read because they are simply more apparent. Here are some examples:

- Does it break easily?
- Can I lease it?
- Do I need specific training?
- Do you install it?
- Do you have a local service department?
- Can I trade in my old machine?

Stephen Neuberth, president of N Systems, Inc., a manufacturing firm based in Columbia, Maryland, knows from experience what kinds of verbal signals indicate a favorable buying decision for his specific company.

"When prospects want to discuss installation schedules and exact details of the equipment, it usually indicates to me that they have moved beyond thoughts about buying to thoughts about owning. In some cases, we provide microwave antennae for special events. In those situations, people typically ask for a quote. If they say, 'We'll need it by date x for the Jerry Lewis Telethon. Can you have it by then?' we believe that the commitment is coming our way. As soon as we say, 'Yes, we can make your delivery,' the purchase order isn't too far behind."

Like Stephen, we should also take time to think about what our customers might say in our unique business that indicates a buying signal. In fact, we may even notice verbal buying (or warning) signals earlier in the sales process during information gathering. This increases our awareness of specific issues we might need to address when we present the solution.

Take, for example, a salesperson selling accounting software to a finance manager. Toward the beginning of her meeting, she could ask, "What is the perception you have of my company's software?" The customer's answer typically provides some type of buying or warning signal.

If he says, "I hear it not only improves the process flow, it helps communication within the department," the salesperson has a good indication that his initial impression is favorable toward her company. She also could assume that process flow and communication are likely important to that person.

On the other hand, if he responds, "I hear it's overpriced for what it does," the salesperson knows immediately that the person is concerned about price and perhaps has a negative impression of her product. Either way, she gains valuable information that affects the rest of the sales discussion.

Trial close questions. Trial closes are evaluative questions. They are useful any time in the process, but especially when it comes to buying signals and warning signals. Here are a few you might use:

- How does this sound so far?
- What are your thoughts?
- What is your reaction to this idea?
- Is this the kind of picture you would like to see yourself in?
- Is that what you'd like to see happen?
- If you were to go ahead, are there any changes you would like to see made?
- In your opinion, does this sound as if it would meet your needs?

Our reaction to buying signals: trial close. Sometimes we don't feel comfortable stopping our solution presentations when we get buying signals. In reality, however, addressing buying signals effectively ensures that our solution is on target. It also allows us to share in our customer's enthusiasm for his upcoming buying decision.

As a general rule, if we get a buying signal, we should not ignore it. We should ask an evaluative trial close question. Remember, some buying signals may not be buying signals at all. That's why trial close questions are so important.

Trial close questions will help clarify where we are in the sales process, what we need to do to keep the discussion moving forward, and whether we are indeed getting a buying signal.

For example, if a prospect says, "Do you have a local service department?" we could respond with an evaluative question, such as, "How would that help meet your needs?" or "Why is that important to you?" The answer to those questions helps us evaluate what the person is thinking. Or what if she says, "Can I lease it?" We could respond with a question such as, "What about leasing appeals to you?"

One important note: When we get answers to these questions, we can often connect them with some aspect of our solution. In fact, if we did an effective job at information gathering, we should already know whether local service and leasing are important factors. However, there are occasions where we haven't been able to get the information, or where the person's needs have changed since we last met. The point is, when we ask an evaluative question, we should use the information we gain to ensure our solution provides what the customer wants and satisfies the emotional need for which they want it.

Leonard Frenkil, Jr., vice president of operations for Washington Place Management in Maryland, has learned the value of evaluative questions firsthand. In fact, he recalls a time when he wishes he had used a trial close question to help him understand his prospect's true position.

"The owner of a local partnership that purchases investment real estate moved into an apartment building while he was attending school. He liked the building and he bought it. But he didn't have any management background or experience. He wanted to know how I'd staff the building and how quickly I could take over. I was convinced I had a verbal buying signal that told me I had the job. In fact, I told him everything. I met with his contractors. We discussed the improvements that could be made within his existing contract parameters. We created operating schedules and budgets. But every time I'd ask for commitment, he put me off.

"Unfortunately, I didn't take the time to evaluate where he actually was in his thought process. I assumed he was giving me buying signals. But in reality, he was not buying. He was trying to get information from me so he could manage it himself."

Len developed good rapport with the prospect nonetheless. But that did little to ease his disappointment at not gaining commitment. From then on, he addressed every buying signal with a trial close evaluative question.

"In another situation, toward the end of my third meeting with the board of directors of a condominium association, the board president gave me a potential buying signal. He wanted to know, if they selected our company, would we ensure that we wouldn't change the specific property manager assigned to his account? My response was, 'If we make that commitment, are you ready to execute a new management agreement?' They said, 'Yes.' And we did."

In this case, the board president's question was indeed a buying signal. By asking an evaluative question, Len was able to determine his level of interest in the solution. Not only that, he was able to enhance the solution to accommodate a request that was important to his customer.

Clearly, buying signals are important and we must learn to read them accurately. In fact, if we're offering the right solution for our customers, we should expect to get buying signals. The key is to respond effectively, in a timely manner, and then move the discussion forward toward commitment.

WARNING SIGNALS

Frowning	Not attentive
Tense posture	Folding arms
Leaning back	Change in tone of voice
Keeping distance from visuals	Change in rate of speech

WARNING SIGNALS

Warning signals are typically anything a customer says or does that may indicate we have lost rapport, trust, or interest. Traditional sales language says to do nothing about warning signals. As professional salespeople, however, we need to realize that they are a common occurrence in the sales process. Just as buying signals indicate a favorable response toward our solution, warning signals typically indicate that the solution we're providing does not fit the customer's wants and needs.

Remember the last time you drove down the highway? Maybe you swerved a bit and hit the "rumble strip"—the silver reflectors down the middle of the lane that make a loud noise when you hit them. If you're familiar with this concept, you know that the rumble strip is designed to wake you up if you fall asleep while driving.

The same is true of warning signals. They serve as a wakeup call to let us know that something is wrong in the relationship between our customer and us.

Just like buying signals, warning signals can be both nonverbal and verbal.

Nonverbal warning signals include:

- Looking at a clock or watch
- Unresponsiveness
- Picking up unrelated papers and files
- Shifting in the chair
- Becoming less friendly
- Accepting telephone calls
- Shifting eyes

When it comes to verbal warning signals, customers may say things like:

- I've heard that before.
- I don't see anything different.
- How much longer is your presentation?
- Can we continue this some other time?

Remember, as we explained in our discussion of buying signals, what we perceive to be a warning signal may not be a warning signal at all. For example, if the customer wants to end the meeting, it could be because he really has another meeting to attend. If he accepts phone calls, he may just be hoping to hear from his boss who's been out of the office all week. If he looks at his watch, he may be admiring a new gift he just received.

Once again, just as we do with buying signals, we need to ask some questions to determine whether the warning signal is real.

For example, if we notice the customer's attention beginning to waver, we could use an evaluative question such as, "It appears as if I'm not addressing your issues. Is there something I missed?"

If we get a verbal warning signal, open-ended questions can be very effective. If he remarks, "I don't see anything different," we could say, "Could you elaborate on that?"

The point is, warning signals demand that we stop the sales process and ask a question to assess where we are with the customer. If we recognize warning signals and handle them skillfully, we avoid damage to the current selling situation and potentially strengthen the trust we have with our customer.

Jeannette Liller recalls a time when she received a warning signal and ultimately asked an associate to evaluate a candidate's position.

"We had scheduled one candidate, Ray, to take a physical at 5:00 A.M. Unfortunately, his appointment was scheduled on the wrong day. So when he showed for his appointment, he was not on the schedule. He had to turn around and go home. We rescheduled for the following Wednesday. Before the meeting that day, Ray tried to call me. But I was on leave. The message fell through the cracks because he called my direct line and left voice mail messages.

"When I returned I had three messages from him on my voice mail. He seemed very upset with me. When I called him back, he was short with me on the phone. He didn't want to talk to me. He kept putting off rescheduling the appointment. So that was a big signal to me that something was wrong. I wasn't able to get him to come in.

"So I had my partner call him. My partner called and got a completely different reaction from this candidate. He was gracious and set his appointment immediately. Had I not recognized the warning signal and stopped my own selling process, this candidate might not have joined."

Jeannette's ability to notice the warning signal helped change her course of action and ultimately helped a young man move forward with a decision that was important to him. Reading our customer's warning signals can produce the same type of positive results.

We owe it to our customers to become good at recognizing and responding to both warning signals and buying signals. Why? It demonstrates that we care about our customers as people. It's also part of practicing good human relations principles and being genuinely interested in what our customers do and say. Top sales professionals make it a habit to understand these signals so they can better see things from their customer's point of view.

Building Emotion in the Sale: The Power of Mental Pictures

In our sales training classes, we often ask, "Why do people buy your product?" The answer we usually get, in substance, is: "Because it is a good product."

In reality, the correct answer should be: "Because they want it." To really set ourselves apart from the competition, we must understand why our customers want what we have to sell. It ties back to the Dominant Buying Motive we discussed in the interview process. What is the customer's emotional payout from buying our product or service? If we can answer this question and use the information skillfully, this factor alone will differentiate us from the competition. Not only that, it improves the odds that the sale won't stall during customer evaluation.

Often, the Dominant Buying Motive is created naturally by a picture the customer creates in his own mind.

Think about some of the major purchases you've made. Chances are, when you bought your last car, you had a picture in your mind. You probably pictured how you'd look or feel driving the new car before you even went to the car lot. Or what about that last major vacation you took? Did you have a mental picture of yourself relaxing on the beach, skiing down a mountain, or doing whatever it is that brings you joy and relaxation? Think about buying a new stereo system. Do you see yourself sitting by the fire, out on the patio, or entertaining guests with your favorite music playing in the background?

The point is, while logic dictates what product and service features we want, most of our final buying decisions are driven by the emotional reason for buying. And this emotional reason typically ties to pictures we have in our minds.

Unfortunately, not all selling environments are conducive to such obvious mental pictures. In those situations, salespeople must paint word pictures—verbal depictions of how our customer feels when using our products and services.

Word pictures are effective after we've identified the customer's primary interest areas and Dominant Buying Motive. Since we can use them at almost any point in the sales process, they are not a specific element of the sales process.

When you think about it, television and radio advertisements rely on word pictures to sell. Yet, as salespeople, we typically resist using them. Why? We're afraid we'll sound unnatural, or come across soft if we appeal to customers' emotions instead of their brains.

It's natural to feel that way. Yet, top salespeople do not let those feelings stand in the way. They try word pictures and then use them consistently and consciously until their subconscious mind takes over and it becomes automatic. Many of the best salespeople in the business have word pictures in their selling toolboxes.

Consider this: You are a prospect who is contemplating the purchase of an in-ground swimming pool for your backyard. You're not sure you're going to make the purchase, because you know it's a huge expenditure. But it's always been your dream to come home from work on a hot summer afternoon, swim laps in the pool, and enjoy recreation with your family.

You ask for bids from two different companies. The first salesperson visits your home. He does a good job of describing the features and benefits of the pool. But when he tells you the price, you start having second thoughts. You don't doubt that you'll make a quality purchase, but you begin to wonder if it's worth the money and the long-term investment of time in maintenance. When he asks you to sign the contract, you stall the sale and tell him you'd like some time to think about it.

The second salesperson, who comes the next day, takes some time to ask you questions. She finds out your concerns about the time and money involved with building and maintaining an in-ground pool. In turn, she knows her solution will have to address those issues. More important, she learns you have an emotional reason for buying—fun times with your family. Simply, the pool is what you want. And the emotional reason you want it is to enjoy recreation and relaxation with the most important people in your life.

Other things being equal, including product features and price, which salesperson stands the best chance of convincing you to part with your money? The one who talks only about features and benefits, or the one who appeals to your mental picture of good times with your family?

Guidelines for Word Pictures

- Make it clear and concise—thirty seconds or less.
- Show the customer as the hero.
- Use present tense.
- Illustrate a direct link to the customer's Dominant Buying Motive.
- Make it believable.
- Tell how the customer is benefiting from your product or service.
- Use language that touches the senses—see, hear, touch, taste, and smell.

While using word pictures may feel uncomfortable at first, it eventually becomes second nature. So how do we get the information to build word pictures? From the information-gathering process, of course.

To best understand how to build word pictures in a sales discussion, it helps to separate the process into five elements:

Remind yourself of what the customer wants and why he wants it.
Before we can create the word picture, we need to understand the customer's primary interest (what he wants) and the Dominant Buying Motive (why he wants it). We can't build a word picture without this information.

Remind the customer what he lacks and get agreement that the lack exists. We need to make sure we're on common ground with our customer by getting agreement that he lacks the benefits to be gained from using our product or service. Of course, we have to be careful not to insult the customer. Take, for example, a person who is buying a new home. If we're selling in this situation, we wouldn't say, "Your current house is unorganized and crowded, right?" It's better to remind the customer of lack by using his own language. In other words, "If I heard you correctly, you said that you are not happy with the amount of space in your current home. Is that accurate?"

Remind the customer your product or service will remedy that lack. (This appeals to what they want—the primary interest.) This statement is related to the features and benefits of our product or service. In our real estate example, we might say, "Buy this house and you have a bedroom for every member of your family."

Paint a word picture illustrating how the customer will feel once the Dominant Buying Motive has been satisfied. The actual word picture is driven by the Dominant Buying Motive. The more we know about that motive, the more effective our word picture will be. Let's continue with the real estate example. Once we've reminded the prospect that the new home will remedy his lack, we can say, "Imagine the peace of mind you'll feel as you watch your two sons go to their own bedrooms and play or do their homework. No arguments, no tension. They're becoming friends, and they're enjoying each other's company instead of fighting over closet space. That means you'll have less stress in your home. Is that a picture you'd like to see yourself in?" How did we know about the stress created by lack of closet space? The customer mentioned it during information gathering. Remember, in this situation, we're painting the picture based on the customer's words. If he had never referred to closet space and stress, we would not build a word picture around it.

Word pictures only work if they are relevant to the customer's situation.

Ask a trial close. Once again, an evaluative question ensures that we understand what our customer is thinking and feeling. In most situations, the evaluative question is fairly standard. We might say something like, "That is an environment you'd like to see yourself in, isn't it?" If the customer hesitates or doesn't agree, we might have misunderstood his Dominant Buying Motive. If that's the case, we need to ask additional Payout questions so we can better understand the Dominant Buying Motive.

These five steps are designed to help us think through the elements of strong word pictures. Once we understand these steps, we can simplify them into a few sentences: "Remind customers they don't have it. Remind them you've got it. Show them what it would be like to have it."

Here's an example of how a word picture might work.

The scenario: The salesperson's company is a national provider of freight services. The buyer wants to alleviate dock congestion so he can leave on time on Friday afternoons to see his daughter play softball.

In this case, the salesperson's word picture may go something like this:

"From what I understand, you are experiencing a lot of dock congestion before the weekend because your current freight provider does not make pickups on time, is that correct?" The prospect agrees. "And, based on the large fleet of trucks we have in our company, I've shared a solution with you that guarantees pickups every Friday by 3:00. Picture this: It's one month from now, it's Friday afternoon at 3:00. Our trucks are here, and all of your shipments make it out the door by 4:00. At 4:30, you're in your car and on your way to the ball field to see your daughter play. Is that a picture you'd like to see yourself in?"

Again, this picture works because it addresses the primary interest and satisfies the customer's Dominant Buying Motive. It's also effective because it uses the same language the customer shared with the salesperson during the questioning process.

Bridges for Word Pictures

These phrases can help you segue into your word picture:
- Let's say we move forward with this . . .
- Let's say you give this idea a try . . .
- Picture this . . .
- Let's assume we do business. Imagine this . . .

Can we use word pictures when we sell intangibles? Certainly. Len Frenkil knows firsthand how word pictures help in this situation.

"When I was first introduced to the concept of word pictures, my reaction was positive because I sell something that is extremely complicated. My product is not tangible. You can't touch it. So it requires the customer to buy me as much as my product. So when I can paint a picture, I can describe verbally what it's like for my customers to enjoy the benefits of my service, and it helps them picture me as the person delivering this service. I don't want them to think about property managers in general. I want them to think about me."

Len recalls one of many situations in which he used word pictures successfully.

"A local real estate broker took back a small apartment community that he previously sold. 'Taking back' generally means the debt is foreclosed (or the deed is offered in lieu of a foreclosure), and the title, or ownership of the property, reverts to the lender.

"By the time it ended up in his possession, it had been abused for over three years. There were maintenance issues, many vacancies, and very unhappy residents. As we walked through the property together, I got agreement from him that vacancies were approaching 25 percent, the roof was leaking, and the residents were unhappy. He also agreed that he was going to have to go into debt to turn this around.

"Then, I painted the picture: 'Let's jump forward to a year from now. We are walking this property that you can be proud of. It's well maintained, the residents are happy, and the property is meeting its monthly debt service. That's where you want to go, isn't it?' He agreed. And today, we have built a solid business relationship."

MORE WORD PICTURES IN ACTION

As with anything in the sales process, using word pictures may not be in your comfort zone right now. But, ultimately, stepping out of the comfort zone is what puts you in the new, more lucrative world of building relationships with customers. In fact, the best way to learn about the power of word pictures is to see how others have used them.

Debra Elmy is an account manager in the cruise business. She works for the Chicago, Illinois, division of Odyssey Cruises. In this particular office, they offer cruises aboard a large boat that tours Lake Michigan alongside the Chicago skyline.

Part of Debra's job is to organize weddings aboard the boat. Even though Debra had worked for Odyssey for several years, the wedding side of the business was new to her. Debra describes one of her earliest and largest sales to a busy bride, Andrea.

"Andrea was really pressed for time and was looking for a one-stop shop for her wedding. She really wanted me to handle everything. I knew I would only get one chance to meet her face-to-face, so I did as much information gathering on the phone as possible. We talked about dates, budget, menus, and all of the typical issues surrounding a wedding ceremony on the boat. Anticipating that I might want to use a word picture, I asked her to describe her ideal day. I learned that a relaxing atmosphere was an important feature to her. I also discovered that she wanted low stress by having things flow smoothly with little effort on her part. Simply, she wanted to enjoy being the bride.

"So when Andrea came to the boat to see what we had to offer, I had my word picture ready. I said, 'Picture this, Andrea. Your family and friends are seated atop the sky deck during your wedding ceremony, with the magnificent Chicago skyline behind you and Robert. The view is incredible, the warmth of the sun is on their faces, and you say your vows. Then, after the ceremony, everyone will come downstairs and enjoy appetizers and cocktails while you, Robert, and the wedding party are taking pictures outside. When you come downstairs and join your guests, they congratulate you on your big day and everyone begins enjoying their lunch.' "

In this case, Debra began her solution presentation with a word picture.

Was it effective? According to Debra, the answer is yes. "I could tell as I talked her through it that she had the picture in her mind. She was becoming convinced that she wanted the picture I painted."

Word pictures come a lot easier to Debra now. In fact, she develops a unique picture for almost every bride depending upon the bride's primary interest and Dominant Buying Motive. Debra believes that using word pictures is one reason she is now one of the top three salespeople in her company.

"I was hesitant to use word pictures at first. I wrote down everything and then practiced it in my head. But now, I think they're pretty easy. It just comes down to knowing your customer."

A sales professional for a company that manufactures pocket tape recorders and transcribers also finds word pictures extremely effective.

In one particular situation, he knew from doing effective information gathering that his prospect's day consisted of both selling and managing. The prospect spent a lot of time out of the office. And when he got back each day, he spent a huge amount of time dictating notes and letters to his office manager. Thus, the prospect's primary lack was time. He had also discovered that the prospect wanted to be able to leave the office earlier at the end of the day.

The sales professional knew that his pocket tape recorder and transcriber could provide an ideal solution for the prospect. The prospect agreed but wasn't really anxious to make the investment. At that point, the sales representative painted his word picture. He said, "Let's look ahead. You purchase our tape recorder and this is what will happen. It's Monday morning at 9:00, and you have just left your first sales call. You immediately dictate your letter into our machine. It's 10:30; you finish your second call and again dictate your letter. You continue this process throughout the day after each call. At 3:30 you walk into your office. Your office manager hands you a stack of messages with telephone calls to return, and you hand her the cassette with your letters on it. As you are returning your calls, you can hear her typing your letters. At 4:45 P.M. she hands you all of your correspondence of the day, neatly typed. You sign all the letters, and together you walk out of the office at 5:00, with a complete sense of accomplishment and peace of mind, knowing you have completed all of your work for the day. Is that something you'd like to experience?"

The customer replied, "How soon can I get the system?"

Again, the word picture appealing to the prospect's emotions is what moved the relationship forward. Before the word picture, the customer saw the logical reason to buy the equipment but didn't have a compelling emotional need to spend the money. After he imagined himself with this new lifestyle, however, he changed his mind.

Frank McGrath from San Diego used a word picture during an impromptu call with a potential customer for radio advertising. McGrath had been trying to get the prospect—a cellular phone provider—to advertise on the radio instead of in the newspaper. As luck would have it, there was a major downpour on the day of his meeting and traffic was terrible. Using his cellular phone, McGrath placed a call to the prospect's office to say that he had been delayed by the weather. The secretary said the prospect was also delayed.

Frank had an idea. He immediately got the man's cellular phone number and called him. After a few pleasantries and an exchange about the traffic, he said: "Tom, you know I've been thinking about the people in these cars around us. They are going to go home tonight and, in the comfort of their own living room, they might read your full-page ad about wireless phones. But picture this: What if you had an ad on the radio? You'd be reaching them right now, sitting here in traffic. You could tell them all the advantages of owning a cellular phone, how they could call ahead if they were late to a meeting, or late coming home."

Frank's word picture gained an informal commitment from the prospect. He agreed to meet with Frank the next day.

Here's another example of the difference a word picture can make—even if the sale already appears lost. Oral T. Carter, a salesperson for a trucking company, and later president of Oral T. Carter and Associates, Inc., had the challenge of convincing a "hopeless" prospect to select his company for his upcoming relocation.

"My boss called me into his office and said, "O.T., do you want to go out on a forlorn hope?' I answered, 'No, I don't want to, but I will.'

" 'Here's the problem,' he went on. 'A man living here in Cleveland has been transferred by his company to Los Angeles. The expenses are being paid by the company for which this man works. They have already selected one of our competitors to do the moving at a price lower than we can quote. Go out and see if you can do anything to get the job for us.'

"I went out, talked with the man's wife. I persuaded her to switch the job to us and to pay, out of their own pocket, the difference between our price and our competitor's. After she signed the contract, I asked this woman what had influenced her to make the change.

"She answered, 'You told me how your truck would back up in front of my new home in Los Angeles and how your movers would carry the containers with my clothes up into my room. Then you had me picture how nice and fresh my clothes would look when they came out of the special containers. That's when I made my decision. I just had to ship by your trucks.' "

Ray Yenkana, who calls himself the "Hard Working Nice Guy" at RE/MAX action realty in Fort St. John, British Columbia, Canada, uses word pictures to sell homes. In one case, he didn't have to paint the word picture himself. Based on his good questioning, the client did it for him.

"I was conducting a needs assessment with my seller. I was at the point in the questioning flow where I asked the seller to describe what it would feel like to have her home sold. She closed her eyes and said to me that she would have a great sense of accomplishment. She could 'see' herself in the future at her new home (not yet built), rocking on her porch in a rocking chair (did not yet own one) with a sense of fulfillment in the attainment of her goal. Needless to say, when I brought her the offer for her home—even though it was much less than what they wanted—the dream that was now in the open encouraged them to accept the offer that eventually sold the home."

Darlene Goetzinger, director of marketing and growth for Omni Eye Specialists in Baltimore, Maryland, actually turned her word picture into the introduction for a successful radio advertisement. While the word picture was not aimed at a specific prospect, it was designed to appeal to potential customers in Omni's target audience.

"You are at the beach and realize that your small child is missing from your side. You jump up in a panic, only to see her playing down by the water. You rush to scoop her up—safe and sound. Aren't you glad you had laser vision correction at Omni Eye Specialists?" This ad generated several new customers for Omni.

Many of the examples we've shared with you do not necessarily follow a mechanical approach to building word pictures. And that's okay.

The salespeople in these stories understand the requirements and fundamentals of the process. Then they adapt the word pictures to their own sales environment and selling styles. You should do the same thing. The idea behind learning how to build word pictures is not necessarily to commit each step to memory. It's more about understanding the impact of mental pictures, leveraging the power of the Dominant Buying Motive, and ultimately improving the odds that you will gain the buying commitment.

Eighty percent of salespeople refuse to close when the buyer is ready, and many customers are ready to close much earlier than the (sales) rep is.
—July 1994, *Sales and Marketing Management*

CHAPTER 9

Negotiation
Finding Common Ground

> When dealing with people, let us remember that we are not dealing
> with creatures of logic. We are dealing with creatures of emotion, crea-
> tures bustling with prejudices and motivated by pride and vanity.
>
> —DALE CARNEGIE

W hen you think of the word "negotiation," what comes to mind? Is it the last time you bought a car? Is it world leaders trying to reach a peace agreement? Do you have visions of manufacturing plants, labor contracts, and picket signs? Or do you think of something simpler, such as trying to buy handmade crafts at a local market on a quaint tropical island?

Whatever the case, it's not likely that most of us view negotiation as something we like to do. We tend to think of it as two sides arguing, with one side emerging as the winner. In fact, we'd probably choose to avoid negotiations altogether if we could. Wouldn't life be simpler if our customers just accepted our solutions without hesitation? Sure it would. But that's not usually the case.

Fortunately, successful negotiations are a positive experience for everyone involved. When we consider the role of negotiation in the sales environment, our approach should be anything but adversarial. Look at it this way: If customers want to negotiate with us, it's a strong indication they want to buy from us. If that's so, why would we approach negotiation from a negative perspective?

We need to approach negotiation from a variety of aspects. We have the qualitative side, which reflects the emotional reaction to the experience. Harsh words, ultimatums, and threats will generally make this a

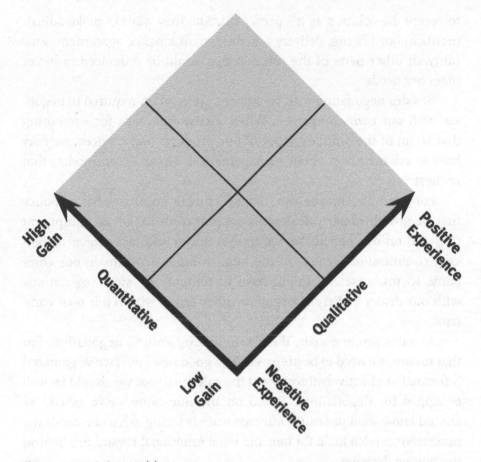

High
Gain

Positive
Experience

Quantitative

Qualitative

Low
Gain

Negative
Experience

Figure 10: Negotiations Model

negative experience for one or both parties. The quantitative axis involves such issues as price, terms, delivery, and value-added services. Higher quantitative gains for the seller will often mean lower gains for the buyer. Buyers and sellers will usually end up on different points of this model.

Negotiation is simply a part of the sales process during which we try to reach common ground. To develop long-term relationships, we want the buyer and seller to feel they both got the best possible deal and that they would do business together again. In some cultures, negotiation is an expected way of doing business. In others, negotiations may not be expected, but they become necessary because the customer doesn't want to accept the solution as it's presented. She may want to make adjustments in our pricing, delivery schedule, maintenance agreement, warranty, or other parts of the solution that could be enhanced to better meet her needs.

Besides negotiating with customers, we're often required to negotiate with our own companies. When a customer asks for something that is out of the ordinary scope of our products and services, we may have to ask members of our management if we can accommodate that request.

For example, maybe our manufacturing company has a policy that we give third-party dealers a 5 percent commission on equipment they sell on our behalf. Yet we have a dealer who asks for a 10 percent commission because of the huge volume it means to our company. In this case, we might have to temporarily stop negotiations with our dealer and try to negotiate other terms within our own company.

As sales professionals, there's no getting around negotiation. For that reason, we need to be prepared. The good news is, if we've gathered information effectively throughout the sales process, we should be well equipped for negotiations. Based on the questions we've asked, we should know what pressures our customer is facing, what she needs the product or service to do for her, and what emotional reward lies behind the buying decision.

Is that all we need? Well, it's a good start. But it also helps to understand some other concepts: 1) the difference between negotiation and objections; 2) the human side of negotiations; 3) types of negotiations; and 4) the role of negotiation tools for both the customer and the salesperson. In this chapter, we'll discuss these concepts in detail.

When all is said and done, negotiating can actually be fun. If we really know a customer's needs and wants, and if we understand some dynamics of negotiation, we can manage the process effectively. As a result, we can develop a strategy for negotiating that creates a positive experience for everyone involved—our customers, our companies, and ourselves.

Guidelines for Negotiation

- Prepare for negotiations by gathering information.
- Negotiation is resolving concerns and reaching agreement.
- Everyone can learn to be an effective negotiator.
- "Winning" means meeting key objectives, not conquering the other side.
- Strive to resolve conflict.
- Use a collaborative, problem-solving approach.
- Remember there may be more than one solution to a negotiations issue.
- Know a lot about your customer so you can anticipate and react to requests.
- Ask questions to determine what the customer really wants.

Negotiation Versus Objection

It's important to understand the difference between a customer's request for negotiation and an opportunity to address an objection. Why? If a customer objects to an aspect of our solution, and we see it as a point of negotiation, we potentially damage our credibility. For one, if we attempt to negotiate, we might appear to be pressuring the customer into a decision when his real issues haven't been addressed. And two, missing the opportunity to address an objection might cause the customer to perceive that we're not listening to his real concerns.

Here's a simple example to illustrate this point.

Let's say you buy a cabinet and you need a television set to place inside it. You decide on a specific brand name and model number. You go to the store and you find the one you want. It has every feature you could imagine. Better yet, the price is less than you thought it would be.

Unfortunately, the television is too large for the space in the cabinet. The space measures twenty-one inches, but the television measures twenty-two inches. You make your requirements clear to the salesperson, yet he proceeds to offer you free delivery, a bigger discount, and even throws in a clock radio if you'll make the purchase today. What is he doing? He's trying to negotiate with you to get your business. What should he be doing? He should be listening to your requirements. He should see that you're objecting to the size of the television. And he should offer you an alternative solution—a television that measures twenty-one inches or smaller.

By attempting to negotiate instead of addressing the objection, he is wasting our time as well as his. Not only that, he's not addressing our real issue—the size of the television. As a result, when he tries to negotiate without acknowledging our objection, we may see him as high-pressure and decide to take our business elsewhere.

Let's look at a business example. A business owner is moving into larger office space. He has two buying criteria: He must be within ten miles of the airport and the office area must be big enough for twenty-five employees.

If the realtor has a space five miles from the airport that can't accommodate twenty-five people, the business owner would likely raise an objection. If the office space can't accommodate the number of his employees, then the realtor is not offering a solution to meet his needs. She has nothing to negotiate, because the office space does not meet the business owner's buying criteria.

If the building does meet his criteria, then it's likely the buyer and realtor will start negotiating. Negotiation points could include the price, the term of the lease, reconstruction costs, landscaping, the occupancy date, option to buy, and a variety of other factors.

Later in this book, we'll learn how to respond to and resolve objections. For now, remember this: As skilled sales professionals, we must be adept at knowing when to handle objections and when to negotiate. Our customers will notice if we aren't. And when we demonstrate that we are listening to their concerns, we establish even more trust in our business relationships.

What You Need to Be a Good Negotiator

- Belief that your solution is the best available
- Commitment to enhancing your expertise as a problem solver
- Eagerness to learn everything you can about your customer's needs
- Courage to walk away
- Willingness to practice
- Desire to create win-win situations

THE HUMAN SIDE OF NEGOTIATIONS: WHAT DO PEOPLE WANT?

The most productive negotiations are aimed at one purpose: the best possible outcome for everyone. We all want to get what we need. Our customers want to feel they got a solution that was in the best interest of their organization or themselves as a result of the negotiating process. We want to feel that we helped our customer and, at the same time, helped our company make a fair and reasonable profit.

Negotiations become adversarial when either party is focused too much on winning. That's why, as salespeople, we need to do our part and practice good human relations skills every time we negotiate with our customers. As in every other part of the sales process, this means that we use good listening skills and try honestly to see things from the customer's point of view.

Tips for Negotiating

- Be enthusiastic.
- Use good human relations skills.
- Use logic, not emotions.
- Be aware of the body language.
- Be persuasive, not manipulative.
- Maintain your integrity.

With that in mind, go back and review the section on building rapport in the interview. While rapport is important throughout the sales relationship, it is critically important during negotiation. The rapport we build directly relates to the level of trust we can achieve in our business relationships. If we negotiate in an atmosphere of trust and respect, we increase the odds that our discussion will be successful for us and for our customers.

Consider the following example. While it's not about negotiation, it does demonstrate how good human relations skills and effective listening can make a big difference in our results.

One day, a fairly ordinary looking couple walked into the president's office at Harvard University, one of the most prestigious colleges in the United States. When they got to the reception area, they told the woman at the reception desk that they wanted to see the president. They didn't have an appointment, but shared with the president's assistant that their deceased son had attended Harvard. The purpose of their visit was to do something on the campus in their son's memory.

The assistant told the couple that the president was too busy to see them. However, the couple wanted to wait. And they waited. And waited. Finally, about two hours later, the president reluctantly agreed to see them.

Before letting the parents talk, the president said that the university would not allow them to establish a memorial. The couple informed him that they didn't just want to build a statue; they wanted to build an entire building. The president doubted that the parents could afford such an extravagant memorial and, in a somewhat arrogant tone of voice, informed the couple about the high cost of what they were proposing.

The mother, put off by the president's attitude, replied, "Is that all it costs?" She and her husband stood up, shook the president's hand, and left the office. At that point, they decided they would build their own building, at what eventually became their very own university.

Today, Stanford University in California is one of the most prestigious schools in the United States.

Do you see how the outcome might have been vastly different had the president practiced good human relations skills? What if he had started the conversation in a friendly way? What if he had seen things from the parents' point of view and been sympathetic to their desires? And, most important, what if he had asked sincere questions, listened attentively, and let the couple do most of the talking?

The point is, if we negotiate from our own point of view, it's difficult to establish any common ground, let alone a mutually beneficial solution.

Human Relations Principles for Negotiation

- Begin in a friendly way.
- Listen attentively.
- Let the other person save face.
- Try honestly to see things from the other person's point of view.
- Avoid arguments.
- Ask questions.
- Be genuinely interested in other people.
- Show respect for the other person's opinion; never say, "You're wrong."

Sometimes, even when the solution may seem to benefit the customer, the end result may leave the customer feeling bad about the buying decision. Remember, it's often said that the customer's perception equals the reality. In other words, if the customer doesn't feel good about the experience, it wasn't a good experience.

Consider a simple example to illustrate this point.

Let's say you want to buy a grandfather clock for your home. One weekend, you walk into the store and you see exactly what you want. You're standing next to the clock. Unfortunately, you notice the price tag says twelve hundred dollars and you have only budgeted one thousand dollars. The salesperson comes up to you and says, "It's nice, isn't it?" You reply, "Yes, it is. What is the lowest price you'll take for it?" And the salesperson replies, "What would you give?" You say, "We'll give you a thousand dollars." And the salesperson says, "Sold."

At first, you probably feel good about the purchase. But what happens when you drive home and start reflecting on your buying experience? Do you, perhaps, think you paid too much? After all, the salesperson took your offer immediately. With that in mind, do you still feel good about the buying decision?

When we see the buying experience through our own eyes, we understand how our customers might feel if we don't handle negotiations in a way that makes them feel good about their decision. That doesn't mean we'll agree on every point. It simply means we both might have to give and take a little bit in order for everyone to feel good about doing business together.

Tom Foglesong, client executive for an information technology services consulting firm, recalls a time when the negotiation process helped one of his customers feel even better about doing business with his company at the time.

"We had a contract, with a Fortune 100 client, through which we billed at an hourly rate. If we had 150 consultants onsite, we billed for 150 people and the number of hours they worked. We successfully built the business relationship in this way, with very little risk on our part.

"The customer informed us that it wanted to go to a fixed-fee contract for our services. We developed a proposal for the fixed-fee contract and presented it to the operations director and contracts officer. They liked our solution, but said they really couldn't afford the price. From there, we had to try to figure out how to share some of the risk with our customer and, at the same time, create a profitable situation for our company as well.

"The negotiations took about five months and were fairly intense. They gave up some things, and we gave up some things. In the end, we were able to reduce our price by finding ways to maintain our level of service and productivity with fewer resources from our company.

"The whole experience was special and really enhanced the relationship we have with this customer. They appreciated our commitment to the project and our willingness to accept some risk. We appreciated the open dialogue we developed with the two key decision-makers. It really was a win-win deal."

Challenges of Negotiating

- Customer not willing to discuss the issues
- Legal issues
- Strong egos
- Lack of relationship
- Fear of losing the account
- Hidden agendas
- Personality conflicts
- Cultural and language barriers
- Unexpected or unknown decision-makers
- Lack of authority to negotiate

TYPES OF NEGOTIATION

Typically, we'll encounter two basic types of negotiation: simple and complex.

A simple negotiation often occurs in a short time frame and is usually driven by an urgent need. The simple style is effective when time is limited, we are working with one buyer, and there is one primary issue. For example, a customer may have a piece of equipment that quits running in the middle of peak production time. Without this machine, the company is going to miss shipments to several key customers. The only way to get a new machine quickly is to have one delivered by private jet from another city. In this case, how much time do you think we'll spend negotiating?

Obviously, the decision-making process will be fast. The customer needs delivery right away, so he won't be in a position to negotiate much on price. And if the suppliers can't deliver within the customer's time constraints, there's nothing for them to negotiate.

With simple negotiations, emotion is often driving the decision. For that reason, the Dominant Buying Motive is usually fairly obvious. In this particular example, the Dominant Buying Motive is clearly survival.

The complex style of negotiation is needed when time is not limited and there are multiple meetings, variables, and decision-makers. For example, suppose a manufacturing company has a twelve-month goal of replacing the entire production line to improve productivity and reduce costs. In this case, the negotiations might be more complex. Complex negotiations typically occur in longer buying cycles. They may consist of several meetings and usually involve more than one company bidding on a contract. In this type of negotiation, the primary interest and Dominant Buying Motive are more likely harder to identify. After all, the plant is not necessarily in danger of shutting down. Management may just want to make the operation more cost efficient.

Why do we need to understand the difference? It improves our effectiveness as negotiators. For example, if we're in simple negotiations, we know we're in a better position to hold our margins and give fewer concessions to our customers. Bear in mind, that doesn't mean we charge customers excessive premiums to take advantage of the situation. But it does mean we have more leverage in pricing and other contract issues.

In complex negotiations, our approach is usually more strategic. We'll need more knowledge about our competitors. We'll have to ask more questions to determine the primary interest and Dominant Buying Motive. We'll likely have to be more creative in developing our solution because more companies are bidding for the business.

Either way, we should be very deliberate in how we approach the negotiation process. We should have a strategy for handling negotiations in a way that makes our customers feel good about working with us.

How to Enhance Communications During Negotiations

- Listen to understand rather than to respond.
- Think logically rather than emotionally.
- Ask specific questions.
- Make eye contact.
- Don't interrupt.
- Respond with specificity.

UNDERSTANDING NEGOTIATION TOOLS

Negotiating is something we've been doing most of our lives. As children, we may have negotiated that extra cookie before bedtime. When we became teenagers, we might have negotiated to stay out past curfew. In our adult lives, we negotiate job offers, automobile purchases, and even some aspects of our personal relationships.

What do these situations teach us about negotiating in the business world?

Most likely, we've learned that there are things we do, or others will do, to move the discussion forward in hopes of finding common ground. In the sales environment, these actions represent a set of well-defined tools that either party might use to elicit a specific response from the other.

In some cases, buyers may use these tools to encourage us to give concessions before gaining commitment. On the other hand, we might need them in situations when customers' requests are not realistic or fall beyond the scope of what we are authorized to offer. What's more, learning about these tools helps us become better prepared with an appropriate response if a customer uses them during the negotiation process.

Historically, these tools have been used as manipulative tactics. Even today, there are salespeople and customers who use them to "win" at negotiations when, in reality, a focus on winning typically creates a hostile atmosphere in which everyone loses.

As professional salespeople, how can we ensure that we don't use these tools to manipulate our customers?

For one thing, we should keep the desired end results in mind. Think about personal examples of negotiation. If we are negotiating for common ground in some aspect of our marriage, we are likely doing so in hopes of creating a lasting relationship with our partner. We want to create an atmosphere of mutual respect and trust.

In the same way, we should also begin business negotiations focused on the end result. For example, if our goal is to write a global contract with a major customer, everything we do in negotiations should be aimed at achieving that goal. That means we focus on the issues, one by one, as they arise. And we do everything in our power to deal with those issues and make our customer feel good about doing business with us. If the customer wants to do business with us, then our goal of writing a global contract is well within reach.

Second, we must keep the right attitude about negotiations. We should never set out to use these tools as ways to manipulate our customers into buying. In today's relationship-focused selling, looking for a "victory" by using hard-nosed negotiation tactics will do nothing but alienate our customers. If our attitude is to focus on the relationship first, then we have a better chance of coming to an agreement that benefits everyone.

On the following pages, we've provided insight into some of the most common negotiating tools.

WALKING AWAY

Have you ever been close to buying a product or service, but then walked away because you lacked agreement on a major issue?

The action of walking away is perhaps one of the most powerful tools of all. For a customer, it says, "I've gone as far as I can go." For a salesperson, walking away says, "I've done all I can do." There's a saying that goes, "You know you're an experienced salesperson when you've made a big sale, lost a big sale, and walked away from a big sale."

Why would we want to walk away from a big sale? In some cases, it's because the customer's request is not in the best interest of our company. In others, it's because we've given every possible concession we can give, and the customer still hasn't agreed to our solution. Keep in mind, walking away doesn't mean we're withdrawing our offer. It also doesn't mean we walk away from the relationship. It just means we aren't willing to change our solution at this point in the sales process.

Eileen Levitt, president of the HR Team in Columbia, Maryland, walked away from a potential customer because the customer did not want to pay a deposit up front to retain her firm's executive search services.

"As a policy, we require a deposit before we begin our search. In one case, I had met with a potential client to fill a high-level position. I asked him to pay a deposit up front, with the remainder upon filling the position. He objected to paying a deposit—or retainer, as we call it in our industry. He wanted to negotiate that point.

"I informed him that it was our firm's policy to require a retainer. I explained to him that, when we're filling a high-level position like his, there are a lot of expenses. If it takes six months to fill the position, and we don't get paid until it's filled, we are basically working for free for that length of time. I also told him that a retainer assured us that he was serious about filling the position. If we don't get retainers, clients could freely change their mind after we've put in work on the project.

"His response was, 'Well, I would think based on the opportunities in this company, where we are going and the people we are connected with, you would want to do this work on a contingency.' I responded, 'So you want us to make a commitment to you.' He said, 'Yes.' Then I asked him, 'How are you making a commitment to us?' He had no answer.

"At that point, I told him graciously, 'Why don't you talk to another recruiter and see if they are willing to do what you want. If they can, then you should go with them. If they can't, and you want us to fill this position, give me a call.' After the meeting, I learned that some of the information he had given me about his company's opportunities and connections was highly exaggerated. So I knew I made the right decision to walk away.

"In our business, we often judge the validity of a customer request by their willingness to make a commitment to us by paying a deposit. Many times, even though it's difficult, we have to tactfully walk away. Otherwise, we'd harm our organization's cash flow and our ability to be profitable."

As Eileen's story demonstrates, walking away is not something salespeople use to manipulate customers. It often comes down to making sure that the customer is as committed to the relationship as we are.

If we are ever in a situation where we must walk away, we must do it without offending the customer. We should be courteous and gracious, as Eileen was in her approach. We could say something like, "It appears as if we've reached an impasse. I appreciate the opportunity to work with you thus far. It looks as if you need someone who's able to go a little further. Unfortunately, it's not us, this time. Please keep us in mind in the future."

Again, the words are up to you. The point is, don't ever use walking away as a tactic to get your customer to buy. Only walk away from negotiations if you've done all you can do, and if it could potentially hurt your company's position to do any more.

Realize that some professional buyers will use walking away as a tactic to gain concessions. They will let us know, in no uncertain terms, they are willing to walk away from negotiations if we won't meet their demands.

What should we do? It depends on the person, the relationship, and the issues. We have to rely on our judgment and experience in dealing with the customer.

PERSUASION

Many times, we use this negotiation tool without realizing we're using it. Why? Because when we are persuading the customer during negotiation, we are simply going back and appealing to the logic behind the emotional reason for buying. We reiterate what the issues are, what the real answers are, and why it's logical to move forward.

If we want to be effective at persuading the customer, we need to remember that the best way to get someone interested in our ideas is to be interested in theirs. In other words, we should ask customers enough questions to know what's important to them. We should be taking good notes and using that information to prepare for possible issues in negotiations. Think about it this way: When you get into the courtroom, which juror is typically most persuasive on the jury? Typically, it's the person who takes the most notes and is most prepared for the discussion.

SILENCE

A lot of times when customers—especially professional buyers—are in the negotiating process, they say things they don't really mean, to elicit an emotional response from the salesperson. It's kind of like a fishing expedition. The customer throws out the bait just to see if we'll bite. For example, in response to our price, a customer may say emphatically, "You have to be kidding, that's ridiculous!"

In a situation like this, the best response is silence. If we remain silent, we are not being manipulative. We are merely trying to prevent the atmosphere from becoming hostile and argumentative. Taking time to be silent allows us to step back from the discussion and think about our next action.

If we have an equally emotional or escalated response, we could make the customer defensive or imply that we believe he's wrong. What's more, we might be inclined to give needless concessions out of fear of losing the business. Remaining silent gives us a few seconds to decide if contract concessions are really the best option.

Silence can work both ways. Our customer may be silent after we offer our latest concession. He may sit there, look at us, and say nothing. Realistically, he may be sincerely contemplating what we've said. But we need to realize, in some situations, customers might remain silent just to see if we'll keep talking—and, perhaps, keep conceding. Why does it work? Silence causes anxiety. And since most of us are uncomfortable with anxiety, we tend to speak. The first person to speak will generally give a concession.

TIME CONSTRAINTS

When we read the newspaper, we often see advertisements that say, "Going Out of Business Sale," or, "Total Liquidation Sale." That's a classic example of time pressure, a negotiation tool used by both parties to create a sense of urgency in order to expedite a buying commitment.

For example, if a business is closing, the seller has time pressure to get rid of inventory by a certain date. On the other hand, the buyer has a limited number of days to make a purchase before the doors close for good.

In business-to-business relationships, time constraints often center on production times and specific events. For example, an introductory offer for a leading-edge software package may only be available for a few weeks, so the customer has limited time in which to get special pricing. Or a certain piece of manufacturing equipment may require a twelve-week lead time, in which case the customer needs to purchase by a specific date in order to meet production requirements.

When it comes to time constraints, we should never create artificial deadlines to force commitment on customers. Remember, these negotiation tools are about creating a positive experience for both parties. If our customers can truly benefit by making a purchase within a specific time frame, then we owe it to them to share that information—even before negotiations start. But if we're just using time as a way to manipulate them into buying, then we aren't operating ethically as sales professionals.

Buyers also have realistic time pressures that may encourage us to shorten lead times or move more quickly on delivery of products and services. However, when the customer's time pressures become a factor in negotiations, it usually benefits the customer.

Here's why. You are probably familiar with the Pareto Principle, also known as the "80-20 rule." In applying that to negotiations, 80 percent of the concessions are generally granted in the last 20 percent of the negotiations.

In other words, if we are dealing with a customer's time constraints, we are more likely to give concessions at the end of negotiations in order to gain quick commitment. When this happens, salespeople have a tendency to overpromise and underdeliver. The key is to be prepared to deal with the customer's time issues in a realistic way that helps the customer but doesn't ultimately damage our company's reputation if we're unable to deliver.

CONTRACTS

This tool is rather common in industries where financing or other issues play a role in the final purchase. Here's how it fits in the negotiation process: Say you're undecided about buying a house. You and the salesperson are at a complete stall because you can't agree on some terms. At that point, the salesperson might want to add some positive momentum to the discussion. She might suggest that you go ahead and apply for the loan or complete some type of paperwork associated with the home purchase. Does this gain commitment? Not necessarily. But it does keep the process moving.

Again, as sales professionals, we don't want to use this tool if we haven't addressed the customer's objections. If unresolved objections exist, trying to complete the paperwork can be perceived to be high-pressure and manipulative. We would only want to use this approach if the conversation is stalled and if we believe that completing some aspect of the paperwork might expedite an inevitable commitment.

Using aspects of the purchase agreement or contract as a negotiation tool can also be effective after the sale, most likely in situations where one party is not living up to terms of the purchase agreement.

For Leonard Frenkil, vice president of operations for Washington Place Management in Maryland, using terms of the contract helped him get better service from one of his suppliers.

"We had a software supplier who was not performing up to the terms of a contract," says Len. "We tried repeatedly to move the relationship forward, but to no avail. Finally, in a meeting with them, we pulled out the contract and simply started reading. When we finished, we said, 'We need you to perform as promised.' The president of the software company said he would work it out and he did. We saw a change in their level of service immediately."

DELAY OR INACTIVITY

Have you ever told a salesperson, "I'll think about it," before you made a purchase? Chances are, the answer is yes. And in many cases, the delay you've imposed is completely sincere. You might need time to review your finances. You might want to shop around with other suppliers. Or you might need to consult a second person, such as a husband or wife, before you make the buying decision.

Our customers are no different. As we discussed in customer evaluation, they often need time to consider many factors before completing the agreement. However, as salespeople, we need to learn to recognize whether or not the delay is real, or is simply a negotiation tool being used to force us into making adjustments to our proposal or price.

So how do we determine if inactivity is genuine? Once again, we ask effective questions. That sounds simple but, in reality, many salespeople respond to the words, "I'll think about it," by saying, "How long do you need?" or "When can I call you for a decision?" Rarely do we probe deep enough to learn the real reason behind the delay. We just accept it.

Instead, we should let the customer know that we understand the need to evaluate the solution, while at the same time probing a little further to see if there's something else causing the delay. For example, we could say, "It's important for you to take the time necessary to evaluate all the facts. Can you tell me what it is that's causing you to hesitate?" Or, "What are some of the factors that are important as you evaluate your decision?"

By empathizing with the customer and asking open-ended questions, we're in a much better position to determine the true reasons behind inactivity. When we learn those reasons, we can better understand what we need to do during negotiation to help the customer make her decision.

AUTHORITY TO NEGOTIATE

If we've done a good job of pre-approach and information gathering, we should know whether our key contact is the decision-maker. We should also know what level of authority the person has to negotiate major points of the purchase. Of course, we don't always have that information. For that reason, we must know how to respond if our customer says she does not have the authority to accept certain terms of the solution.

For example, let's say we're selling contract employment services for temporary workers. We provide our customer, the manager of human resources, with a one-year contract to staff the company's customer service function. After we submit our proposal, she informs us that the dollar amount of our contract exceeds the amount of money she can approve.

Does that mean our customer is not the decision-maker? Does it mean she is the decision-maker, but simply can't put her signature on the contract? Or does it mean she's using a negotiation tool in order to make us think about lowering our price?

With several possibilities, how do we know the answer? Again, we need to ask the right questions to determine her true situation. For example, we could say, "When you talk to your boss, you will recommend us to her for the job, won't you?" Or, "Is that going to create an issue for us going forward?"

Again, these are just suggestions. We need to develop questions that fit our style, yet still get the kinds of specific answers we need.

What if it turns out that the customer really is on our side and is sincere about consulting the decision-maker? At that point, we should try to work with the customer and anticipate some concerns the decision-maker might have. From what she says, we can then coach her on how our solution addresses these issues. Armed with this specific information, she will be ready to respond to the decision-maker if and when these points arise in conversation.

If we determine, after questioning the customer, that she's using her authority to negotiate as a stalling technique, then we may want to handle the situation differently. We can let her know that we appreciate her need to refer the decision to others. Then we should ask more questions to determine the real reason she's hesitating.

When it comes to the authority to negotiate, it's also important for us to know our own guidelines for negotiation. For instance, what percentage discounts are we allowed to offer without asking a higher authority? What "throw-ins" (covered later in this chapter) are we allowed to include without approval? The answers to these questions are important. In order for us to handle negotiations effectively, we must know exactly what our limitations are relative to what the customer wants.

What happens if the customer asks us for something we don't have authority to give? Obviously, it's time for us to step back from the negotiation and consult our management. If we don't, we risk giving up too much. Sure, we want to help the customer. But enthusiastic salespeople often have the habit of doing what it takes to meet customer demands at the expense of their own companies. We should never hesitate to say that we have to check with our office before we complete the details. Customers will respect our willingness to try, and our companies will appreciate our efforts.

YOU GO FIRST

In an old model of selling, salespeople and customers often argued over who went first. Why? The theory is that whoever goes second has an advantage.

Here's what we mean. Remember the grandfather clock example? We went first in giving our price. Since we did, we were never able to find out if the salesperson would have accepted less for the clock. He already knew we'd pay one thousand dollars. Why would he tell us he would sell it for nine hundred dollars if he knew we were willing to spend one thousand dollars?

So what happens when we give our customer a proposal? Aren't we, in effect, going first? Is it possible that a customer might use this tool to lock us into a specific price or contract term? It could happen, but only if the customer doesn't trust that we'll provide him a unique solution at a fair price.

In the context of the Sales Advantage, going first should not be an issue. Throughout the sales process, we are building an atmosphere of trust and mutual respect with our customers. If we're doing our jobs effectively, we're gathering information along the way so we understand the customer's financial limitations. We also are building a solution that's designed to meet a need, not a price.

Say, for example, you're an interior decorator. Your customer wants to remodel the inside of his entire two-story office building in a one-year time frame. You give him your proposal. He informs you that his budget cannot absorb the cost. But because of the trust and rapport he has with you, he really wants you to do the work. Unfortunately, you can't lower your price, because you already gave him the best possible price you could, knowing he might have a problem with the cost. The solution? After negotiating, you both agree that he will remodel the first story of his building this year, and the second story next year. He agrees, and you sign the contract.

Did going first mean anything to anyone in this situation? Absolutely not. In an atmosphere of trust and respect, it doesn't matter. All that matters is that everyone feels good about the end result and both companies benefit from the solution.

ULTIMATUM

Some people confuse an ultimatum with walking away. But indeed, they are very different things. When we walk away, we're saying we've gone as far as we can go, but we leave the offer on the table. On the other hand, when we give an ultimatum to a customer, we're basically saying,

"Do this, or else." For example, "Unless we sign the contract by Thursday, I'm going to have to withdraw the offer." Or, "This price is only good if you buy these items in quantities of one thousand."

Whatever the case, the ultimatum is not a tool commonly used in relationship sales unless absolutely necessary. Ultimatums force our customers into a corner. They attack a customer's ego and make him defensive. And they potentially shut down any hopes of having a productive conversation with our customers to develop creative solutions during the negotiation process.

So why do we bring them up? For one, customers may give us ultimatums, so we need to recognize that these statements may be designed to encourage us to give further concessions. If that's the case, we should respond by sincerely appealing to the customer's ethics and sense of fairness. If we still think, after the ultimatum, the customer is a good business prospect, we should consider keeping the door open.

We also bring up ultimatums because, sometimes, we have honestly done everything within our power to move the commitment forward. Basically, there's nothing left to negotiate, and there's no point in continuing the conversation. Instead of walking away and leaving our solution on the table, we choose to withdraw the offer completely, mainly because we've determined that the business relationship is not going to be good for our company. In these situations, we owe it to our company and to ourselves to withdraw the contract and move on.

We should never use the ultimatum just to force commitment. The ultimatum is merely a tool for ending negotiations so we can focus our attention on more productive business activities.

THROW-INS

Have you ever been offered something for "free" just to encourage your purchase? That's a tactic known as throw-ins—additional items or services that make us feel that we're getting a better value for our dollar.

Should we just offer throw-ins up front and hope to bypass the negotiation process? Not unless it's part of a special promotion that's available to all customers. Typically, we wait and offer throw-ins when we get closer to the commitment. In some cases, we don't need throw-ins for negotiation, and we can add them anyway just to show appreciation to our customer.

Esther Hanlon is an account manager with CMS Hartzell, a custom manufacturer of die-casting and injection moldings. Esther relates a story about negotiation in which a throw-in helped her secure a $9.4-million contract—one of the largest single contracts ever awarded to her company.

"We had been contacted by an existing customer who had the opportunity to get a rather large contract to supply a government agency with their particular product. There were all kinds of parts they needed in order to fulfill this contract, and we had the capability to manufacture all of them. They asked us, along with several other suppliers, to bid on it.

"When we got into negotiation, the biggest issue was the timeline. This was especially important to our customer because, for each day they missed the ship date to the government agency, they would have to pay a penalty. And if we missed our ship dates to them, we could potentially affect their ability to ship on time.

"Even though the timeline was extremely tight, we agreed to it. But they still hesitated to give us the order. This contract meant a lot to our company, and we knew we needed an answer in order to meet an already aggressive production schedule. So we gave them added incentive to do business with us: We offered to throw in a rebate of fifty thousand dollars. Essentially, the plan was to return to them a percentage of the value of their invoices each month until we reached fifty thousand dollars.

"They signed the contract and it turned out to be a win-win situation for everyone. By offering a rebate, we did not have to pay out any money until we were actually receiving money from the customer. Our company was able to profit and we were able to provide a lot of work for our employees at all three manufacturing plants. In fact, we actually beat our delivery dates thanks to a lot of teamwork in our own organization.

"But most important, it was a good deal for our customer. They were able to deliver on a huge contract for their company. The whole project was very successful for them."

Characteristics of Successful Negotiation

Everyone feels a sense of accomplishment.
Both parties feel the other party cared.
Everyone believes the negotiations were fair.
Each party wants to do business again.
Both parties feel each one will keep its promises.

Just as throw-ins were effective for Esther, they can be effective negotiating tools for you as well. Give sincere thought to what throw-ins you can offer your customers. Adding value to your solutions is always a way to show customers you appreciate them and care about the relationship.

COMPLETING THE NEGOTIATED AGREEMENTS

We've successfully negotiated the terms of our solution. The customer is happy because he is getting exactly what he needs and wants at a fair price. We are happy because we are now on the verge of building a new customer relationship and making a sale for our company.

However, before we sign the contract or get the purchase order, we must make sure we've worked out all of the details and documented key points from our discussion in writing. If we ignore this step, we may regret it later. If we don't have details in writing, we might forget a promise we made to our customer, only to find out that it's one of the most important factors influencing her buying decision. If this happens, our credibility will be damaged, along with the relationship.

Keep in mind that the desired outcome of a successful negotiation is no different than that of any other aspect of the sales process. When all is said and done, our goal is to establish profitable business relationships with our customers—profitable for them and for us. That's why we must approach negotiations with the same level of human relations skills, integrity, and professionalism as we would any other part of the sale.

As with anything in the sales process, negotiation takes practice. But the ability to negotiate seemingly minor issues related to the sale can become significant when multiplied over many years of a sales career. When we recognize the role of negotiation tools in the sales process, we are better prepared to meet the challenges of negotiating with skill and confidence.

Remember, we know what we need to make the sale successful. The key is finding what the customer needs, then looking for where our mutual needs overlap. When we find the overlap, we find the key to negotiating successfully.

Planning for Negotiations

- Is the negotiation simple or complex?
- What is the competition?
- What are the issues to be negotiated?
- What issues should be avoided?
- In what order should we address these issues?
- What time constraints exist?
- When must my customer make a decision?
- What are the things my customer must have?
- What are the things my customer would like to have?
- What is the Dominant Buying Motive?
- What is my authority to negotiate?
- What is my customer's authority to negotiate?
- What do I know about the customer's negotiation style?
- What outside influences will affect negotiations?
- What is the minimum price I can accept?

CHAPTER 10

Commitment
Moving from Prospect to Customer

> Most sales have been won or lost long before we ask for a commitment. Trying to make up for a poor sales presentation by coming up with a magical close is like nailing Jell-O to the wall. It doesn't stick, and it makes a mess.

The entire sales process is really a series of incremental commitments that start with the initial meeting with a customer. We gain commitment for the first appointment. We get commitment to present our solution. We might get commitment to interview others involved in the decision-making process. And the list goes on. If we see commitment as something that happens only at the end of the sales process, we may not have a full understanding of what it means to gain commitment in our customer relationships.

Thinking of the commitment as the one big step in selling is just like saying that putting is the one big step in golf, when that's really not the case. If it takes a golfer eleven strokes just to get to the putting green, sinking the ball in one putt is relatively unimportant to the outcome of that hole.

The process a pastry chef might go through in preparing a fabulous dessert illustrates the same concept. The final step of the preparation process might be to bake the dessert in the oven. But if all of the ingredients aren't right in the first place, it doesn't matter whether the oven temperature is correct. The end result will, most likely, be disappointing.

Both of these illustrations demonstrate the importance of recognizing the role of commitments in building solid customer relationships. If we haven't handled the rest of the sales process effectively, then trying to gain commitment at the end is most likely a futile task.

Gaining commitment is not just about closing the sale. In fact, we need to change our perception that getting commitment requires some mysterious miracle phrase or technique that only the best salespeople know. Nothing is farther from the truth.

Even so, many salespeople look for the magic wand they can wave to gain commitment. But in reality, there's no magic involved. Remember: Gaining customer commitment is nothing more than the logical outcome of a strong sales process. When a salesperson says, "I have trouble getting commitment," he or she really means, "I have trouble selling."

In relationship selling, we want to take the word "close" out of our vocabulary, period. Why? It sounds too final, and it implies that the relationship is over. On the other hand, the word "commitment" says that we're in this together for the long term.

If we think of ourselves as working toward a series of incremental commitments instead of final closes, it virtually changes our approach to selling. Some people argue that it's just semantics. We contend that when a person says yes to a commitment, a whole new window of opportunity opens.

Remember that there is no magic formula for closing. The magic is in doing everything else well, then having the confidence to ask for a decision.

Even today, we see employment ads for good "closers," and we wonder why. An overemphasis on closing can lead to manipulative tactics and strained customer relationships. Any experienced buyer will recognize these tactics and take offense when we use them. In fact, purchasing agents go to seminars where the leader says, "Here's what the salespeople are going to try to use on you. And here's how to respond to it."

When we are truly focused on helping our customers, gaining commitment is not a heavy-handed process. Top sales performers do not manipulate customers into commitments they later regret. The rest of the selling process is equally, if not more, important. We're establishing rapport, listening effectively, developing creative solutions, and building trust along the way. If we do these things well, we will gain commitment by providing the best information, the best analysis, and the best solution, all completely targeted to our specific customer.

Clearly, if one keeps the focus on the customer, gaining commitment is like a partnership. So instead of wondering, "How do we close the sale?" a better approach is this: "How do we tie up the loose ends of the sales process to make the customer comfortable with the buying decision?"

Human Relations Principles and Buying Commitments

- Let the other person feel the idea is his or hers.
- Establish common ground by asking questions that evoke a "yes" answer.
- Talk in terms of the other person's interests.

Ways to Gain Commitment

When customers make a commitment to buy a product or service, they are in reality placing their trust in us to deliver solutions to their needs. Asking for customer commitments doesn't involve hard-nosed tactics. It simply requires us to ask the right questions or, in some cases, further explain the solution we've presented.

Methods to Gain Commitment

Direct question
Alternative choice
Next step
Minor point
Opportunity
Weighing alternatives

USE A DIRECT QUESTION

Once we've generated interest, presented a solution, and appealed to the Dominant Buying Motive, the best way to gain commitment is to simply ask for it. So why don't we? Mostly because of fear, reluctance, and uncertainty.

Realize, however, that our customers are probably experiencing the same emotions. They may be afraid of spending the money. They may be reluctant to switch suppliers. They may be uncertain that our company will deliver. Even though customers may know it's a good decision, it involves change, and most people are uncomfortable with change.

Recognizing that we share these emotions with our customers often makes them easier to overcome. Why shouldn't we expect to get the commitment, after all? If we have handled the sales process well, if we know that our solution addresses the person's primary interest and Dominant Buying Motive, why shouldn't we expect the customer to do business with us? And since we expect that outcome, why not ask for it? Maybe that's all the customer is waiting for. One graduate from Michigan told us, just by asking for the order, he increased his closing ratio by almost 200 percent. Can we have more customer relationships just by asking for commitment? Chances are, the answer is yes.

PROVIDE AN ALTERNATIVE CHOICE

If you do a lot of shopping in department stores, you can probably recall a time when you took your purchase to the counter, and the clerk asked you, "Cash or credit?" This is a good example of what we mean by providing alternative choices.

When we ask for commitment in this way, we simply ask the customer to select one of two options, both of which are minor in nature. This assumes that the customer is going to make a buying commitment in our favor.

Here are some very basic examples of alternate choice questions:

- Would you rather take the cash discount, or do you like the payment plan better?
- Which of these do you prefer, this one or that one?

- How do you prefer paying, weekly or monthly?
- Which color do you like better?
- Where do you plan to use it, here or there?

Marco Poggianella, an Italian entrepreneur with Energheia, a company in the field of biological products for agriculture, uses this method frequently with his customers.

"Instead of stating the total price to the customer, I often give them a choice of monthly installments. I might say, 'Is $150,000 a month all right with you, or perhaps $100,000 a month is better?' "

REFER TO THE NEXT STEP

Asking the customer about the next step takes us beyond the actual commitment to the next action we need to take after we gain commitment. The next step is not, "When can I stop by and get the order?" When we refer to the next step, we should do so in a way that's relevant to our specific customer.

Next-step questions should not have "yes" or "no" answers. For example, if we use the question, "Do you think the first of the month would be a good time to install this new machine?" the customer may think of numerous reasons why that particular date is not satisfactory.

On the other hand, if we ask, "Ms. Gonzalez, when would you like me to schedule the installation team?" we leave the door open for more positive discussion.

GET AGREEMENT ON A MINOR POINT

If we use this approach, we are asking the customer to make a minor decision that indicates the larger buying decision has already been made. Making a decision on a minor point is generally easier for the buyer. By getting agreement on a minor point, we are making it easier for our buyers to do business with us.

A minor-point question goes something like this: "Do you want to invest in the extended warranty for this copier?" Clearly, if they want to buy the warranty, then they plan on buying the copier.

Other examples: "Should I mail you the documents or would you like to pick them up?" Or "Mr. Geffert, in whose name should the title be drawn?" Whatever the case, a minor-point question assumes that the customer wants to do business with us and allows us to help the customer move the relationship forward.

PROVIDE AN OPPORTUNITY

In most of today's selling situations, the opportunity approach is particularly helpful with customers who are ready to buy, but who are clearly procrastinating. Simply, it presents the customer a brief window of opportunity during which time a certain deal or option is available.

Toby Leach, sales manager with Thermal Science Technologies in Hanover, Maryland, used this approach successfully to gain commitment from a customer who appeared to be putting off his buying decision.

"My boss stopped me in the hall and asked if I had gained commitment with a particular customer," said Toby. "After I told him I hadn't, I went back to my office to think about what I could do to get my customer to commit. I was selling this particular customer removable insulation blankets for manholes on his campus. Typically, once the customer commits, we then bring in a team of engineers to measure the piping within the holes before manufacturing the blankets.

"I knew I would have a team of engineers in the Philadelphia area, where this customer is located. So I called him and let him know that our team of engineers would be happy to stop by the university and do the 'final measurements' on his manholes. The customer responded by saying, 'Sure, have them come by and do the final measurements. I'll send the requisition up to purchasing.' Simple as that, I gained the commitment."

Toby used this approach effectively and sincerely. But there are many salespeople who misuse it. They create false opportunities just to create pressure on the customer. For that reason, we must ensure the opportunity is legitimate and truly relevant to the customer's situation. If it's not, we risk damaging the trust and credibility we've established in the relationship.

WEIGH THE ALTERNATIVES

Remember a time when you had a difficult decision to make? Did you ever take a piece of paper, draw a line down the middle, and list the pros and cons on either side? That's what we call weighing the alternatives— a commonsense approach to reminding our customer that the reasons for making the commitment in our favor outweigh the reasons for not moving forward.

While this approach is effective in certain selling situations, we offer some words of warning about it: The weighing method has been around a long time. Experienced buyers know it well and will often see it as manipulative, even when we are being sincere. We should only use this approach when 1) the customer is inexperienced in making buying decisions and will sincerely appreciate our help in clarifying the situation, or 2) we're in a selling situation where a lot of information has been exchanged and everyone could benefit from a summary of the issues.

For example, the weighing approach could be helpful with written proposals or in a stand-up presentation to a buying team. In these situations, we can use this method to compare our products with those of our competitors, if we know who is bidding.

Some salespeople feel it's dangerous to bring up any reasons why the customer should not do business with us. They seem to feel that, as we get closer to the buying decision, we have hypnotized the customer into forgetting the reasons for not wanting to buy.

In reality, we have nothing to lose, because the customer is thinking of the disadvantages anyway. By weighing the alternatives, we're simply evaluating what's already been discussed.

While we don't want to sound mechanical in our discussion, it does help to understand the fundamental process of approaching the "weighing" conversation.

Take a few words to connect the end of your solution presentation with the beginning of the weighing statement . . . and ask permission to proceed. Say, for example, "Mr. Rashad, we've discussed a lot of issues. And we've talked about many reasons for and against this buying decision. To help you make the best decision, maybe it would help to take a blank piece of paper and write down the pros and cons of moving forward. Would that be okay with you?"

Don't simply repeat the solution presentation. Remember, before we've reached this part of the conversation, we have already shared the important facts, benefits, and application information relative to our product and service. We should have identified and responded to all objections by this time. We also should have appealed to the Dominant Buying Motive. Now is the time to simply summarize, as concisely as possible, the points for and against making the buying decision in our favor.

Don't gloss over the summary of our product and service advantages on the grounds that we've already covered them. Again, we don't want to be repetitive, but we do want to list the advantages with force, sincerity, enthusiasm, and brevity.

Keep a friendly attitude. We want to think of ourselves as friends, presenting the customer with the points for and against buying, so he can make up his own mind.

As sales professionals, we owe it to our customers, our companies, and ourselves to ask for commitments. Our customers expect us to ask. Some experienced buyers will even be disappointed if we don't. They know it's part of our jobs. We should never end a meeting without asking for or giving some kind of commitment—whether it's a commitment for another meeting, to a proposal, or for an opportunity to present a solution. Asking for commitments is part of showing we are proud to be sales professionals. It also demonstrates the confidence we have in our ability to provide unique solutions for our customers.

The Power of Persistence

Winston Churchill got up to give a graduation speech at Oxford University. He began speaking and said, "Never, never, never give up." Then, he sat down.

Asking for Referrals

Referrals fall outside the sales process sequence because they can happen anywhere in the sales process. Any time we are confident we have rapport with the other person, we can ask for a referral. We have nothing to lose and everything to gain. After all, the purpose of referrals is to give us more opportunities. And more opportunities generally mean more commitments.

You'll recall we discussed the value of referrals in new opportunity and initial communication. So why do we bring them up again? Because commitment is another appropriate time to ask for names of people who might be interested in what our company has to offer. Clearly, if the customer is excited about the buying decision and we've exceeded expectations, there's never a better time to ask. On the other hand, we can ask for a referral even when we're turned down. If a customer doesn't have the need for our product or service, perhaps he'll know someone who does.

We'll rarely get referrals unless we ask for them. With that said, why do many sales professionals overlook this opportunity?

For one thing, we get caught up in the moment and forget to ask. Think about it: What do many of us do after we shake hands and sign the contract? We focus on getting the paperwork together to move the sale through. And if it's a big sale, we go out and celebrate. The point is, rarely do we turn around and ask for a referral.

Another reason we don't ask for referrals may be that we feel uncomfortable asking for business leads after a long sales process with a tough customer. This is only natural. It's up to us to assess the rapport we have with our customers and the appropriate timing for the request. In some cases, we might wait a week or two after gaining commitment before asking. Or maybe we ask the customer immediately, but he wants to wait and see if our relationship is successful before sharing the names of others. No matter what the case, we shouldn't be discouraged. That we don't get the referral right away doesn't mean we won't get it at all.

Even though opportunities from referrals are among the best new opportunities we can find, it's not likely we'll get customers from each referral. But if we get more referrals than our competitors do, who do you think will make more sales? Remember, everything we don't do gives the competition an opportunity to help more customers than us.

When Asking for Referrals

- Think of your customers as partners who can refer you to a steady stream of new business.
- Don't underestimate the power of a satisfied customer's goodwill or influence.
- Remember that people who are referred to you are more likely to meet with you than cold call prospects.
- Recognize that a referral represents a higher-quality prospect who is more inclined to consider your offerings.
- Bear in mind that people who buy are more likely to refer others.

METHODS OF GETTING REFERRALS

How you obtain a referral is really up to you. Typically, however, we get referrals in one of two ways:

The customer initiates contact. The customer's personal introduction adds to our credibility early in the sales process with the new prospect, so it's typically easier to schedule that first appointment. If the referral is in the same building, we can ask our customer to introduce us. If the person is not nearby, perhaps the customer could place a phone call while we're in his office. Or, if he feels more comfortable, we can ask if he'll place the call at his own convenience at a later time. Either way, this method usually has the most impact on the person to whom we're being referred.

We get the name and initiate contact on our own. In some cases, the customer is willing to give us the names but doesn't have the time or the sense of urgency to call the referrals. If this is the case, it's a good idea to have the customer write the referral's name on the back of her business card and give it to us. This will help us keep a record of where the referral originated.

Regardless of what method we use, we should do pre-approach and follow the logical steps of initiating communication before making contact with the referral. However, for some reason, it's human nature for many salespeople to jump right into the initial communication without doing these. Obviously, we can do some pre-approach research with the customer who provides us with the prospect's name. But we can't stop there. Remember, while referrals are powerful door openers, they don't guarantee a sale. We should put as much effort into working with a referral as we would any other prospect.

Also, when we get referrals, it's a good idea to send a thank-you note to the customer who provided the referral. In addition, be sure to call the customer and let him know the outcome of your conversation. Not only is it common courtesy, the customer is likely interested in the results. If the results are positive, the customer will feel good. If the outcome wasn't favorable, you've at least acknowledged that you value the customer's time and appreciate his willingness to help. Who knows, a simple acknowledgment may result in even more referrals.

REFERRALS THAT COUNT

For sales professional Philip Crane, the relationship he built with a top national company in the corporate financial consulting business helped him gain entry into another company with existing supplier relationships. Just twelve months from getting the referral, Philip's company became the preferred supplier for this company and the business represented a significant amount of sales volume.

"In my opinion there is nothing magical about a relationship sale or getting a referral," said Philip. "The Sales Advantage taught me how to position myself as to how I would want my supplier to work for me. In a nutshell it helped me understand the customer's point of view and to provide what they need as opposed to what I wanted."

Gianluca Borroni, a financial marketer for Banca Mediolanum in

Italy, depends solely upon referrals as the basis for his sales activity. Gianluca does not leave a meeting without asking for the names of other potential customers.

"Asking for referrals is one of my strong points," says Gianluca. "As soon as the contract is signed, I congratulate the client and then proceed to ask a few questions leading up to my request for referrals. I ask them questions such as, 'What did you like the most about doing business with me?' 'What were the reasons that prompted you to become my client?' On the basis of those responses, I reinforce some of the positive points we've discussed.

"Once I establish a positive line of questioning, only then do I ask, 'What other people do you know to whom we could provide these same advantages? Let's concentrate on people who are very close to you and who listen to you, because subsequently I will call them on the telephone and give them advance notice of my visit.'

"If they say they can't think of anyone, I say, 'Let's begin with the people closest to you.' If I know the person well, I've even been inclined to ask them to go through their address book, starting with A—but I only do that if I know the person well. The point is I am persistent in requests for references."

Gianluca's persistence paid off. He was recognized as the company's Global Award Winner, honoring him as the firm's top salesperson in Italy. He achieved the results necessary to receive this award in only four months, thanks mostly to his ability to ask for referrals.

"I actually told my clients about the competition. I told them, 'I want to be the best. May I ask for your help?' When they asked how, I asked for references. They were anxious to support my efforts in being one of the best financial consultants in Italy.

"After I won the award, I invited all of my clients to a meeting and showed them a film of the prize award ceremony. I then thanked them because their trust and confidence were the reason I achieved these results."

David Michael, owner of Michael Mortgage Group, has built 100 percent of his business on referrals. For that reason, David starts strategizing about them early in the sales process. So when he gets to the commitment stage, he already knows he will get referrals.

"I am committed to giving all of my customers a high level of service," says David. "There are often times, however, when I make a conscious effort to identify certain customers who I know can provide me with a good referral network. For those customers, I go above and beyond my typical level of service to make sure they will refer me to their friends and associates. In fact, they will even say to me, 'Do you do this for everyone?' In that case, I'll reply, 'No, I'm doing it for you.' Then I tell them I would appreciate their referrals. They are more than happy to help out.

"In one instance, I was helping a gentleman secure a home mortgage. I knew this man was influential and trusted in the business community. I identified right away that he was someone who could help my business, so I wanted to give him special treatment. In his case, because of some past credit issues, I knew that his interest rate would be higher than usual and that the fees associated with the loan would be higher. And I also knew he wouldn't be happy about it. He had already experienced some bad service from our industry.

"So I ended up giving up all my fees on this transaction, just to reduce the fees he would have to pay. We also conducted the closing at his office, rather than have him come to our office or to the title company's office. And I visited him at his house afterward to make sure he was really happy. Since then, I've gained over $20 million worth of business that I can track to that one person. Although it has been over five years since I helped this customer, I still get at least two calls a month from people he has referred to me."

Going the extra mile is an important element in any selling relationship. As David's story illustrates, however, consciously identifying people who can provide good referrals ensures that we have a long list of satisfied customers who are willing to share their experience with others.

Referrals are so important to David's business that his firm even sponsors a monthly referral contest for existing customers. "Customers submit their referrals via e-mail, and we enter their names in a drawing," says David. "At the end of the month, we award a prize. It can be anything from a gift certificate to concert tickets. Then, at the end of the year, we award a bigger prize, like a weekend vacation.

"The contest is just one more way we can build our business on referrals, because in this business, you have to have raving fans. We want to identify and create as many raving fans as possible through referrals. It's the best way."

What do David, Gianluca, and Philip all have in common? For one thing, they know the importance of referrals, and they aren't afraid to ask for them. But, most important, they know the value of strong customer relationships when it comes to asking for referrals. If we are successful in developing mutual trust and respect, getting referrals is simply the next logical part of the commitment.

CHAPTER 11

Follow-up
Keeping Our Commitments

> When you get right down to the root of the meaning of the word "suc-
> ceed," you find that it simply means to follow through.
>
> —F. W. NICHOL

O nce we gain commitment, the door opens for an even bigger opportunity: repeat business. Numerous studies about today's sales environment support the idea that it's much more diffi- cult and expensive to get a brand-new customer than to keep a current customer satisfied.

That's why keeping our customers happy is in our best interest. What's more, further sales and referrals will only happen if we follow through on our commitments and ensure our company provides the outstanding products and services we've promised.

Consider the importance of follow-up from your own point of view. Remember a time when you bought something that didn't live up to your expectations? In some cases, it may have been because the per- son who sold it to you misrepresented the product or service capa- bilities. But in many cases, it wasn't the salesperson's fault at all. It was an experience after the sale—such as poor treatment from a customer service representative or inadequate technical support—that stopped you from making further purchases with that salesperson or his com- pany.

One salesperson shared with us that he lost his biggest account because of his company's delivery driver. In fact, the company lost several accounts because of this person, but didn't realize immedi- ately that he was the cause. Then, one day, a customer was direct with the salesperson and said, quite simply, "Your delivery driver is a jerk."

While it wasn't the salesperson's fault that the driver angered his company's customers, it was his responsibility to find out why his customers were unhappy. The same goes for us.

While we can overcome poor after-sale results, it's usually tough. Whether we like it or not, our reputation as a salesperson is tied closely to how our organization performs after the sale. This is hard for most of us to accept. After all, unlike other parts of the sales process, after-sale activities require us to relinquish some of our control.

But even if we don't have total control in how the product or service is delivered, we can help generate good results. Successful salespeople do everything they can to ensure effective follow-up. This not only includes contact with customers on a regular basis, it also means building good relationships inside our own organization. If we do well at follow-up, we help ensure the customer's lasting impression of our product or service delivery is not the last impression.

Following Up with Customers

Staying in contact with our customers is the best way to ensure they remain satisfied. In long selling cycles, following up encourages long-term relationships and loyalty. In transaction-based sales, good follow-up keeps our name in front of customers so they remember to refer friends and relatives when the need arises. Whatever the case, consistent and relevant follow-up demonstrates that we really do care about our customers and that we aren't just there to collect commissions.

CURRENT SALE FOLLOW-UP

With those considerations in mind, here are several actions you can take to maintain the all-important after-sale contact with customers:

- Deliver products or paperwork personally to the customer's home or office.
- Check with internal personnel to be sure that all components of your solution have been delivered as promised.

- Let customers know that your team is following up to ensure timely delivery of orders.
- Assure yourself that the installation is done properly and the product functions as promised.
- Be available to support any technical issues.
- Send letters or make phone calls to thank customers for their purchase and reiterate that their satisfaction is important.
- Keep customers updated on new technology or new applications for the products or services they currently use.
- Remind customers of your other products and services. (Remember the Opportunity Chart? This is a good way to remind yourself of other solutions you can possibly offer customers.)
- Know when it's time for them to reorder.

AFTER THE SALE AND BEYOND

If we don't follow up with our customers after the sale is over, we risk losing them, even when we've had good results. Why does this happen? Because we leave room for our competitors to come in and give our customers attention that we're no longer providing. We've shifted our focus to more urgent customer needs or brand-new business. To an extent, this is necessary. But remember, in our noticeable absence, the customer may decide the competitor cares more about his business than we do.

For that reason, we should always find opportunities to let our customers know we care about them and appreciate their business. One of our trainers shared a story about a sales professional who made weekend "thank-you" calls. He placed these calls to his customers' voice mail on Saturday. As he left his message, he played a tape recording of applause in the background. He would tell customers how much he appreciated their business and that the applause was for them. Come Monday morning, his customers would arrive at the office with a pleasant voice mail message to retrieve.

One of the most effective things about these calls is that the salesperson used them to follow up with all customers, regardless of how much or how frequently they ordered.

When we make an honest effort to communicate with all of our customers consistently, we establish a relationship that goes beyond sales-person and customer. When the customer sees us or hears our name, she doesn't think, "I wonder what that salesperson is pushing today." She's more likely to be receptive to our calls and visits and to believe that we have something positive to share with her.

In some cases, we have opportunities to create follow-up that's more unique to a specific customer. Susan Harkey, national account executive for Old Dominion Freight Lines in High Point, North Carolina, saw firsthand how personal follow-up enhanced trust and loyalty in an important customer account.

"I had frequent contact with a decision-maker from one of our cus-tomer companies," says Susan. "She was not very open around me, so I was having trouble getting to know her as a person.

"One day, when we were having a business lunch, this woman men-tioned that she didn't have enough humor in her day and that she'd like to laugh more. So the very next day, I started forwarding her some jokes I received through a daily e-mail service.

"She called me immediately and thanked me for thinking of her. I continue to send her the jokes and, ever since then, our relationship has become much more open and comfortable."

Susan's success in enhancing the relationship with this customer demonstrates the value of follow-up that's more personal. Clearly, how-ever, if the woman had never mentioned a desire for more humor, Susan's daily e-mail jokes would not have been as meaningful. In fact, they could have been unwelcome.

A STRATEGY FOR FOLLOW-UP

As Susan's story illustrates, e-mail is an efficient way to follow up. In fact, e-mail and other technology make it easier than ever for us to stay connected with our customers. With that in mind, here are some im-portant elements of an effective follow-up strategy:

> *A current and active database.* The foundation of any good follow-up effort is a well-organized and frequently maintained customer database. For follow-up to be rather effortless, we need

to have telephone numbers, fax numbers, and e-mail addresses easily accessible. This is best accomplished through an electronic contact management system. Many of these systems will even prompt us with alarms as a way of reminding us to call the customer on a specific day. Whether we have an electronic or a manual database, it's important to keep it updated. Entering pertinent information after each conversation with a customer ensures that we accurately retain every issue and concern so we can refer to the information during subsequent contacts.

Good lines of communication. There is very little that is more irritating to a customer, especially after the sale is made, than being unable to reach the sales representative. For that reason, it's imperative that, when customers want to reach us, they be able to do so easily.

We need to establish a process for continuing communication that works well for everyone. We should make every effort to inform our customers of pager numbers, cellular phone numbers, e-mail addresses, or any other way they can reach us in an emergency. Not only should customers have this information on hand, they should also know the best way in which to communicate with us.

What happens if they don't? Well, say, for example, a customer sends questions to us via e-mail. Yet, during active travel weeks, we aren't able to check our e-mail frequently. That means it may not be possible for us to respond as quickly as the customer hopes. Chances are, the customer will experience some frustration and interpret our lack of response as lack of caring. In turn, we'll be frustrated because we do care. Establishing communication guidelines up front usually eliminates these misunderstandings.

Another piece of advice: If you are on the phone often or frequently out of the office, make sure there is someone in your office who can alert you when customers call. This person doesn't necessarily handle the situation, but he or she should be able to get us a message if important issues arise.

A Strategy for Follow-up

- Keep a current and active database.
- Establish clear lines of communication.
- Send interesting information.
- Provide new product updates.

Interesting information. We can become a valuable resource to our customers by providing them information about issues that affect their people or their businesses. We should keep them abreast of new technology, emerging markets, market trends, and other industry information.

New-product updates. This is a good way to let customers know that we're aware of their future business needs. And it's another great way to keep our name in front of customers after the products or services are delivered. We can mail brochures about new products or upgrades to their existing equipment. We can send faxes with technical tips. We can write e-mail that discusses new product applications. These are all time-efficient and cost-effective actions that require minimal effort on our part, yet provide added value to our customers.

IMPORTANT REMINDERS FOR CUSTOMER FOLLOW-UP

No matter what your follow-up strategy, there are two important things to remember:

Always be conscious of "next steps." Develop a system that allows you to evaluate what the customer has and what that product or service is doing for the customer. Continually ask yourself what you can do to move their company to a new level of success. Become a member of their team. Think about their business issues and how you can become a part of their solutions.

Exceed their expectations. Never stop at just providing what your customers request—do a little more. Although we may provide exactly what they ask for, we leave a window of opportunity for our competitors when we fail to exceed their expectations.

Consider this: You're dining in one of your local restaurants. You order your favorite appetizer. The waiter knows you well. When he brings your appetizer, he informs you that he asked the chef to give you a larger portion than usual because he knows how much you enjoy this particular food. What is he doing? He's exceeding your expectations and most likely enhancing your loyalty as a customer.

FOLLOWING UP WITH OUR OWN TEAM

Customer follow-up is just one part of the equation. As we mentioned earlier, one of the greatest challenges salespeople face today is inside our own organization—the challenge of engaging our internal support teams toward the common goal of customer satisfaction. In today's sales environment, it's very hard to be completely successful without the efforts of people in our own company.

It's often said that we can judge the morale in any organization by looking at the lowest-paid employee. In some cases, those people represent a part of our support staff. With that in mind, it's essential that we do our part in making sure their morale is high.

To do that, we must start seeing things from the support staff's point of view. Typically, there are two general reasons why they may be less than enthusiastic to help us:

Resentment and perception. Perhaps the salesperson has neglected to show gratitude or appreciation for the support staff's efforts. Subsequently, these people—not fully understanding the challenges of selling—may resent the salesperson for getting all the credit, let alone all the commission.

Too much work, not enough hands. It's often hard to engage the internal team simply because they're overworked and understaffed. They not only have to help us, they have to help ten other salespeople. So even though they take pride in doing a good job, time and workload aren't always on their side.

Ways to Show You Value the Team

- Call on the weekend and leave a voice mail message, so they get it first thing Monday morning when they come to work.
- Thank them in front of other people.
- Send letters of appreciation to team members.
- Send copies of appreciation letters to their supervisors.
- Bring doughnuts or bagels in to work.
- Order pizza or sandwiches for lunch.
- Present humorous awards.
- Take them out for dinner.
- Buy simple, yet meaningful, gifts.
- Get to know them as people.

HUMAN RELATIONS SKILLS MAKE THE DIFFERENCE

Treating the support team with the respect and courtesy they deserve is the best way to motivate them toward the common goal of customer satisfaction. It's also important that we demonstrate a sincere interest in their opinions.

Steve Wedderburn is one of the top salespeople for Lexus automobiles in the state of Texas. "While I have a very good understanding of the workings of a Lexus, I am not an expert on the more sophisticated aspects of the engine or computer systems. I would be insulting my customers and ruining my integrity if I pretended to be. I can explain to the customer how everything works, how it will benefit them, and what makes it the cutting-edge car it is. That's what they want to know if they are going to invest in a luxury vehicle.

"On the other hand, if customers have a question about how the computer system is configured or how many parts are in the engine, I will bring in one of our mechanics to talk with them. After all, the mechanics are the experts under the hood. Our customers respect their opinion and so do I."

Clearly, Steve recognizes the importance of building rapport with his mechanics. If you want to know the secret of building rapport with your support team, go back and review what it takes to build rapport with customers. Those same human relations principles are key in creating good relationships inside the organization.

Team-Building Principles

- Create a shared sense of purpose.
- Make the goals team goals.
- Treat people like the individuals they are.
- Make each member responsible for the team product.
- Share the glory, accept the blame.
- Take every opportunity to build confidence in the team.
- Be involved, stay involved.
- Be a mentor.

We have nothing to lose and everything to gain from respecting our internal team. Since it's usually up to them to ensure we keep our promises to customers, it's important they have a mutual respect for us. They don't necessarily have to like us (although that helps!), but they do have to value our role in the company.

If we are successful in creating a positive relationship with people on the inside, we make our jobs on the outside a lot more fun. Why? Because we can focus more on building customer relationships and less on solving problems that arise due to our company's failure to keep its commitments.

TEAMWORK WITH OTHER SALESPEOPLE

Building relationships with our support team is critical in creating successful customer relationships. But what about enhancing communication and teamwork with other salespeople in our company? By sharing ideas and building rapport and trust with one another, we not only improve results for our company, we can serve our customers better. How? By communicating information about common challenges and learning ways in which our fellow salespeople have solved problems similar to those our customers might be facing.

Ian Smith, sales manager for Airborne Express in Manchester, England, saw firsthand how building teamwork within the sales organization affected his company and his customers.

"In my industry, it's almost impossible to get potential customers to switch from their current express carrier. Why should they? They have no problems, great rates and, usually, great relationships. All salespeople in our company face this challenge.

"I work regularly with our European headquarters office in London and, in particular, the sales manager for national accounts, who came from North America. We agreed that working together as a 'unit' within the United Kingdom marketplace would benefit us greatly. She had experience selling in North America and I knew the United Kingdom market and competition. For that reason, we both had great knowledge to share with one another.

"We agreed to meet and discuss strategies we could both implement with our respective sales teams. Six months after having worked as a unit and using the same strategic approaches, we saw results. We achieved a national increase of 11 percent in our customer base and had two successful corporate account bids in just the first phase of competing for the business."

Ian's story illustrates the benefits of working closely with other salespeople in our company. While it seems like common sense, it's not necessarily common practice. In today's sales environment, many salespeople work alone either at home-based offices or in isolated locations away from other salespeople in their organizations. Not only that, in our push to get more new business for ourselves, we simply may not take the time to develop this important alliance that can enhance our sales effectiveness.

Next time you encounter a seemingly unique customer situation or gain insight into a specific market challenge, remember the resource that's at your fingertips: your fellow salespeople. Pick up the phone, send an e-mail, and communicate with them. What you learn just might enhance your ability to develop unique solutions and provide better follow-up to your customers.

CHAPTER 12

Objections
Opportunities to Communicate

One of the surest ways of making friends and influencing the opinions of others is to give consideration to their opinions, to let them know their feelings are important.

—DALE CARNEGIE

R emember the first time you drove a car? You excitedly got behind the wheel and anticipated that first drive around the block. But as you looked at the dashboard in front of you, a little bit of reality set in. "What are all those buttons and gauges?" you might have thought. "How will I ever learn to operate all of them? Is it even possible to watch the road and turn on the windshield wipers at the same time?"

Of course, reading this scenario now, it's hard to imagine that driving an automobile ever seemed complicated. Once we practiced our skills, driving became second nature. And today, when we get into the car and turn the key, we don't think twice about what it takes to drive from one point to the other.

Handling objections is much the same way. It appears complicated at first, and we have to do a lot of things simultaneously. But once we practice the tools and commit to using them whenever necessary, the process of handling objections becomes second nature. Just as with driving a car, we won't think about what to do next. We do it naturally.

In the perfect world, if we've gathered information effectively, we should know exactly what objections the customer might have before we present our solution. Armed with that knowledge, we can address these issues in presenting the solution and minimize the chance that they will surface as objections later on.

On the other hand, selling is not a perfect world. Even when we've done a good job of gathering information and getting to know our customer's needs and wants, it's still possible that we'll miss a key point. It's also possible that something occurred in the buyer's environment in the time between our latest meeting and the solution presentation. If that's the case, the customer may object to parts of our solution based on new information that's become available.

That's why objections can be so frustrating. We don't know if they'll happen. We don't know when they'll happen. And when we do get objections, they aren't always clear. The customer may appear to be objecting to one aspect of the purchase when, in reality, he has a completely different reason for resisting the buying decision.

Clearly, we can't change the fact that objections will occur. So the best thing to do is to change our attitude about them. Instead of seeing objections as roadblocks to gaining commitment, we should see them as opportunities to build even stronger relationships with our customers.

In reality, a genuine objection is usually a sign that the person is thinking seriously about buying from us. Look at it this way: Let's say we're walking through the appliance section of a department store. We pass by a washer and dryer. Will we stop a salesperson and start raising objections about those products if we're not interested in buying them? Probably not. If we don't want that new washer and dryer, what's the point of objecting?

On the other hand, what if we need these appliances? Before we spend the money, chances are we'll talk with a salesperson and expect him to address our concerns and questions to the point that we'll be comfortable with the buying decision.

The same goes for our customers. If they're not interested in our product or service, chances are we won't get far enough in the sales process to get objections. But if they are interested, they want enough information to make a decision they feel good about.

When we look at objections from this point of view, we realize they usually represent nothing more than the customer's indecision or a lack of information. With that understanding, we can stop fearing objections. We can start appreciating them for what they really are: opportunities to communicate with our customers in a way that makes them feel good about their buying decisions.

Since objections can happen at any time, they are not a specific as part of the sales process. In this chapter, we will examine a process that gives you a blueprint to help resolve objections more effectively, no matter when they occur.

> **Resolving objections rule.** To resolve objections, build trust, credibility, and value, always treat the customer with respect.

Human Relations and Objections

Objections often create emotional and mental roadblocks for many sales professionals, even the most experienced. They can even cause us to experience feelings of animosity toward our customers. When that happens, we might make the mistake of handling objections in such a way that we offend the customer. This type of reaction is not always our fault. In fact, many of us have been trained to believe that handling objections is much like going to war with our customers. But nothing is farther from the truth.

When dealing with objections, as in all stages of the sales process, the relationship comes first. Good human relations skills, sincerity, and empathy are all essential to preventing the customer from becoming defensive and destroying much of the good work we have done up to this point.

Therefore, establishing and maintaining a warm relationship with the customer is key in this environment. Dale Carnegie's human relations principles provide some good suggestions. Here are just a few:

- Begin in a friendly way.
- Never tell a person he or she is wrong.
- Avoid arguments.
- Make the other person happy about doing the thing you suggest.

Of course, the driving philosophy here is the principle of seeing things from the other person's point of view.

Ernie Kyger, a successful new-home salesperson in the Washington, D.C., area, recalls a rare time when not seeing the objection from the customer's viewpoint actually cost him a sale.

"Sheila Walker seemed like the easiest buyer in the world for me. She answered every question without hesitation, and I was sure that I had the right house for her. I was thoroughly familiar with her wants and needs and emotional motivations. I made my presentation with confidence, knowing that I knew everything important about Sheila's dream house.

"But Sheila wasn't so easy, not yet anyway. 'I really love an open foyer, and this house doesn't have one,' she said. She then proceeded to tell me of a house that my competitor had, a house that didn't have most of the things she wanted. There was even a drainage ditch in the backyard. She wasn't keen on the drainage ditch because she thought her kids might be tempted to play in it. 'Still,' she said, 'I'm not sure. It's either your house, or the other house.'

"I thought this was only a minor delay. I assured her she was better off without the open foyer. 'An open foyer means high energy bills because you are heating space that you'll never use,' I said. 'Also, the closed foyer is the reason our house has bigger bedrooms upstairs than the other one.' A convincing argument, if I say so myself.

"Of course, she bought from my competitor. I was mystified. I was friendly with my competitor, so I called her. 'Why did Sheila buy your house?' I asked. 'What were her hot buttons?' My friend told me. 'Sheila wanted a brick front and gas fireplace.' Now, I was really mystified. I had a brick front and gas fireplace to offer, too. My friend never mentioned the open foyer.

"I then realized I had broken the most important human relations principle of all. I never looked at the situation from the customer's point of view. I never asked her, 'Why is an open foyer so important?' I tried to talk her out of it. I talked about my own point of view, not necessarily hers. If I had asked that question, I would've had better information to work with, and I might have gotten the sale. I will never forget Sheila Walker, nor will I ever forget to use human relations skills to understand and clarify the objection."

As Ernie said, he learned the hard way how important it is to see things from the customer's point of view when we handle objections. It's not always easy. But we must make the effort.

Are we saying that salespeople need to be mind readers? Absolutely not. Remember what Ernie said: "I never asked her why an open foyer was important." The key word in his comment is "asked." We need to remember the importance of questioning our customers throughout the sales process, and then really listening to their answers.

Andrew Winter, a top business development manager at Ignition Group in Toronto, Ontario, Canada, realized this critical point when he received a price objection while working for a previous employer.

"After spending a tremendous amount of time developing a customized display fixture for a retailer's new cosmetics department, I got a call late one afternoon from the customer saying he had found a cheaper price for a similar product. I was shocked. I believed I had the best solution. Our design was original. And I also believed I was the only supplier they were considering.

"After dealing with the initial shock of their comments, I was able to revise the pricing slightly through a different manufacturing process. I resubmitted the quote. I had feared that my design had been knocked off by my competition. In reality, I was competing against myself because I failed to ask enough questions.

"Fortunately, later the next day, I got the order for a test program of twenty-two units. If the designs prove to be effective, the order for the rollout could be two hundred to four hundred pieces.

"Things easily could've gone the other way, which is why I believe good questioning skills are necessary throughout the process. If I had continued to ask questions regarding the customer's purchasing policies, I would have learned that they have a policy requiring them to get quotes from three suppliers. Since I hadn't thought to ask this question, I foolishly believed that I was the only one they were dealing with. I made the mistake of seeing things from my own point of view, not the customer's."

Clearly, if we remember the importance of seeing things from the customer's point of view, then we should remember the importance of asking questions throughout the sales process. That's the only way we'll be able to truly understand and relate to the customer's world.

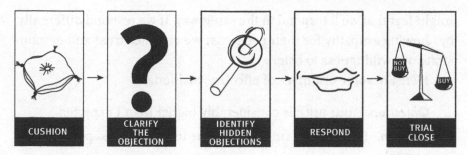

Figure 11: Resolving Objections

Taking Action: Five Steps to Resolve Objections

Dealing effectively with objections requires us to practice careful, sensitive listening skills along with positive, factual responses to customer concerns. Of course, as with any part of the sales process, it helps to have a strategy. And just as with driving a car, this strategy becomes second nature if we understand it, practice it, and are committed to using it in every situation when objections occur.

RESOLVING OBJECTIONS STEP 1: CUSHION

In the real world, what does a cushion do? That's easy. It softens and comforts. That's also the role of a cushion when resolving objections.

Suppose our customer raises an objection. Then suppose we say something like, "Ms. Davis, that's not so. You are crazy to think that!" Obviously, even if we don't agree with the customer, we would not answer her objection in that way. On the contrary, our goal is to find a point of agreement—or "cushion"—between the customer and us before we address the objection.

Simply, a cushion indicates that we hear the customer's concern and we understand that it's important to her. A cushion does not agree, disagree, or answer the objection. An effective cushion communicates to customers that their objections are not just giving us excuses to sell harder or close more aggressively. A cushion lets them know that we are still prepared to see things from their point of view.

What a tremendous way to lower resistance and differentiate ourselves from the competition. After all, customers often deal with salespeople who take an objection as a declaration of war. Naturally, they might fear that we'll respond in the same way. If we respond differently, by showing empathy for their concerns, we enhance trust and demonstrate our willingness to listen.

Here are some examples of effective cushions:

Objection. Your price is considerably higher than I expected.

Cushion. Being concerned about the investment is perfectly normal.

Objection. Our deadline is the last week of this month and we can't consider anyone that can't meet that schedule.

Cushion. I can understand how important delivery schedules can be.

Objection. We don't have the time or resources to retrain our staff to operate a new system.

Cushion. Knowing that your people can make it work is a key issue.

Objection. We simply can't afford the loss of production the installation you are proposing would require.

Cushion. Downtime is always a serious consideration.

Objection. We really like the house, but conventional financing will require a 10 percent down payment. That will make things very difficult for us.

Cushion. The amount of the deposit is a significant factor.

A word of warning about cushions: Avoid the natural tendency to cushion the objection and then follow it with the word "but." Here's what we mean: "The amount of the deposit is a significant factor, but the return on your investment will be high." Do you see what happens? In this situation, we found a point of agreement. However, if we follow it with a "but" statement, the reply appears argumentative. So, instead of creating an atmosphere of trust and mutual respect, we've probably added some tension to the discussion.

Unfortunately, it's human nature to use the "yes-but" method. Why? It's not because we're purposely trying to be argumentative. We're simply trying to link our cushion with our next statement.

Here are three suggestions for avoiding the word "but" in your conversations:

Use the word "and." It's still a linking word, but doesn't send an argumentative message.

Use the customer's name. "I really appreciate your concern, Angela, downtime is always an issue."

Take a breath. "Downtime is always an issue [breathe]. Let's talk about that further.

Remember, when we use a cushion, we don't use it as a launching point to argue with the customer and immediately talk about our point of view. We use it as a way to establish common ground before asking questions to clarify the real objection.

RESOLVING OBJECTIONS STEP 2: CLARIFY THE OBJECTION

Some of the best examples of clarifying an objection come from children. Consider this typical conversation:

"Mom, can I go over to my friend's house for a couple of hours?"

"No," replies the mother.

"Why?" says the child.

"Because it's getting kind of late," says the mother.

"Why?" repeats the child.

"Because dinner's going to be ready."

Again, the child says, "Why?"

And the mom replies, "Because I'm making meatloaf, your favorite meal."

Then, the child says, "Okay, I got it. You want me to stay home for some meatloaf."

Had the child stopped asking questions, he never would have learned about the meatloaf dinner. The point is, in clarifying objections, we need to approach the customer with childlike curiosity. Why? In most cases, we are not asking enough questions to fully understand the customer's issues.

For that reason, one of the most effective things we can do after we cushion an objection is to ask a question, or a series of questions, in order to clarify our understanding and our customer's understanding of the objection.

To illustrate this concept, think of a time when your friends invited you to join them for an event, but you didn't want to go. Rather than be specific about your reason for not attending, you might have said, "I'd love to, but that time doesn't work for me."

In giving that response, you were just giving them a general reason you declined their invitation. You responded by sharing the information you consciously—or subconsciously—wanted to communicate.

Your objection was, "It's a bad time." But that could mean a number of things. Maybe you've been working a lot and you needed time alone. Maybe the season finale of a favorite television show conflicted with the time your friends suggested. Or maybe you didn't particularly like one of the people attending the event. The point is, your friends never really knew why you objected, so they didn't have a chance to adapt their plans to accommodate your real issues.

Our customers have the same tendency. They may appear to be objecting to one aspect of our solution, when they're really objecting to something completely different. That's why it's so important to really understand the message behind the words.

Sounds easy to most of us. But in reality, it's one of the most challenging steps of the objection process. Why? Mainly because there are many elements in our communication environment that make it difficult to interpret the real message.

When a customer voices an objection, there are four factors we have to consider:
- What they actually say
- What we hear
- What we interpret it to mean
- What they really mean

To better understand why we can't rely on our own interpretation of the customer's issues, consider this exercise we sometimes do in our training: We give the trainees a word or sentence, and then we ask each person to tell us what it means.

For example, let's say we use the word "deep." Some people interpret that word to mean ten feet of water. Others say it is one thousand meters of water. Some people don't think about water at all. To them, the word "deep" means a person who has profound thoughts about simple things.

Try this exercise with some of your friends or coworkers. You'll hear for yourself the variety of interpretations people can have. Where do these interpretations come from? From many sources: past experiences, other people's opinions, or what we've always thought the word meant. There are an infinite number of reasons why we interpret things the way we do.

So how does this relate to objections? Well, think about it. Is it possible that when a customer gives us an objection, we might interpret what they mean incorrectly? It happens to hundreds of salespeople every single day!

For example, a customer might say, "I have a problem with the price." Most salespeople will start handling that "price" objection based on what they think the customer means. If the salesperson interprets it to mean, "The customer wants a better price," he will respond one way. If he interprets it to mean, "The competition has a lower price," the response will again be different. Or if the salesperson believes the customer is really saying, "I don't like you and I'm just using price as an easy way to get you out of my office," there will be yet another type of response.

Which interpretation is correct? We have no way of knowing unless we clarify the objection. Sure, we could guess, as many salespeople do, but then we might respond to what we think the objection is and not be responding to the real issues.

Here are some examples of questions we can ask to help clarify the objection (in each case, the objection has already been cushioned):

- I think we may be looking for something else.
  What exactly are you hoping to find?

- I'm not convinced that your company is the one that can help us.
  If you did partner with us, what major concern would you have?
- Your price is too high.
  What is it about the price that concerns you the most?
  Would you please tell me more?
- Since our last meeting, there have been some changes and we would like you to call us in six months.
  Can you please tell me about those changes?
- I don't have time to talk about this right now. Can you just put something in the mail?
  Sure. What kind of information do you need?
- I don't think that piece of equipment will work in our plant.
  What is it about the equipment that worries you?
- We are still evaluating options at the moment.
  Can you please tell me more about your specific needs to see if we have a good option for you?
- Your competition has come in with a better proposal.
  What specifically makes it "better"?

These are just a few examples of the hundreds of questions we can use to help clarify objections. Take some time to write out the most common objections you hear. Then, develop some questions you can ask to help the customer clarify objections in your own selling environment.

Most Common Objections

- Price doubt—doesn't see value
- Product or service doubt—doesn't think performance will meet expectations
- Happy with current supplier—not motivated to change
- Peers or influencers in the company—worried about their opinions
- Time frame—doesn't think company can deliver when needed

You might think, "How am I going to remember to ask these questions?" The answer is, "Practice, practice, practice!" When we apply this line of questioning faithfully, it becomes second nature—a logical flow in response to our customer's statement.

Tim Fitzgerald, a financial advisor for Ferris Baker Watts in Columbia, Maryland, describes how he uses this approach. "In one situation, I was speaking with a potential client and her objection was about the fee structure on the investments I had recommended to her. Instead of going to great lengths to justify my fees (which is what I used to do), I asked her, 'What specifically within the fee structure concerns you?'

"Upon questioning her further, I discovered that her main concern arose from some articles she had been reading in financial magazines. These articles stated that investors shouldn't pay fees. It also said that many stockbrokers who charge fees actually have been underperforming in the market. These conclusions had made her a bit suspicious about the fee structure.

"After she answered my questions, I could tell the main thing she needed was reassurance. So I took the time to discuss with her that our ultimate goal, fees or no fees, was to increase the value of her portfolio over time. I then showed her the performance of the investments that I had recommended for her. On the average, the overall portfolio had, in fact, outperformed all of the major indexes over the past twenty years. So even with the fees, she made more money than she would have in other no-fee options. Her concern about the fees then disappeared because she saw the value behind them. We decided to work together and she has been very pleased with the performance of her investments."

A salesperson for Dale Carnegie Training admits—even though he knows better—he learned firsthand the power of clarifying the objection. "I was at an appointment with a person from a web hosting company in Northern Virginia who was interested in taking the sales training course. Her sales were okay, but for the past few years she was always hovering around the 100 percent of quota mark. Not bad, but below her personal standards. She thought if she could fine-tune her selling skills it would help her break through that barrier.

"Everything was going well at the appointment until I mentioned the price of the course. Her body language changed noticeably and she seemed to withdraw and became very quiet. 'That's more than I expected,' she said.

"Since I had prepared for this objection, I proceeded to re-emphasize the value and benefits she would realize based on the experience of thousands of graduates. I told her how she could expect her sales and income to increase. I started to get excited and became more enthusiastic. I showed her testimonials of salespeople who had increased their incomes by 50 percent or more. I showed her the manual and some more brochures. In my mind, I had created such incredible value that there was no way that she could object to the price.

"The trouble was, the more excited and 'convincing' I got, the further she retreated. Then I started getting frustrated. After about ten minutes I literally ran out of things to say and there was an awkward silence.

"At that point, she said to me: 'My company typically only spends half of that amount on sales training.'

"I was stumped. Surely this was a hopeless objection if ever there was one! The awkward silence continued. I was thinking of ways to leave her office and move on to my next appointment when she said, 'How do I sign up?'

"Now I was totally confused. I asked her about the price issue. She mentioned that all she needed to do was ask her manager to approve the extra investment, which wouldn't be a problem because he was the one who recommended the course to her. In reality, the reason she became quiet was that she was thinking of when she could meet with her manager so she could discuss the issue with him.

"I quickly realized that I was answering the objection based on my interpretation. I was enthusiastically helping her see the value of the course, which was a mistake, because she was already sold on the value. She just needed to think through how she could get the funding. If I had just asked her (after I had cushioned her objection) a question such as, 'What do you mean?' it would have clarified my understanding and saved both of us a lot of time."

Categories of Objections

Genuine. This type of objection blocks the orderly flow of the sale. Unless resolved, this issue will probably stop the sale from proceeding.

> **Example.** We have twelve square feet of office space available for the installation and this equipment has a footprint of almost eighteen square feet.

Skepticism. The person is not convinced that our solution meets his needs. He probably needs more evidence or a different kind of evidence.

> **Example.** I'm not sure this will really work for us. Our needs are somewhat unique.

Misconception. This objection is based partially on fact and partially on fallacy. Typically, misconceptions are more opinion than fact, so they don't block the sale.

> **Example.** I understand that your piece of equipment doesn't retain its value as well as that of some of the big-name companies.

Delay. This type of objection either gives the buyer more time to decide or may even indicate that the commitment will not go forward. In some cases, delays are created when the customer doesn't have the authority to make the buying decision or when he feels pressured into making the decision.

> **Example.** Let me think about it and I'll get back to you.

Hopeless. A hopeless objection that cannot be overcome at this time. Many salespeople give up on objections that are not truly hopeless.

> **Example.** We signed a contract with the competitor. In fact, the equipment was installed yesterday.

RESOLVING OBJECTIONS STEP 3: IDENTIFY HIDDEN OBJECTIONS

Should we really keep asking our customers for more objections? Yes. Here's why. In many cases, there is an underlying objection that has not been addressed, one that represents a further obstacle between our customer and the commitment. By getting to the hidden objection through effective questioning, we can get it out in the open sooner. In some cases, customers may not even realize why they are hesitating. We can be doing a service by asking questions that bring out all those concerns.

We can identify hidden objections by asking two simple questions:

"In addition to your concern about [objection], is there anything else causing you to hesitate?" If the client says yes, then we can keep probing. If she answers no, we can say:

"So, if we can resolve your concern about [objection] would you be ready to move ahead?"

The answers to these questions allow us, in a nonthreatening way, to assess the seriousness of the objection. They also help us understand where the customer's thinking is relative to the commitment.

Here's how these questions might work if we are selling Internet access:

SALESPERSON: "Other than the connection speed, is there anything else causing you concern at the moment?"

CUSTOMER: "No, it's primarily the speed that I'm worried about."

SALESPERSON: "So if you felt more comfortable about the connection speed, you would be ready to move forward, is that correct?"

CUSTOMER: "Yes."

If the answer is yes, we must try to resolve the objection about connection speed. What if the answer is no? That gives us some valuable information as well. Why did the customer say no? We could guess (like most salespeople), or we could put the question back to the customer:

SALESPERSON: "So if you felt more comfortable about the connection speed, you would be ready to move forward, is that correct?"

CUSTOMER: "No, probably not."

SALESPERSON: "Obviously, there is something else causing you to hesitate. Could I please ask what that is?"

If the customer gives us another objection, we go back to the beginning of the process. We cushion the objection. We ask questions to clarify the objection. Then what? We look for another hidden objection. After all, there might be more than two concerns we need to resolve before the customer feels comfortable making the commitment. Often, even though the customer voices more than one objection, we find there is only one major factor causing him concern. Nevertheless, we still need to go through the process thoroughly.

Remember, objections aren't always rational. So if we don't recognize them, clarify them, and then look for more, we risk that they will remain an issue. This could delay, and even prevent, a buying commitment in our favor.

Greg Jacobson, a successful salesperson for American Power Conversion in the Washington, D.C., area, recalls a time when uncovering the hidden objection helped him gain a major commitment with the United States federal government.

"I was trying to add a few more of our products to one of our largest resellers on the State Department contract. The addition of these products would mean some significant business for my company. The reseller requested that I send information as soon as possible. He indicated that receipt of the information was the key to moving the sale forward quickly.

"After providing the reseller with the things he requested, such as data sheets, pricing information, and other terms and conditions, I noticed that the sale of these additional products still was not moving forward. I asked the person responsible and he told me that they 'just needed a little more information.' He sent me to get that.

"Again, upon fulfillment of this information request, the product addition still did not move forward. When I asked about it, they again specified that they didn't want to move forward yet because the information I had provided them was incomplete. When I clarified what they meant by 'incomplete,' they provided me with a request for some further information.

"At this point, I got the sense that the information wasn't the real issue. So I stopped and said, 'If I get you this last piece of product information, will there be anything else keeping you from adding this product to the contract immediately?' Well, guess what, there was.

"As it turns out, they recently had some pretty significant revenue losses with other products on this contract. So, they decided that they could only add new items to the contract if the margin was very healthy. They were looking for more margin with our product, which meant I'd have to sell it to them for less than I was offering.

"I asked them, 'Why didn't you just say that to me up front?' As it turns out, this was not a buying criterion earlier in the sales discussion. So they were hesitant to bring it up to me late in the process.

"After uncovering this additional information, we were able to compromise on the pricing and found a level that was healthy for everyone. The product was added immediately after that."

When to Respond to Objections

Now. As a rule, the most common time to answer an objection is as soon as the customer brings it up. This shows you're using good listening skills and being responsive to their needs.

Before they are expressed. It usually pays to answer an objection before it comes up. However, the only time you should answer an objection in advance is when you feel reasonably certain that it will be raised. This knowledge comes from doing your homework, asking the right questions, and truly listening to your customer during every phase of the sale.

Later. The answer to some objections should be postponed. Here are a few guidelines for making that decision:

- The answer to the objection is so long and involved that it interferes with the orderly flow of the sales process. Tell the customer that you'll address it at the appropriate time.
- It's included later in your presentation, which means you should continue with your presentation and tell the customer you'll be covering it later on.
- You aren't equipped with the facts necessary to provide a truthful and convincing answer. If so, tell the buyer you will get the facts.

Never. Some objections don't need to be answered. They merely represent the customer's opinion on some aspect of the product or service. If an objection does not influence the outcome of the sale, or if other factors will outweigh the objection, we may choose not to address it at all.

RESOLVING OBJECTIONS STEP 4: RESPOND TO EACH OBJECTION

To understand the importance of the first three steps in handling objections, let's consider the sport of volleyball. When the ball comes over the net and goes to the player at the back of the court, does she try to hit a winning shot from there? Usually not. Instead, she passes the ball to the player standing in front of her. When that player receives the ball, does she try to hit a winning shot? She could. But she'll probably get better results if she passes it to the player standing right next to the net, because that person is in the best position to hit a winning shot.

In much the same way, the first three steps of the resolving objections process set up our response so that we can be more successful. Remember, if we go straight from hearing the objection to attempting to resolve it, we risk answering the wrong objection or missing other hidden issues that create barriers to gaining commitment.

On the other hand, if we cushion the objection, clarify it, and then identify any hidden objections, we are well positioned to resolve the customer's real issues.

How to Respond

- Reverse
- Explain
- Educate
- Provide evidence
- Provide value justification

Reverse. Many sales professionals believe that the reasons customers say they won't buy are ultimately the reasons they will buy. Therefore, let's turn the objection into the reason for buying.

Consider a person who is hesitating in registering for a self-defense class. In this case, the customer might say, "You know, now that I think about it, I really don't need a class like this—I rarely go out alone." The response in this case could be, "That's the very reason you ought to take the course. You said you rarely go out alone because you don't feel safe. After you take the course, you'll become more confident and going out alone won't worry you as much."

Here's another example. The objection: "Your price is too high." The answer: "The fact that our price is higher than those of some of the other products you are considering is probably the very reason you should select our product."

Explain. When we provide explanations in response to objections, we are simply sharing with our customers some insight, information, and ideas that directly relate to their concerns.

If we use a reversal like the one above, we need to follow it with an explanation:

"You are probably wondering why I say that. Well, rather than see how cheaply we can build our products, we made the decision to see how well we could build them. We could use smaller motors, lighter wiring, and less durable materials and then reduce the price of our equipment. But we don't. When you buy our machine, you are getting one that's designed to meet a need, not a price."

As with all of the suggested language in this book, the idea is not to be mechanical in your communications. It's to understand the types of questions and answers that are most effective in certain selling situations. Remember, adapt the suggestions to your style and use only the ones you feel comfortable using.

Educate. Sometimes, we just need to provide our customers with factual information in response to an objection. We might show them brochures, specification sheets, photos, our website—anything that helps them better understand our product or service.

Raymundo Alejandro Acosta F. relates a story about selling sporting goods at Acosta Deportes in Mexico City. In one situation, he recalls a mother who wanted to buy tennis shoes for her son. The customer wanted leather shoes and objected to Raymundo's suggestions of other types of shoes. Raymundo knew, in this case, tennis shoes made from synthetic materials would be a better alternative. Once he educated the mother on the benefits of synthetic shoes, such as breathability and durability, the mother understood why they would be more suited to her son's activities. She was happy with her purchase and was pleased that Raymundo helped her make a good decision.

Provide evidence. A lawyer wouldn't go to court without evidence to support her case. In the same way, we shouldn't go into an objections discussion—or any part of the sale, for that matter—without evidence that supports our facts and claims.

Evidence is a critical tool in addressing almost any type of objection. Take a few minutes and review the discussion on evidence in the previous chapter. Remember, evidence includes demonstrations, examples, facts, exhibits, analogies, testimonials, and statistics.

Hank Haaksma from Oakpoint Oil (a distributor of Chevron), Winnipeg, Manitoba, Canada, found himself providing evidence almost by accident. "I made my first call to R. L. Trucking. They own some tractors and trailers that would be ideal for one of our products, Chevron Delo 400 (diesel engine oil). The manager showed a little interest, but price was a major objection. He was using a competitor's product at the time.

"I invited him to a Delo dinner to give him more information. Then, on my second call, my business manager went with me and we further discussed the advantages of the Delo 400 product. However, the customer was still uncomfortable making the switch. We did agree, however, that he would be a good customer for our lower-priced Chevron RPM product. We suggested this to him. The next day, he ordered a drum of RPM. Unfortunately, we didn't have any in stock, so we sent him a drum of Delo 400, but charged him the lower RPM price.

"About five weeks later, he ordered a second drum of oil. Assuming he meant a second drum of RPM, I delivered that. When I got there, he noticed which oil I had brought him and he told me to take it back because he wanted the Delo oil. I asked him what changed his mind? He told me, after using the Delo oil, he realized he could achieve significant cost savings. The performance of Delo oil meant he had to buy less oil because he had to change the oil less frequently. So even though it was higher-priced up front, the longer change intervals enabled him to run his fleet of trucks more efficiently. This was enough evidence for him to overcome the price objection. The customer is now trying other products in the Delo line."

Hank used some creative thinking in this situation. Had he not sent the customer the premium oil at the standard oil price, he would've missed the opportunity to provide a strong piece of evidence that eventually overcame a price objection.

Jerry Rodier, a commercial real estate agent from Saskatchewan, Canada, used a simple demonstration and some showmanship to overcome his customer's objection.

Jerry was preparing to sell a four-hundred-thousand-dollar commercial property to an institutional client. He had carefully rehearsed the many reasons why he felt this property was certain to soar in value over the next ten to fifteen years. It was a pretty convincing argument, he felt. But there was one likely stumbling block: Jerry suspected the client would balk at his commission. So Jerry brought a big bag of poker chips along with him as he entered the boardroom to make his presentation.

Jerry made his presentation about why the property was about to soar in value and the client looked convinced. But the client voiced an objection about Jerry's commission, as expected. At this point, Jerry dumped all the poker chips on the boardroom table.

"This is the amount of money you stand to make on this building over the next ten or fifteen years," he said. "And this," he said, picking up a single poker chip from the pile on the table, "this is what we are arguing about, isn't it?" The client smiled. "Where do I sign?" he asked.

John Robertson and John Stinson, of Stinson Robertson Custom Builders, relate a story of how they ultimately used an analogy—comparing the familiar to the unfamiliar—as evidence in answer to a price objection.

"We were approached by an architect, with whom we had done business previously, about pricing a job for an entertainer who had recently moved into the area. The entertainer was planning to build an elaborate entertainment building on his riverfront estate outside town.

"The architect explained that another contractor had completed some major renovation work on the prospect's house a few years earlier. However, for personal reasons, the prospect had decided to select another contractor for the new job. We were given a preliminary set of plans for pricing to give the owner a better idea of the project costs. We were asked to provide this price in a relatively short time period, which we did.

"When we met with the prospect, he indicated that the price was somewhat higher than he had hoped it would be. We then suggested some minor changes in the design of the building and in the materials to be used as a way to help lower the costs. However, we stressed to him that if he deviated significantly from our recommendations, he could jeopardize the overall quality and image of the new building.

"During the meeting, the prospect happened to share with us that he was also principal owner of a food products business whose products he actively promoted for their quality and value. He emphasized that he was a good businessman and knew the value of a dollar.

"A week later, as agreed, we sent the prospect our final price, which was lower than our preliminary price but in the general range of what the prospect said would be acceptable. The next day, we were shocked when the prospect called us and said that, unknown to us, he had also sent the final drawings to his previous contractor for a price. His previous contractor gave him a price somewhat lower than our price. So, he informed us that he subsequently awarded the job to the other contractor.

"My partner and I were very disappointed to hear this, and we were totally frustrated about what to do next.

"Later that same day, I went in to a local grocery store and looked at the prospect's food products prominently displayed on the shelves beside competing brands. I noticed that his products were priced significantly higher than his competitors. That gave me an idea about how to help him understand the quality of our business.

"I returned to the office and immediately wrote him a letter. I explained how I had visited the grocery store and had noticed that his products commanded a much higher price than his competitors. They were packaged and presented well and, more important, tasted better than his competitors' products. The reason for his products' success was they represented a better value to the customer.

"I proceeded to use an analogy and explain to the customer that this was exactly how my partner and I perceived our services relative to our competitors. We may have a higher price than our competitors, but our overall quality, service, and craftsmanship create better value for our customers.

"A few days later, we received a call from the prospect saying that he had received our letter and that, after some thought, he had reconsidered his decision and was going to award the contract to us after all. We entered into a formal agreement with him the next day and proceeded with the work."

Provide value justification. We all need to be aware of key points that make our products and services special. To do that, we should ask ourselves one basic question: What does our organization bring to the customer that would make him do business with us rather than do business with the competition? The answers to this question will help us create our company's value proposition.

Sometimes, the value proposition includes unique services. Product features can also bring value to customers. In some cases, it's the sales professional himself who makes a company stand out from its competition.

Such is the case with Jonathan Wax, a financial advisor in Tampa, Florida. With the increase of online Internet trading, Jon realized that he needed to demonstrate his value to customers more than ever before. His value proposition? Jon is very timely in communicating with his customers when he sees changes in their portfolios. What does that mean to his customers? If there's a change in their stocks, bonds, or other offerings, Jon informs the customer immediately. Jon's prompt calls often save customers thousands of dollars in losses. Jon knows that this level of personal service is something the electronic trading companies can't offer.

What is your value proposition? Take some time and create one for yourself. Having a value proposition is not only important in responding to objections, it can also make you a more effective and confident salesperson throughout the entire process.

RESOLVING OBJECTIONS STEP 5:
EVALUATE THE CUSTOMER'S POSITION WITH A TRIAL CLOSE

When we bake a cake, how do we know it's done? Often, we stick a toothpick in the middle to see if it comes out clean. If the cake is finished, we remove it from the oven. If it's not, we bake it a little bit longer.

Just as we use a toothpick to determine whether a cake is ready, we should use a trial close to evaluate whether our customer is ready to move forward with the buying decision.

The trial close evaluative question is critical in helping us determine our next steps. Why? If we proceed to try to gain commitment and the customer still has objections, we may be perceived as putting pressure on the customer, when, in fact, we don't mean to pressure him at all.

On the other hand, if we've satisfied the objections, then asking for the commitment is completely appropriate.

Esther Hanlon, with CMS Hartzell, was dealing with a rather complicated objection. She used a trial close that addressed the customer's issues and ultimately moved the sale forward to gain commitment. "My customer placed different purchase orders throughout the year, all for the same product. The orders would be for different quantities and different delivery dates. The customer's objection was that the price would vary from one order to the next, which gave them problems in controlling their costs.

"I realized I needed to educate the customer on why the price would vary. I reminded him that all our products are customized, with tooling developed for each specific customer job. Each order involves procuring inventory, tooling setup, coordination in the manufacturing process, and so on. I explained that higher-quantity orders and more consistent delivery schedules help us keep our costs down, and we pass those savings on to our customers. Now he could understand why our pricing appeared inconsistent.

"I came up with a unique solution that would benefit both companies. I asked the customer for a one-year forecast, and committed to produce their material every six weeks and hold it for them. They would give us a release when materials were needed.

"To move the sale ahead, I asked a trial close. 'What will be the results when you get more consistent pricing and the added benefit of having material available exactly when you need it?' That was all it took. The customer was delighted. We got the business."

Esther did many things right in addressing the customer's objections. She asked enough questions to determine the customer's real issues. She offered a unique solution that would accomplish some things important to the customer. And she evaluated the customer's position before she asked for commitment.

Asking evaluative questions before asking for commitment is just part of the relationship-building process. If we proceed without knowing where our customers stand, they might perceive that we don't care about their issues. When that happens, we damage our credibility and ultimately risk losing the commitment.

Guidelines for Resolving Objections

- Get into the right mental attitude—and stay in it.
- Never argue with a customer. Of all the ways to lose a buying commitment, this one's almost guaranteed.
- Never treat a customer's objection with contempt.
- Answer briefly, and don't waste too much time on objections.
- Be confident and thorough in your response. If you seem unsure or don't address the objection fully, the customer will pick up on it.
- Only provide answers you know for certain are true. If you don't know an answer, find out and call the customer back immediately.
- Develop standard answers for common objections and commit them to memory.

CHAPTER 13

The Biggest Sales Advantage
Our Attitude

> Some people hear opportunity knocking and complain about the noise. Others wait, patiently or eagerly, to hear the knock. Don't do either. Go out and keep knocking on the doors of opportunity until they open under your persistence.

Dale Carnegie once said, "It isn't what you have, who you are, where you are, or what you are doing that makes you happy or unhappy. It is what you think about it. Two people may be in the same place, doing the same thing; both may have about an equal amount of money and prestige—and yet one may be miserable and the other happy. Why? Because of different mental attitudes."

Think about Mr. Carnegie's statement. Can you recall a time in your life when a bad attitude kept you from being productive? Or what about a situation in which a positive attitude helped you overcome adversity?

Take, for example, a man named Fred Smith. When he was in college, he got a C on a paper in which he described the concept of an overnight delivery company. If he had not kept a positive attitude about his idea, he might have given up on his dream. And today, we probably wouldn't have a company called Federal Express.

We are no different from Fred Smith when it comes to the power of attitude in our lives. Without a doubt, it has a huge impact on whether we achieve our personal goals as well as our sales goals.

At the beginning of this book, we introduced attitude control as one of the five drivers of sales success. While all of these drivers are important, attitude is unique. Why? Unlike the other four drivers, attitude is developed internally. Selling skills can be taught. Communication and people skills can be improved through education. Organizational skills can be enhanced through technology. But attitude comes from within.

Consider this: Thousands of people across the world have participated in our sales training program. If everyone had the same attitude about the course, every graduate would be equally successful. Of course, that's not the case. Some people don't believe in the power of the tools and principles. Therefore, they listen with a closed mind and maintain a negative attitude throughout the learning process. Others are enthusiastic while they're in the classroom. But when they get back to their daily routines, they become complacent and aren't motivated to make changes.

While we'd like to think that a good understanding of the buying and selling process could overcome these unproductive attitudes, it's highly unlikely. Certainly, the right sales tools can improve our attitude about selling, but it doesn't create a positive attitude. We must find that within ourselves.

For example, instead of viewing prospecting and pre-approach as monotonous work, we should see them as opportunities to build better customer relationships from the very beginning. We shouldn't let fear stop us from stepping out of our comfort zone to use word pictures or ask for referrals. We should always be receptive to new ideas for improving our selling skills, no matter how successful we become. Instead of seeing problem customers, we should see customers with problems to solve. By having the right attitude about building relationships with customers, we create a win-win situation for everyone involved.

Consider Hong Kong entrepreneur Grant Craft, owner of Craft Projects. Grant and a business associate were in the middle of negotiations for a large construction contract with a major international company. They felt confident they would gain commitment. So confident, in fact, that Grant moved forward with his previously scheduled plans to vacation in the Philippines.

When Grant's plane landed in the Philippines, he retrieved a phone message from his associate. The customer wanted to see more evidence that Grant's small company could handle the job. Realizing he needed to be there personally to present evidence, Grant immediately bought another plane ticket and prepared to make the four-hour flight to Singapore.

Grant made a successful presentation. The result? His company established a new business relationship that had significant impact on Craft Projects' bottom line.

That's what we mean by attitude coming from within. While Grant knows how to use a variety of selling tools, his "do whatever it takes" attitude is something he developed in his own character. And he's certainly seeing the rewards.

In just four years, his company grew from zero income to $25 million. Estimates for fifth-year revenues exceed $100 million. Craft Projects has offices in Hong Kong, Singapore, and Australia. In 1999, his company was recognized as one of the top businesses in Australia.

For entrepreneur Paula Levis Suita of Smith & Suita, cofounder and principal of a PR, investor relations, and marketing firm in the Boston, Massachusetts, area, the combination of Sales Advantage tools and a positive attitude made the difference between anxiety and developing a winning approach. It's also what helped the young firm gain one of the biggest accounts in its history.

"It all started when we got a call from a harried marketing person at a high-profile company who needed investor relations assistance immediately. The chief financial officer had recently left the company, as had the company's investor relations person. There were a number of upcoming activities in which they needed immediate help. Meeting 'next week' was not sufficient; they wanted to see us the next morning.

"We prepared for the next day's meeting with a two-hour refresher course on the Sales Advantage process the night before, and did as much pre-approach work as we could. We met with two people and developed great rapport. Our primary contact asked for a written proposal and said the company would get back to us immediately following its receipt. We sent the proposal that night. We felt very confident that we had gained commitment—even before we sent the proposal. Then we didn't hear from them for two months.

"During that two-month period, we called our primary contact and then followed up with the secondary representative. We e-mailed them individually and then together. We found relevant reasons to call. We sent copies of articles they might find of interest as a subtle reminder. But no matter what we did, we never got a call back.

"As the lead person on the opportunity, I started to doubt my skills, question my abilities, and generally take it way too personally. My confidence began to decline. Nevertheless, I tried to maintain the 'smile across the telephone' and show my eagerness to help and solve their problems. After weeks of being persistent, we finally connected with our secondary contact. She told us that the company had indeed liked our proposal but that the primary contact had transferred to another position. She also said that they had been in the midst of several changes and had simply not had the time to call. We started our assignment with them not long after that conversation.

"The lessons learned from this sales situation include: 1) Small business owners can't just rely on their specific skills, services, or products to land the assignment. They must learn the fundamentals of sales in order to survive. 2) Successful salespeople—and particularly women who have been trained to be supportive and not assertive—have to get over the 'I'm-being-too-aggressive fear' and just keeping making the call—again, and again, and again. 3) A positive attitude makes all the difference."

MORE WINNING ATTITUDES IN ACTION

Ed Porter, an account manager with an information services company in Gaithersburg, Maryland, feels he absolutely must keep a positive attitude given the nature of his inside sales position. Ed deals with corporate inbound and outbound calls. Customers call for a wide variety of reasons, and they expect immediate results.

"In one case, an insurance company had been contacting us regarding information on our software services. While we have a good reputation for responding to customers, this one somehow fell through the cracks. To top it off, on this particular day when they called in, I happened to be the seventh person they talked to. The call went like this: 'This is what I want. I want to talk to you about your enterprise systems. I need somebody onsite next week. If you can't do that, then we are going to take our business someplace else. We will take you out of consideration.'

"This represented a small dilemma for me. I am in inside sales and I don't go onsite. We have outside sales people, but they are not always immediately available. I knew I would not be able to meet this customer's demand immediately if I spent time trying to find answers. So what did I do?

"I accepted responsibility for making sure this customer's needs were met. I asked more questions to determine her specific issues. Then I told her we could do what she wanted us to do. I got her name and phone number. I promised her I would call her back that afternoon and let her know when we would be there. I told her I would be her personal point person. I told her to bypass the 800 number and gave her my direct line. As soon as I got off the phone, I called my manager and explained the situation to him. I told him that we needed someone onsite. He assured me we would have someone there, and he gave me a specific date.

"I called the customer back. We went ahead and scheduled the appointment for the next week."

Ed's attitude made all the difference. Had he taken the approach, "It's not my job," his company might have lost the opportunity to do business with a customer that represented significant revenue, but Ed took responsibility for the situation and saw things from the customer's point of view. He then saw to it that his company lived up to the commitments he had made to the customer.

Patricia Ferráez, a store manager for Acosta Deportes in Mexico City, is yet another salesperson whose attitude about taking responsibility made all the difference.

"One morning, a customer who had bought a gym station for his home called to claim his merchandise. Unfortunately, because our delivery vehicles were either booked or out of order, we were not able to deliver his product on time. He wanted his money back or a next-day delivery. When I put myself in his shoes, I could certainly understand why he was upset.

"Later that same day, another customer from a lighting company came along. When this customer was about to leave, I got an idea. I said, 'Please help me. I need to deliver this gym equipment, and I see you have the truck from your company. Would you please deliver this equipment for us? Meanwhile, I will prepare your order and give you a special discount on this order and future ones.' "

Not only did Patricia please the customer who ordered the gym equipment, she impressed the customer from the lighting company who saw firsthand her commitment to customer service. Both remain loyal to Acosta Deportes thanks, in large part, to Patricia's creative thinking and ability to see things from the other person's point of view.

James, a successful salesperson in Florida, has the same great attitude when it comes to seeing things from the customer's viewpoint. "I've never really been focused on the commission. I am always focused on treating other people the way I want to be treated. I believe if we do that, everything else falls into place."

When James started in sales with his current employer, he inherited a customer who had only made a few small purchases in the past. The person responsible for making the buying decisions was often short on time and didn't express much interest in building a relationship with James's company.

After doing some pre-approach, James discovered that this customer came into the office at 4:30 A.M., and typically didn't leave until 8:00 P.M. As he put himself in his customer's shoes, he realized he might have an opportunity to meet with this gentleman if he accommodated the customer's work schedule. So what did he do?

"I would go see him at 4:30 in the morning. Or, I'd go see him at 8:00 in the evening. Sometimes, when I saw him in the evening, I would end up staying until 11:00, because we would start talking about the business. The relationship started growing from there.

"Over time, I started to get about 98 percent of his business. And I was never the cheaper product. As we were making deals, we got to the point where we just trusted each other and made decisions to help each other out. Whatever he needed, whether it was service, parts, the availability of credit, I would work with him to meet his needs.

"Eventually, this customer had to make a very significant order. My company's bid was about $1.5 million more than the next-closest competitor. Despite the price difference, the customer chose to do business with us. This sale represented half of our total sales revenue that particular year.

"When the customer came to a meeting at our facility, I was curious about why he selected us in light of the huge price difference. To my surprise, he looked across the table at everyone, pointed at me, and said, 'Relationship.' Even though I knew we had a good relationship, I never expected him to say that. He wasn't the type of guy that verbally expressed his gratitude. Needless to say, his answer to that question made everyone in the room sit up and take notice."

To James, having the right attitude about serving customers is one of the biggest advantages a salesperson can have.

"Attitude is key. Always focus on how well you can do your job, what you can give to your customers, and what you can show your customers as the benefits of doing business with you. I've seen people who are basically concerned about the money aspect of sales, and the customer always seems to see that. I feel you have to have a good attitude above everything else.

"I first started with my employer pumping gas in cars when I was sixteen years old. I decided I didn't want to do that all my life. So in my own mind, my theory became to do what is asked of me, to the best of my ability and do it at 110 percent. Always treat people the way you want to be treated. I kept that attitude through every job I had at the company, and it has made all the difference in my career."

ANOTHER PERSPECTIVE ON ATTITUDE

In talking about attitude, we're not implying that top performers like James never feel fearful or frustrated. Of course they do. Salespeople with good attitudes have bad days. They get angry. They feel hurt. They even feel rejected. The difference? The best performers use these emotions as steppingstones, rather than barriers to success.

In his book *Wisdom, Inc.*, author Seth Godin states: "If one out of 10 sales calls leads to new business, a pessimist would call that a 10 percent success rate. A successful salesperson realizes that all he has to do is be turned down nine times before he's virtually guaranteed a sale. By viewing rejection as a steppingstone to acceptance, salespeople are able to persist until they achieve their goals."

Take, for example, the typical reaction of salespeople when it comes to rejection. As sales professionals, we've often been taught not to view a rejection personally. After all, people are rejecting our products or services, not us.

Those are comforting words, but unfortunately, most average salespeople find them a little too comforting. They use them as an excuse for not improving their selling skills. If they can blame rejection on their product, service, or proposal, then there's little motivation for change.

Top performers are typically different. They understand the logical reasons why the customer didn't buy. But emotionally, they are more inclined to take the rejection personally. That's what makes them top performers.

Why? Instead of blaming the product, service, or proposal, they take responsibility. Their attitude says, "What can I learn from this experience?" Or, "What can I do differently?" If they don't get past a gatekeeper, they ask themselves why. If a prospect doesn't want them to participate in the bidding process, they find out why. If they lose a sale, they analyze the situation so they will succeed next time. They don't make excuses or fall back on old sales clichés, they hold themselves accountable for their results. And they use that accountability to propel them out of their comfort zones to look for ways to improve.

Generally, the best people in any profession are very emotional and passionate about what they do. The best nurses usually get emotional about creating comfort and caring for their patients. The best public speakers are those who feel passionate about inspiring each audience. The best managers usually care about the people they manage. The best athletes are most often found crying on the bench when they lose, but exuding extreme joy when they win.

We should expect nothing less of ourselves as top sales performers. We need to realize that it's okay to get emotional if we have passion about what we do. Fear, anxiety, and frustration are just normal feelings in the profession of selling. The key is that we can't let these negative emotions keep us from getting out of our comfort zone and making positive changes in the way we sell.

ATTITUDE MOTIVATES US TO SET GOALS
AND MANAGE OUR TIME EFFECTIVELY

Abraham Lincoln was once asked how he, a man with limited education from a rural area, became an attorney and, ultimately the president of the United States. Mr. Lincoln replied, "The day that I set my mind to it, the job was about half done."

In 1960, when President John Kennedy announced that the United States would put a man on the moon in the 1960s, it was estimated that only 10 percent of the technology necessary to accomplish that task even existed. However, in July 1969, from the surface of the moon, Neil Armstrong uttered the words, "That's one small step for man, one giant leap for mankind."

Those two events, roughly one hundred years apart, started with goals that seemed impossible. Both became a reality.

No matter what the situation—whether it's traveling to the moon or simply meeting our sales objectives—having specific goals and timelines is important to our success.

Ron Scribner, vice president of Marsh & Company Hospitality Realty in Toronto, Ontario, Canada, believes that setting time-specific goals with customers often helps him generate the best results.

"One of our customers, Shoeless Joe's (a chain of sports-theme restaurants and bars in Canada), wanted to develop its brand name through franchising. We knew that the target had to be more specific. So we developed a goal of growing from four locations to twenty locations in a three-year time frame, with all franchisees making a profit.

"With that as our mission, we developed a five-year business plan and marketing package. I made a personal commitment to do whatever it took to help the customer achieve his goals. We interacted on a daily basis in the spirit of harmony and a common cause. By the end of those three years, we had twenty locations built or under construction, with projections of adding eight locations annually each year thereafter. We accomplished this without incurring any debt or personal liability.

"The payoff for my customer has been wealth and happiness. The payoff for me was being able to provide added value to the business relationship that helped achieve the customer's goals. The bonus for me is that the customer and I have become friends as well as business associates."

Would Ron have been able to achieve those results in three years without a specific goal? Perhaps. However, knowing exactly what he had to accomplish, and when he had to deliver, greatly improved the odds that he would achieve success in such a short time.

Hideo Suzuki, president of Cyberland Corporation in Japan, attributes his career success to personal goal setting. When he was an employee of a computer company, Hideo set a goal that he wanted to start his own company within five years. In preparation for his long-term goal, he set several short-term targets. He started saving money to build capital. And, before work and on the weekends, he taught himself how to create graphics on a Macintosh computer.

As a result of his focus and dedication to his goal, Hideo resigned his job with the computer company and started his own firm after just three years of working toward his goal. His first year in business, sales were $225,000. Just two years later, Hideo's sales increased to over $1.75 million. During a time when many businesses in Japan were losing money, Hideo's was making a profit.

We are all capable of accomplishing great things when we set our minds to it. Salespeople with specific goals and deadlines consistently accomplish the impossible. How? By focusing a winning attitude on managing their time and setting goals in a way that helps them meet the challenges of selling in an increasingly competitive market.

Selling requires a toolbox of skills that can often seem overwhelming and virtually unlimited. If we don't clearly define our goals, or find a way to manage multiple priorities, we will not reach our potential as salespeople. Having the right attitude about goal setting and time management makes all the difference.

Positive Attitude and the Sales Advantage: A Winning Combination

We firmly believe that the Sales Advantage tools and principles can energize your selling efforts. They can empower you, challenge you, and give you a new level of confidence in your sales abilities. But the key word is you. Your attitude makes all the difference in whether the tools will motivate you to build the solid customer-focused relationships you need for long-term success in selling.

How can you maintain a positive attitude even when things aren't going your way? Here are a few ideas:

Get around people who are passionate about selling. Mr. Dale Carnegie often liked to quote Mark Twain, who said, "Keep away from people who try to belittle your ambitions. Small people do that, but the really great ones make you feel that you, too, can become great."

Read, watch, and listen to inspirational material. Use driving time to listen to motivational or educational tapes. Read business magazines, newspapers, and trade publications. Get on the Internet. Watch television programs and videos that add to your knowledge and motivation.

Talk to customers who love the product or service you sell. Reward yourself by calling customers who are satisfied. We sometimes find we're constantly dealing with problems and putting out fires. Our satisfied customers will help us remember the rewards of being in our business.

Write out your vision and invest yourself emotionally in your job. If you have goals and invest yourself emotionally in your work, not only will you enjoy it more, but the people you work with will enjoy it more, too. You will start to look forward to the next day, the next call, or the next order—no matter what the outcome.

As you embark on your new adventure in selling, armed with the Sales Advantage tools and principles, here are three things to keep in mind:

You get the sales advantage by learning how to use the tools and principles.

You keep the advantage by committing to practicing the use of the tools, day in and day out, until they become second nature.

You sell more than ever by having the right attitude about selling, by building customer-focused relationships, and by looking for ways to get out of your comfort zone and try something different.

In sales, it is easy to give up. It's easy to do a little less and then try to explain why we are not producing the kinds of results our companies expect and deserve. We can blame the market, the competition, our products, pricing, advertising, and the unethical practices of people in our industry. But as we do this, we should keep in mind that others are succeeding in the same market. Some of them are even selling inferior products for higher prices, without even advertising, and they're doing it in an ethical way. How are they doing it? They have the right attitude about improving their skills, trying new sales tools, and doing what it takes to really serve the customer.

So when things seem to be going against you, remember these words from Mr. Carnegie: "Don't let anything discourage you. Keep on. Never give up. That has been the policy of most of those who have succeeded. Of course, discouragement will come. The important thing is to surmount it. If you can do that, the world is yours!"

Our Thanks

Dale Carnegie & Associates, Inc., would like to extend a special thanks to contributors across the world who provided stories, analogies, and input for the book's content. We couldn't have done it without you! We would like to extend special appreciation to Kathy Broska, whose tireless efforts and devotion to quality made this effort a success. We'd like to recognize specific Dale Carnegie Training sponsors and trainers who went above and beyond the call of duty to support this landmark initiative. The people listed below unselfishly shared their time and knowledge to ensure that we created a book that complements our sales training and truly provides value to sales professionals in any field.

Joe Brinckerhoff
Rick Gallegos
Rob Haines
Greg Hock
Kevin Kinney
Scott Laun
Mike McClain
Chris McCloskey
Tom Otley
Dr. Earl Taylor
Ron Zigmont

Index

Accenture, 123

Acosta F., Raymundo Alejandro, 254–55

Acosta S., Raymundo, 83–84

Acosta Deportes, 83, 254, 265

Acquisitions, 10

Adler, Ronald B., 113

Advertising, radio and billboard, 29

Airborne Express, 234

Alternatives, commitment and, 217–18

American Hospital Association, 63

American Power Conversion, 105, 251

Analogies, 140–41

Andersen Consulting Italia, 123

As Is, Should Be, Barriers, Payout
    model of questioning
    description of, 107–10
    examples of, 110–13

AT&T, 118

Attention getters, 70–74, 91–92

Attitudes
    controlling/changing, 14–15
    examples of winning, 264–69
    importance of, 261–64
    Sales Advantage and, 270–72
    setting of goals and, 269–70

Authority to negotiate, 204–5

Auto Meier AG, Strengelbach and
    Zofingen, 162

Azizian, Eddie, 128–29

Baek, Sook Hyun, 31–32

Banca Mediolanum, 221

Barriers questions, 108, 110–13

Berti, Gualtiero, 79

Bertolet, Bill, 30–31

Bettger, Frank, 1

Biernat, Sharon, 96

Blalock, Cheryl, 91

Borroni, Gianluca, 221–22

Bridges, 132

Broska, Jay, 90–91

Bruss, Deborah, 7

Building directories, use of, 29–30

Business/social functions, 31–32

Buying
    criteria, 99
    word/mental pictures and reasons
        for, 175–85

Buying motives, dominant, 100–104,
    175

Buying signals
    nonverbal, 167–69
    reactions to, 171–72
    trial close questions, 170–72
    verbal, 167, 169–70

Call reluctance
    See also Prospects/prospecting
    tips for overcoming, 20–21

Calls, making alternate, 33–34

Canada-wide Magazines and
    Communications Ltd., 30

Carnegie, Dale, 17, 59, 62, 71, 80, 84,
    113, 116, 148, 158, 186, 236, 261,
    272

Carrara, Marco, 123–24
Carter, Oral T., 183–84
Challenges, types of, 8–13
Chambers of Commerce, 31
Champions, 25–26
Charles Schwab, 111
Chevron, 255
Choices, commitment and alternative,
    214–15
Churchill, Winston, 218
Cintas Uniforms, 140
Clarity
    guide to, 152
    resolving objections and, 243–
    248
CMS Hartzell, 208, 259
Cole's Printery, 118
Commitment
    how to gain, 213–18
    importance of, 211–12
    referrals and, 219–24
    use of term, 212
Communication
    enhancing, during negotiations,
    196
    follow-up and, 229
    skills, 15
Communication, effective
    be animated, 148
    conciseness, 151
    evidence, use of, 152–53
    involve audience/customers, 154
    speak directly, 149–51
    summarize frequently, 153–54
    use of audiovisual equipment/props,
    154–55
    words to avoid, 148
Communication, initial
    attention, getting, 70–74
    credibility statement, 52–56
    follow-up telephone call, 60–61

methods of, 56
pre-approach and, 39–40
preparing for, 47–49
quality versus quantity, 50–51
reasons for being turned down,
    50–52
by telephone, 61–70
two-step approach, 56–61
written, 56–60
Community organizations, use of,
    30–31
Competence, pre-approach and, 43–
    44
Complex negotiation, 195–96
Compliments, use of, 71
Conciseness, importance of, 151
Contact list, managing, 36–37
Contractors Sales Co., 110
Contracts, 202–3
Correspondence, referring to previous,
    67
Courage, pre-approach and, 44–45
Craft, Grant, 262–63
Craft Projects, 262–63
Crane, Philip, 221
Credibility statements
    attention and, 70
    developing, 53–56
    elements of, 53–54
    role of, 52–53
    sales discussions and use of, 92
Cucullo, Susan, 118–19
Cushion, resolving objections and,
    241–43
Customer evaluation
    buying signals, 167–72
    reasons for stalling by customers,
    166–67
    warning signals, 172–75
    word/mental pictures and reasons
    for buying, 175–85

Customers, follow-up and, 226–28, 230–31

Cyberland Corp., 270

Daewoo Electronics, 32

Databases, follow-up and use of, 228–29

Delay/inactivity, 203–4, 249

Demonstrations, 135–37, 162–64

Direct questions, commitment and, 214

Dominant buying motives, 100–104, 175

Dooley, Liz, 112–13, 140

Edison, Thomas, 13, 68

Educate
attention getter, 72
responding to objections and, 254–255

80–20 rule, 202

Elmy, Debra, 181–82

Emerson, Ralph Waldo, 21

Employees
follow-up of, 231–32
human relations skills and, 232–33
ways to show you value, 232

Endagraph, 154

Energheia, 215

Enthusiasm, use of, 62

Evidence
analogies, 140–41
book, creating, 142–45
demonstrations, 135–37
examples, 137
exhibits, 139–40
facts, 137–39
responding to objections and providing, 255–58
solution development and, 134–145

solution presentation and, 152–153
statistics, 142
testimonials, 141–42

Examples, 137

Exhibits, 139–40, 162–63

Explain, responding to objections and, 254

Facts, 137–39

Fannon, Kevin, 73–74

Federal Express, 261

Ferráez, Patricia, 265–66

Ferris Baker Watts, 247

Filtering, 116–17

Fitzgerald, Tim, 247

5 Great Rules of Selling, The (Whiting), 22, 72, 135, 148

Foglesong, Tom, 194

Follow-up
customer, 226–28, 230–31
importance of, 225–26
internal/company, 231–32
strategies, 228–30

Foltz Concrete Pipe Co., 160, 161

Foster, Lisa, 118

Frenkil, Leonard, Jr., 171–72, 180–81, 203

Gatekeepers
voice mail, 68–70
working with, 9, 65–68

Geiger, Molly, 127–28

General Foods, 161

Genuine objections, 249

Goals, attitudes and the setting of, 269–70

Godin, Seth, 267–68

Goetzinger, Darlene, 184–85

Going first, negotiations and, 205–6

GSI Lumonics, 89

Haaksma, Hank, 255–56
H.A. McLean Travel, Inc., 118
Haas, George, 110–11
Hanes, Bob, 58–59
Hanlon, Esther, 208, 259–60
Hanlon, Jeff, 29–30
Hann, Larry, 61–62
Harkey, Susan, 228
Hei, John, 44
Hendricksen, The Care of Trees, 150
Herlong, Gayle, 139–40
Hermann, Bill, 73
Hill-Rom, 63–64
Holden, Andrea, 63–64
Holman, W. C., 19
Hopeless objections, 249
How to Win Friends and Influence People
    (Carnegie), 80
HR Team, 198
Hughes, Bruce, 7
Human relations
    commitment and, 213
    interviews and principles of, 77–
        80
    negotiations and, 191–94
    objections and, 238–40
Humor, use of, 63
Huntimer, Randall K., 32–33

Ignition Group, 25–26, 240
Important, making people feel, 84–85
Incoe Corp., 88–89
Information
    follow-up and use of interesting, 230
    gathering, 96–101
    overload, 8–9
Initial communication/contact. See
    Communication, initial
Interest
    genuine, 80–82
    primary, 98–99

International Promotional Ideas,
    96
Internet, taking advantage of, 34–35
Interviews
    building rapport, 76–77, 86
    drawing on human relations
        principles, 77–80
    guidelines, 77
    information gathering, 96–101
    interest, genuine, 80–82
    introductions, 83
    listening, importance of, 88–89,
        113–19
    pleasantries, making, 90–91
    sales discussions, starting, 91–96
    smiling, 83–84
    stop, look, and listen, 82–83
    talk in terms of the other person's
        interests, 85–88
Introductions, 83
Ireland, Brett, 87–88

Jacobson, Greg, 105, 251–52
Jamieson, Scott, 150–51

Kennedy, Ian, 79–80
Kennedy, John F., 269
Kinney, Kevin, 135–36, 139
Kopf, Brian, 78
Kuthrell, Robert, 111–12
Kyger, Ernie, 239–40

Ladbrokes Racing Corporation, 154–
    155
Larson, Eric, 14
Leach, Toby, 216
Leader in You, The, 113–14
Legge, Peter, 30
Leleu, Elisabeth, 105–6
Leonard, Jeff, 159–61
Levitt, Eileen, 198–99

Lewis, E. St. Elmo, 166
Lexington State Bank, 103, 149
Lexus cars, 232–33
Liller, Jeannette R., 168, 174–75
Lincoln, Abraham, 269
Listeners, speaking directly to, 149–51
Listening
  importance of, 88–89, 113–19
  levels of, 114–15
  tips for better, 115–17
Lists, keeping updated, 27, 36–37
Looking Out, Looking In (Adler and
    Towne), 113
Lowe, Mike, 74
Lu Li Fung, 143–44
Lynx Golf Co., 16–17

Maloy, Jack, 6–7
Manca, Ignazio, 129
Marr Scaffolding, 120
Marsh & Company Hospitality Realty,
    269
Maxwell, Rob, 43–44
Maynard, Linda, 149–50
McCann, Chris, 86–87
McCann, Jim, 86–87
McCarthy, Jarrad, 154–55
McCarthy, Mary, 89
McClain, Mike, 41
McCloskey, Chris, 78
McCloskey, Kevin, 6
McGrath, Frank, 73, 183
McGrath, Paul, 136–37, 140
McLean Travel, Inc., H.A., 118
Meier, Heinz, 162–63
Mental pictures. *See* Word pictures and
    reasons for buying
Mergers, 10
Merrill Lynch, 117
Michael, David, 222–24
Michael Mortgage Group, 222

Minor decisions, commitment and,
    215–16
Misconceptions, 249
Mistakes, how to avoid making, 40–
    41
Mold Makers, Inc., 89
Money Group, 23
Monk, Sandy, 95–96
Motley, Red, 1
Muller, Beat, 80–81

Neal, David S., 88
Negotiation
  agreements, 209–10
  challenges of, 195
  characteristics of successful,
    209
  communication enhanced during,
    196
  defined, 187–88
  guidelines for, 189
  human side of, 191–94
  model, 186–87
  planning for, 210
  tips for, 191
  tools, 197–209
  types of, 195–96
  versus objection, 189–90
Negotiation tools
  authority to negotiate, 204–5
  contracts, 202–3
  delay/inactivity, 203–4
  going first, 205–6
  persuasion, 200
  silence, 200–201
  throw-ins, 207–9
  time constraints, 201–2
  ultimatums, 206–7
  walking away, 198–200
Negotiator, qualities needed for,
    191

Networking
  guidelines, 31, 32
  referral, 35–36
Neuberth, Stephen, 169–70
Next-step questions, commitment and, 215
Nichol, F. W., 225
Nonverbal buying signals, 167–69
Nonverbal warning signals, 173
N Systems, Inc., 169
Nugent, Kathleen, 14–15

Oakpoint Oil, 255
Objection(s)
  anticipating, 236–37
  categories of, 249
  clarifying, 243–48
  common, 246
  cushions, 241–43
  human relations and, 238–40
  identifying hidden, 249–52
  negotiation versus, 189–90
  resolving, 238, 241–60
  when to respond to, 252–53
Odyssey Cruises, 181
Old Dominion Freight Lines, 228
Omni Eye Specialists, 184–85
Onama S.p.A., 129
1–800 Flowers.com, 86–87
Opportunities
  See also Prospects/prospecting
  categories of, 122
  commitment and, 216
Opportunity analysis, 43, 120–24
Opportunity chart method, 23–25
Organizational skills, 16
Overstreet, H. A., 125
Owen, Ted, 31

Pareto Principle, 202
Payout questions, 108–9, 110–13

Pearce, Russ, 158–59
People skills, 16–17
Persistence, power of, 218
Persuasion, 200
Pleasantries, making, 90–91
Poggianella, Marco, 215
Porter, Ed, 264–65
Pre-approach step, 3, 5
  benefits of, 39–45
  defined, 39
  reasons for ignoring, 38
  sources of information on, 45
  what you can learn about prospects
    during, 46–47
Presentation of solutions. See
    Solutions, presentation of
Price buyers, 10–11
Priganc, Robert, 23–25
Product knowledge, solution
    development and, 133
Products
  complex, 12
  follow-up and use of new product
    updates, 230
Proposals, 156
Prospects, methods for finding new
  advertisements, 29
  building directories, 29–30
  business/social functions, 31–32
  Chamber of Commerce, 31
  community organizations, 30–31
  existing customers, 22–28
  Internet sources, 34
  lists, 27
  new customers, 28–37
  referrals, 26–27, 35
  telephone directories, 30
  trade shows, 33
  while driving, 29
Prospects/prospecting
  changing our view of, 20–22

qualifying, during opportunity
    analysis, 43, 120–24
qualifying, during pre-approach,
    41–43
reasons for avoiding, 19–20
what you can learn about, during
    pre-approach, 46–47
Purchasing agents, 2–3

Quantum EDP, 6
Questioning process
    examples of, 110–13
    role of, 104–6, 109–10
    starting off right, 106–7
    types of questions, 107–9

Rapport, building, 76–77, 86
Referral(s)
    asking for, 26–27, 219–20
    example of getting, 221–24
    methods for getting, 220–21
    network, 35–36
    using, 67, 72
RE/MAX, 184
Renaissance Executive Forums, 117
Repro Tech, Inc., 7
Reverse, responding to objections and,
    253–54
R. L. Trucking, 255
Robertson, John, 256–58
Rodier, Jerry, 256
Ross, Carl, 16–17

Sales Advantage, attitudes and, 270–72
Sales discussions, how to start
    attention getters, 91–92
    credibility statements, 92
    why talk statements, 93–96
Salespeople
    importance of, 1
    qualities of successful, 13–17

Sales philosophy, 2
Sales process
    overlap in, 4–5
    reasons for understanding the
        whole, 5–8
    steps in, 3–4
Sales success, qualities needed for,
    13–17
Sanderson, R. G., 161–62
San Diego Business Journal, 31
Saunders, Karp, and Co., 118
Saunders, Tom, 118
Schwab, Charles, 111
Scribner, Ron, 269–70
Selling skills, need to improve/update,
    15
Selling Solutions, 158
Shoeless Joe's, 269
Should Be questions, 108, 110–13
Showmanship, 157–65
Siemens Italy, 79
Silence, 200–201
Simco Electronics, 14–15
Simple negotiation, 195
Skepticism, 249
Smiling, 83–84
Smith, Fred, 261
Smith, Ian, 234
Smith & Suita, 263
Solution development
    product knowledge and, 133
    role of, 125–29
Solution development, steps for
    application, 134
    benefits, 133
    bridges, 132
    evidence, 134–45
    facts, finding, 131–32
    trial close, 145–46
Solutions, presentation of
    communicating, 147–55

Solutions, presentation of (*cont.*)
  methods for, 155–57
  showmanship, 157–65
  words to avoid, 148
Sonatex Laminating Canada, Inc.,
  105
Stallings, Mary Sue, 103–4
Standard Register, 127
Stand-up presentations, 155
Startling statement, 72–74
Statistics, 142
Stinson, John, 256–58
Stinson Robertson Custom Builders,
  256
Stundis, Tom, 120–21
Suita, Paula Levis, 263–64
Sullivan, John, 126–27
Support, role of internal, 12–13
Suzuki, Hideo, 270

Taylor, Earl, 81–82
Team presentations, 156–57
Teams
  building, 234–35
  development principles, 233
  follow-up of, 231–32
  human relations skills and, 232–
    233
  ways to show you value, 232
Technical presentations, 157
Telephone calls
  attitude and, 61–62
  barriers to, 65–70
  clarity and brevity, 62
  effectiveness of, 61–65
  follow-up, 60–61
  humor, use of, 63
  making presentations by, 155–56
  selling principles using, 61
  tone of voice, 62
Telephone directories, use of, 30

Tenuto, Jim, 117–18
Testimonials, 141–42
Testing Machines, Inc., 126
Tetra, 6–7
Thermal Science Technologies,
  216
Throw-ins, 207–9
Time, challenge of, 11
Time constraints, 201–2
Tone of voice, 62
Total quality management, 9–10
Towne, Neil, 113
Trade shows, 33
Treasure Island Aquarium and Pet
  Center, 6–7
Trial close, 145–46
  questions, 170–72, 179
  responding to objections and,
    259–60
Two-step approach, 56–61

Ultimatums, 206–7
U.S. Postal Service, 105

Value justification, responding to
  objections and providing, 258
Varian Vacuum Technologies, 14
Verbal buying signals, 167, 169–
  170
Verbal warning signals, 173
Verge, Jyoti, 65–66
Viesta, Gene, 82
Voice mail, 68–70

Walking away, 198–200
Warning signals, 172–75
Washington Place Management, 171,
  203
Wax, Jonathan, 258
Wedderburn, Steve, 232–33
Western Pacific Distributors, 128

Whiting, Percy, 22, 72, 135, 147, 148
Why talk statements, 93–96
Winter, Andrew, 25–26, 240
Wisdom, Inc. (Godin), 267–68
Wolfson Maintenance, 79
Word pictures and reasons for buying,
   175–76
  bridges for, 180
  elements of, 177–79

examples of, 181–85
  guidelines for, 177
Written communication, 56–60

Yenkana, Ray, 184
Yu-Ling Enterprises, 44

Zastrow, Lloyd, 88–89
Ziglar, Zig, 148

MICHAEL CROM is the Executive Vice President of Dale Carnegie & Associates. He works closely with the team supporting their worldwide network of Dale Carnegie Sponsors with particular focus on North American operations. He also serves as part of the senior management team of the company as well as the Board of Directors for Dale Carnegie. He lives in Huntington, New York.

J. OLIVER CROM is the Vice Chair of Dale Carnegie & Associates. He advises the senior management of DC&A on policy matters and strategic planning, and he is available to all departments for counseling and advice. He is active on several committees on the board of DC&A. He lives in Sands Point, New York.